Fatal Flight

The Maltese Obsession with Killing E

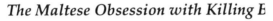

The fate of migrating birds in the Mediterranean has for a long time caused anguish and dismay amongst bird and nature lovers. Malta is a particularly bad offender – although other Mediterranean countries such as Italy, Spain, Greece, Cyprus and even France are not entirely guiltless.

Natalino Fenech grew up in Malta within the cult of shooting and trapping but long ago 'saw the light'. Since then, with his cool and scientific mind, he has been collecting information to launch for the first time a clear and irrefutable exposure of the whole appalling business.

The facts are easy to read for those with eyes to see. Annual figures show that 3 million finches are trapped while 80,000 golden orioles, half a million swallows, 13,000 shearwaters, over half a million thrushes, 1000 stilts, even ospreys and 50-80,000 birds of prey are gunned out of the sky. And why? Not for the pot or to control marauders but for the fun of it, for stuffing and for display. There are over 40 taxidermists in Malta, stuffing thousands of birds a year. People are taking boats out to sea to shoot the migrants before the land shooters can get at them. People are regularly using live birds as decoys and as 'clay' pigeon targets. People miss work to satisfy their craze.

As the endorsements to this book show, the practice has got to be stopped and, with Malta's wish for stronger ties with the EEC, now is the ideal time to publish and to encourage the power of the written word to galvanize us into action.

Fatal Flight is a riveting book. It holds the reader transfixed throughout a methodical and unsentimental exposure of a whole strange way of life. The world of the Maltese shooter and trapper may be abhorrent to us, but if we are to move in the right direction, it is essential to understand the situation in all its gory detail.

Can we remain idle once we know that the birds we protect so dearly are being shot and trapped on their way to their winter quarters – or, even worse, on their way to their breeding grounds within the European Community?

NATALINO FENECH started his conservation activities at 16, first as a young member of the Malta Ornithological Society; he then served on a number of posts within the MOS council. He left the organization and helped from Żgħażagħ għall-Ambjent – a youth movement for the protection of the environment.

The new group had a baptism of fire when, on their first street action against the destruction of the countryside, they were savagely attacked and beaten in front of the police on the streets of Valletta by thugs who were linked to speculators, several of whom were later convicted due to the group's perseverance. The movement carried out a number of actions to stir up public opinion.

Natalino was employed by the local telephone company, and later studied at the University of Malta, from where he obtained a diploma in Journalism, a BA and a Post-Graduate Certificate in Education. For three consecutive years he worked at the Environment department, a job he recently left to take up teaching. Currently he is studying for a Master's Degree as a part-time student at Durham University.

Natalino runs a bird hospital at home. On an island bristling with guns, patients are not lacking and the treated birds, including some rare birds of prey, are sent to the Italian League for the Protection of Birds (LIPU) for rehabilitation and eventual release.

His articles and photographs, bringing the indiscriminate shooting of birds to the public attention, have appeared in a number of specialized publications throughout Europe. He is a regular contributor to the Maltese press on matters related to environmental protection and has been among the leading spirits who stirred the environmental consciousness of Malta in the mid-eighties.

Fatal Flight

The Maltese Obsession with Killing Birds

NATALINO FENECH

QUILLER PRESS
LONDON

DEDICATION

To those who strive for
conservation without seeking
personal gain

First published 1992
by Quiller Press Limited
46 Lillie Road
London SW6 1TN

ISBN 1870948 53 X

Photo credit: Front cover photograph of osprey by David Cottridge.
Back cover photograph of alpine swift by Natalino Fenech.

Produced by Hugh Tempest-Radford *Book Producers*
Printed in Great Britain by St Edmundsbury Press

Contents

Foreword   vii
Other Opinions   viii
Preface   xii
Map   xvi

Chapter 1   **An Overview of the Local Situation**   1

*The socio-economic situation and cultural attitudes; Hunting,
democracy and conservation; Tourism and hunting; Shooting and
religion; Of saints and legends; Of saints and men; Shooters' arguments;
The political situation; No official action; Flagrant abuses; Bird stuffing;
Shooters' excuses; Bird trapping; A not so different situation; The myth
of tradition*

Chapter 2   **Hunting Practices in Malta**   22

*Falconry; Game hunting; Firearms make an appearance; The song
remains the same; Birds at the market; Shoot less to kill more; Trap
shooting; Shooting for the pot; The real shooters*

Chapter 3   **Changes in Shooting Paraphernalia**   39

*Early firearms and hunting; Breech-loading guns appear; Changes in
guns; Better gunpowder; Plastic wads; Special cartridges; Locally made
cartridges; Heavy guages; Calls and decoys; Use of tape-recordings;
Other decoys*

Chapter 4   **Shooting from Sea-craft**   51

*Shearwater shooting; The current trend; Nothing is spared; Inadequate
legislation*

Chapter 5   **Taxidermy**   57

*Types of collections; Early collections; Importation of bird skins – the
current situation; Bird stuffing today; A list of birds in some private
collections (Table 6); Estimated numbers of some species of birds killed
annually (Table 7); Average number of birds shot or trapped*

Chapter 6   Metaphors of Superiority, Masculinity,
              Virility and Machismo   84

A symbol of status; Social factors; A day in the life of a shooter; Shooters'
rituals; Talk of the town; Shooters' language; The shooting mania; Other
attitudes; Images of sexuality; Macho images; The Rambo mentality;
Shooters and the law; Marked changes: wordage on cartridges; Other
changes; Time off for hunting; Number of sick claims per month (graph);
Killing sprees; Exporting shooters

Chapter 7   **Trapping**   102

Finch migration; A day in the life of a bird trapper; A historical
perspective; Finch trapping; The use of clap-nets; Number of finches
trapped; Number of trapping sites in the Maltese Islands; Intensive
trapping; Live decoys; Use of hybrids; Fluttering decoys; Importation
and sale of birds; New methods; Pipits, wagtails, sparrows and other
birds; The use of vertical nets; The use of vertical nets today; Flap-traps
and cage-traps; Robin trapping; Other trapping methods; 'Game' bird
trapping – quail trapping; Turtle dove trapping; Plovers and lapwings;
Other birds in captivity; Nests and nestlings stolen

Chapter 8   **History of Hunting and Bird Protection**
              Legislation   128

The earliest hunting laws; Hunting laws under the order of St John;
Hunting and bird protection laws under British rule; Closed-seasons
appear; The trail to the laws of 1980; The first draft; Back-tracking; The
act and regulations of 1980; For better and for worse; The current
situation; The conservation movement; Malta and the EC; Malta and the
Maltese

Selected Bibliography   141
List of References   143
Tables   155
Plates   between pages 96 and 97

Foreword by David Bellamy

Malta is a group of five islands which together cover an area of 320 square kilometres. Lying midway between two continents at the centre of modern civilization, these islands and their deservedly proud people have always played a strategic role in the development of human affairs.

Malta's population stands in excess of 350,000 people, a number which is swollen by hoards of visitors during a long tourist season. They come to soak up the sun; to enjoy peaceful tranquillity and clear unpolluted waters; to eat well thanks to the farmers who ensure agricultural self-sufficiency for the island; and to savour the George Cross spirit of the people. Malta is a paradise, except for one vice of some 5% of her population who at regular intervals down the tools of their various trades to shoot and trap more than four million wild birds every year. This senseless slaughter includes two thousand five hundred little bitterns; sixteen thousand herons and egrets; three thousand honey buzzards; ten thousand marsh harriers; six thousand five hundred hobbies (a total of over fifty thousand raptors in all); eleven thousand five hundred assorted owls; sixteen thousand hoopoes; five thousand bee-eaters; eighty thousand golden orioles to name but a few. If that list doesn't make you sick then add seventeen hundred kingfishers; fifty-five thousand cuckoos; one hundred thousand robins; two hundred thousand skylarks and at a rough guess over two million finches. Many of these birds arrive on Malta tired from long migration flights and even those who make it to the few so-called nature reserves – even churchyards with trees – find guns and traps in wait.

Why does it happen? Why does the church appear to condone it? The answers are long and complex, revolving around the miscarriage of ancient Roman Law which in effect states 'if it hasn't an ownership label around its neck, it's fair game'.

Whatever the real reason, please, please, it has to stop, for that attitude has no place in the civilized world!

David J. Bellamy

Other Opinions

Greenpeace

Greenpeace does not so far have a bird-protection campaign. This is not because the organization considers this an unimportant matter or one of low priority. It is just that we cannot work on everything at the same time. There are several organizations we have full confidence in, who are presently campaigning for the protection of birds.

As the Greenpeace Mediterranean campaign co-ordinator, and the former chairman of a Mallorcan bird-protection organization, I cannot avoid being aware of the importance of bird-protection in the Mediterranean. This region is a veritable cross-roads for all sorts of bird species migrating from Africa to Europe and vice-versa. Malta is one of the natural stopovers for these creatures and has to be seen as part of a chain of havens essential for migrating birds. Seen in this dimension, bird-protection in Malta takes on more than local significance.

Natalino Fenech's book clearly sets out the importance of Malta for migrating birds; it also sets out the problems the bird population has to face in this country. Hunting is clearly shown to be a catastrophic problem for birds of all sorts of species traversing the archipelago of Malta, Gozo and Comino. Malta is not the only place where hunting has proved a severe problem in the Mediterranean. This fact cannot, however, ever be seen as any sort of justification. On the contrary the frequency of hunting practices throughout the region gives this problem the unenviable importance it holds.

The process of extinction cannot be calculated over a couple of years in isolation but is normally a slower process resulting from a culmination of causes. Once a species is extinct it is extinct forever. Such phenomena create imbalances in nature which are often not easily noticeable or of immediate importance.

In the last half a century, hardly the time to wink in nature's terms, imbalances in nature have accelerated to a very noticeable and alarming rate. One should therefore heed the kind of scientific information presented by Natalino Fenech in his book. The facts he presents us with demonstrate that there are grave problems for bird-conservation in Malta. It is vital that those responsible take heed and take the proper remedies before it is too late.

Xavier Pastor
Greenpeace International,
Mediterranean campaign co-ordinator

Malta Ornithological Society (MOS)

The publication asserts and highlights what the Malta Ornithological Society (MOS) has been stating since its inception in 1962; that the Maltese Islands are one of the worst black spots for birds in the Mediterranean. There is no other place where the shooting and trapping of birds is so intensive and extensive. This is indeed a national problem which should be treated urgently as such by the Government. The onus rests on the political parties occupying the seats in the highest institutions of these islands. MOS has left no stone unturned to lobby against the destruction of birdlife by Maltese shooters both locally and abroad. This it has done through public actions, use of the media and a continuous educational campaign. As a result, public awareness has rapidly increased during the last years, so much so that MOS can boast to be the largest conservation body on the island. Although MOS has to date, never called for the abolition of all hunting and trapping, it cannot tolerate the continuous widespread killing of birdlife in these islands.

MOS endorses with pleasure this publication by Natalino Fenech. It urges the authorities to act forcefully and eliminate this sad state of affairs by aligning Malta with the rest of Europe in this respect.

Joe A. Doublet
President, MOS

Royal Society for the Protection of Birds

The sight of thousands of gliding birds – storks, buzzards, kites and eagles has fascinated man for centuries. Our wonderment has been heightened by the knowledge of the huge distances covered and the wide diversity of the places in which they nest and winter.

Migratory birds are our shared international heritage; they may be protected in some countries, but there are still alarming dangers to be faced on the long migration flights. Malta represents a microcosm of all that is wrong with man's attitude to wild birds, so graphically described here by Natalino Fenech.

The Royal Society for the Protection of Birds was in the forefront of the battle to end the evil of the plumage trade – a battle which lasted nearly forty years; indeed the roots of our organisation are firmly based in international activities.

We have been privileged to work side by side with Malta's growing army of bird protectors for over 20 years, and together we hope to win the hearts and minds of Maltese people, so as to make Malta, and indeed all Europe, a safer place for birds.

This book is one more step towards bringing the problem to a wider audience both on Malta and elsewhere in the world.

Through such knowledge we can finally end the destruction of Malta's rich heritage of bird life.

Barbara S. Young
Chief Executive, RSPB

International Council for Bird Preservation (ICBP)

Bird-shooting and trapping in Malta have been the subject of many writings, campaigns and protests. Given such a high number of shooters and trappers in such a small country, as well as an ever increasing awareness of bird conservation, the discussion of the issue is bound to be lively and sometimes controversial.

Along the years the conservation movement has been accused of magnifying the problem and of overestimating the killing. In this book Natalino Fenech shows through sound facts and figures that the number of birds trapped and killed is even more than previously estimated. He argues forcefully, and quite rightly, that such practices of destroying bird-life have no place anymore in a modern European society.

Natalino Fenech needs no introduction in the local field of bird conservation. His strong arguments in the defence of birds helped to galvanise the conservation movement. His enthusiasm and concern for nature, which he showed through joining the Malta Ornithological Society at the early age of fifteen, is clearly seen in his book in which he gives us insight into an intricate socio-political problem which, sadly, this country has not yet been able to resolve. His excellent photography enhances this further.

The International Council for Bird Preservation is pleased to endorse this book, hoping it will serve as an eye-opener to the authorities and an encouragement to the public to act and help remedy this deplorable situation which is harming Malta's otherwise excellent international image.

Joe Sultana
Chairman
ICBP European Continental Section

Farley Mowat Limited

Natalino Fenech is one of the new heroes of our time. A conservationist dedicated to trying to stop the unbelievable slaughter of birds that annually takes place on his native island, he has been fearless in his efforts to bring the truth to the public eye and ear. As an example of what we should all be doing, he must be regarded with awe and admiration. The book itself is an account of our disastrous and totally destructive attitude towards other living creatures. To read it is to weep – but also to become angered to the point where one has to do something about it.

Farley Mowat

Scottish Wildlife Trust

Malta has become Europe's Jekyll and Hyde country. Visitors to these fine islands can bask in the warmth of the friendly welcome and climate and appreciate the rich Maltese history and culture. They can also see migrant birds slaughtered with pump-action shotguns in public parks and terror-struck finches crammed into paper bags and sold like candy in street markets.

Natalino Fenech's book is a major achievement. Lifting the mask to reveal a face of contemporary Maltese life that the tourist guides would rather ignore. Through careful analysis of the history of bird shooting and trapping on the Maltese Islands he has given the lie to the idea that these activities are somehow part of a noble Maltese tradition. He has exposed them for what they really are – a type of modern barbarism supported by a powerful and aggressive minority.

This book should be essential reading for anyone who cares about bird welfare and for anyone who might be considering a holiday in Malta. If it makes the growing band of green tourists reject these islands as a holiday destination until birds are properly protected there, then perhaps the Maltese government will, at long last, see that Jekyll and Hyde belong to last century and have no place in the modern Europe.

Dr. Kenny Taylor
Northern Officer
Scottish Wildlife Trust

The Game Conservancy

What happens in Malta is unjustifiable on any grounds. Shooting in spring and shooting of scarce and internationally protected migratory species for ornamental display has no connection whatsoever with responsible and sustainable hunting of quarry species for the table. It is really a case, as described in the book, that *'in Malta there are only shooters and shooting and not hunters and hunting'*.

We utterly condemn it and call upon the Maltese Government to back only the law-abiding hunters and the environmental groups in bringing it to an end. Unless they can do this, one must question their ability to enforce any other conservation legislation which is part of the structure of the European Community Malta has applied to join.

Richard Van Oss

Preface

In the Maltese Islands, hunting was never an important activity related to man's survival. The first communities which settled within our shores would not have survived long had they depended solely on hunting. If any large wild animals existed, these would have been wiped out in a very short time, and had these people been only hunters, they would have had a tough time to survive.

The only weapons, found in local archaeological sites, which could possibly have been used for hunting, amount to only two spear-heads. This, coupled with the fact that finds of bone remains of wild animals are few and far between, confirms that hunting was not an important part of daily life in pre-historic Malta. Hunting may have been a source of additional food.

During the Middle Ages, it evolved into a recreational activity for the upper classes, who used trained falcons at first and, later, firearms.

The invention of gunpowder gave man powerful new weapons, and the development of efficient breech-loading guns in the middle of the last century transformed the situation radically. In the last century, the use of guns for hunting purposes was still relatively restricted but, since then, the rising standard of living has enabled more and more people to own guns.

I have grown up in an environment which, at best, can be described as hostile to birds. Grandfathers from both sides of my family, were shooters. So were some of their children, my uncles, who followed in their fathers' footsteps. Unfortunately for them, and for many others like them, they did not know any better. Bird shooting was part and parcel of their daily lives.

At a tender age, I was used to seeing guns, cartridges and dead birds in my grandfather's house. I recall, as a young boy, going to my grandfather's, and watching him clean the guns after the morning shoot. Then I used to help him feed the birds and rabbits he reared. I used to spend hours sitting and watching while he loaded cartridges for the next migratory season.

I was not more than six years old when my grandfather made me a wooden gun to play with. It even had two shaped pieces of tin in which I could load (spent) cartridges. I remember myself playing, pretending to be a shooter, tossing a dead swift in the air and pretending that I was shooting it myself. Some time later, my uncle, who is a shooter, bought me a toy rifle which shot plastic bullets. Needless to say, aspiring to be a shooter, this was my favourite toy. It was the closest thing to a real gun. I used to take it with me whenever I went out shooting with my grandfather or uncle.

Shotguns were always present on family outings. The Sunday afternoon family outings were never without a gun or two. Being brought up in such an atmosphere, I could not but aspire to become a shooter and to have a large collection of stuffed birds. At school, environmental education was unheard of and, although I was very interested in birds and loved animals, I used to think that the gun was the only means with which to enjoy birds.

At the age of fifteen, I was introduced to the Malta Ornithological Society (MOS) thanks to my mother. It did not take me long to realise that the gun is anything but the right way to appreciate birds. In no time I found myself occupying various posts, including that of PRO and, later, assistant general secretary, within the MOS council. A few years later, I left the MOS and, together with a few other people, formed a pressure group for the protection of the environment, Żgħażagħ għall-Ambjent, which has now evolved into an environment movement called Moviment għall-Ambjent.

Having lived on both sides of the fence – brought up in a pro-hunting environment and, later, active in the conservation movement – I set forth in preparing this study on bird hunting and trapping in the Maltese Islands so that the reader may get an idea of the destruction of bird life which takes place under the guise of hunting.

Most of those who shoot have a licence to hunt. Indeed, they pay for such a licence so that there is nothing illegal about them carrying a gun. When they are in the field, they are just shooters and they shoot at all kinds of birds, and not only at the ones which they are allowed to shoot by law.

Throughout this study, it will be noted that most of the time I use the words 'shooters and shooting' and not 'hunters and hunting'. This is so because in our islands, there are no hunters and hunting, but only shooters and shooting – a difference bigger than words can tell. This is confirmed by a handbook written for local shooters by a keen Maltese shooter. The book is entitled The Maltese Shooter's Handbook and was written, as the author puts it, 'with the Maltese shooter in mind'.

I wrote down all I have found out about the phenomena of shooting and trapping. I have tried to write down most of that which local shooters and trappers tend to 'forget' to say. When writing about how shooting and trapping are carried out, it is impossible to write without treading on emotional grounds. However, what is written is supported by scientific evidence which proves facts objectively.

Those who are not familiar with the way in which bird shooting is carried out in our islands are going to find it hard to believe some of the facts, especially if they have only read about them without experiencing any of them.

I invite the reader to wake up early in the morning in April or May and to take a stroll along Dingli Cliffs, Buskett Gardens, or any other place in the countryside, and to note the number of shooters or the number of shots which he would hear or, for that matter, count the number of spent cartridges which litter the countryside. Then the reader will start to comprehend the gravity of the problem which has been ignored for far too long, especially by politicians and decision-makers. The readers too can do their part if, after reading this book and no doubt confirming its contents, they use their influence in the struggle to help stop this wanton destruction of life.

It is only when the silent majority speaks out loud and clear that the decision-makers will realise that it is time to do something about a problem they have always conveniently ignored. Then, maybe, one will be able to walk in the countryside and enjoy the song of a golden oriole or the call of a cuckoo while watching a honey buzzard soaring above, a kestrel hovering a few metres away, or a harrier gliding effortlessly over a field of swaying silla.

Then Malta too would be a safe place for birds, but only if you, the reader and others who are against the destruction of bird life, will decide to do something more active than just reading this book.

Yes, the killing of birds will go on . . . only if we want it to.

ACKNOWLEDGEMENTS

I would like to thank Clive Cohen, without whose sterling help this book would not be yet in print. Clive helped by crashing through barriers which came from the least expected quarters as well as by commenting about the contents of the various drafts. He also put me in contact with the publisher, Jeremy Greenwood, who went far beyond the normal activities and obligations of a publisher and laboured with love for over two years to see the book in print. I am also indebted to Mr Derek Rayner who contributed towards financing the project, and to Rosamund K. Cox, editor of *BBC Wildlife Magazine*, for her constant support and sound advice.

My thanks are also due to Prof. Patrick J. Schembri, Charles Gauci and Alfred E. Baldacchino who read the various draft manuscripts and to Rev. Prof. Peter Serracino Inglott, Dr Kevin Aquilina, Joe Sultana, John Azzopardi, Tony Mallia, Evarist Bartolo, Saviour Catania, Kjeld Hansen and Roger Arnhem who read one of the drafts. Their remarks, comments and suggestions were invaluable to me in many ways.

Most sincere and grateful thanks to Joe Attard Tabone for his remarks regarding the chapter dealing with legislation; Dr Paul Sant Cassia, Charles Cassar and Jeremy Boissevain, with whom I discussed some aspects of a socio-anthropological nature and to Prof. Godfrey Wettinger, Prof. Anthony Bonanno, Dr Mario Buhagiar, Dr George Zammit Maempel, Gużè Cassar Pullicino, Stephen Degiorgio and Angelo Dougall who were more than keen to discuss various historical and other aspects.

I would also like to thank Joe Sultana for making available literature, some of which is not available in local libraries and Alfred E. Baldacchino who, besides being my strongest supporter and sternest critic, made available his personal file of press cuttings for the years 1974–8 which would have otherwise taken me quite some time to locate. Thanks are also due to Roger Mathieu, Carlo Consiglio, Renato Massa and Joan Mayol Serra for information regarding hunting in their respective countries.

I must also thank, albeit anonymously, Taxidermists A, B and C and the shooters who gave me their bag records. Unfortunately I cannot mention their names. I had agreed to this before the information was given to me and I doubt very much whether I would have published their names, even if they did not mind it themselves. I fear that the risks would have been far too great for them. Thanks are also due to Alex Casha, Charles Coleiro and Vincent Sammut who gave me individual lists of collections of stuffed birds.

The list of acknowledgements would be incomplete if I did not thank the wives of those mentioned above, for bearing with me while I monopolised their husbands' time.

The staff of the National Library, in particular John B. Sultana, the Librarian, as well as Gawdenz Coleiro, Charles Vella, Anthony Bugeja, Tony Debono, Saviour Camilleri, Saviour Schembri, Charles Debattista, Lawrence Chetcuti, Gaetana Ellul and Joe Caruana and Charles Farrugia of the Palace Archives, deserve a word of thanks as much as anybody else. They were all very helpful during my hours of research.

Writing is essentially a solitary activity, and last, but not least, I would like to thank my parents who had to put up with me during the compilation and writing of this study, my brother for helping me by writing some computer programmes to sort and analyse the data made available by the taxidermists, and my girlfriend Rose, whose constant encouragement, understanding and inspiration made me want to write this book even more.

Natalino Fenech
March 1992

Bird Sanctuaries of The Maltese Islands

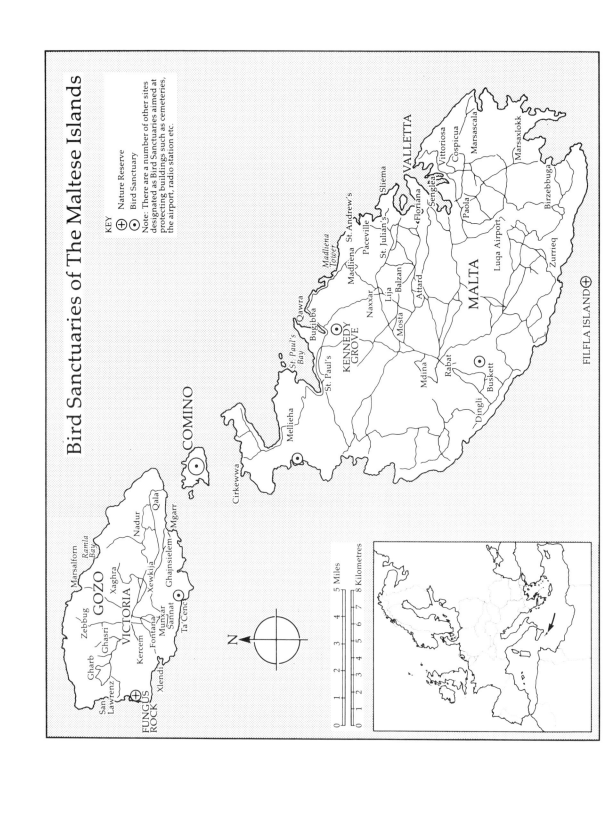

KEY

⊕ Nature Reserve

⊙ Bird Sanctuary

Note: There are a number of other sites designated as Bird Sanctuaries aimed at protecting buildings such as cemeteries, the airport, radio station etc.

GOZO

Marsalforn
Ramla Bay
Zebbug
Xaghra
Nadur
Qala
VICTORIA
Gharb
Ghasri
Fontana
Kercem
Munxar
Sannat
Xewkija
Ghajnsielem
Mgarr
San Lawrenz
Xlendi
Ta Cenc ⊙
FUNGUS ROCK ⊕

COMINO ⊙

Cirkewwa

Mellieha

St. Paul's Bay
Qawra
Bugibba
St. Paul's
KENNEDY GROVE ⊙

Madliena Tower
Madliena
St. Andrew's
Paceville
St. Julian's
Sliema
VALLETTA
Floriana
Senglea
Vittoriosa
Cospicua
Marsascala
Marsaxlokk

Naxxar
Lija
Balzan
Attard
Mosta
Mdina
Rabat
Buskett ⊙
Dingli

MALTA

Paola
Luqa Airport
Zurrieq
Birzebbuga

FILFLA ISLAND ⊕

N

5 Miles

0 1 2 3 4 5

8 Kilometres

0 1 2 3 4 5 6 7 8

Chapter 1

An Overview of the Local Situation

A number of visitors to the Maltese Islands during and after the 15th century commented briefly about the shooting and catching of birds. The main ornithological works on the Maltese Islands, such as those of Wright and Despott, mention the destruction of birds. More recently, Woldhek and Magnin have scraped the surface of the problem of bird shooting and trapping. Many ornithologists, journalists as well as tourists who visit Malta, frequently write about the uncontrolled large-scale shooting and trapping which goes on unabated.

There are a number of factors which have led to the current situation of shooting and trapping. One can say that this situation has very specific historical and cultural roots in our islands. In simpler words, three essential factors are involved: cultural attitudes towards nature, the socio-economic situation and changes in the natural environment.

Since hunting essentially involves the killing of birds and other animals, one must examine whether hunting adds anything to the welfare of mankind. As things stand, hunting is the privilege of a very small minority, as it satisfies only the hunters.

The socio-economic situation and cultural attitudes

The rise in the standard of living is among the reasons why bird shooting and trapping have become popular pastimes. It brought guns, ammunition and cars within everyone's reach. It also brought more free time. But the main reason why shooting evolved in such a way is the lack of proper education about how to use one's free time. Towards the end of the 1800s, Cooke[1] noted that bird shooting 'is a common Sunday pastime'. Closer to our times, in the fifties, shooting took place mainly after work in the evenings and on public holidays.[2] Nowadays, shooting takes place all day long and all year round. Irrespective of the time of day or year, somewhere there is a shooter in wait or roaming in the countryside. *Bang* seems to be ubiquitous in Malta; indeed it is the most popular noise. Bird shooting has become a way of life for shooters.

Hunting, democracy and conservation

Hunting is not democratic. All over the world, and more so in the Mediterranean region, hunters are a small minority of the population.

Yet they are privileged. They are allowed to do things which most people cannot do, such as keeping, carrying and using firearms. They roam freely in the countryside. In Malta, they trample fields in pursuit of birds to shoot and they often cut trees (which they call *pruning*) so that they have a clear view for shooting. Some shooters plant trees; but they do not plant trees to protect nature. They plant non-indigenous fast-growing ones such as acacia and eucalyptus which do not contribute anything to the Maltese environment. Trees are planted to attract birds nearer to the shooting hides, which are built in strategic positions along these small plantations. Shooters also build rooms and shooting hides in the countryside where one is not normally allowed to build, and they build these hides and rooms illegally, without applying for any building permits.

One must also mention the damage done to overhead electric and telephone cables when shooters shoot at birds which perch on them, as well as the inconvenience and nuisance caused by the sound of guns and by showers of lead pellets which hit glass panes and fall on roof tops as a result of shooting in close proximity to inhabited areas.

On top of all this, there is the pollution resulting from lead shot and the litter from spent cartridges. In a study entitled *Fate of Lead in Maltese Soils*, Cachia and Taliana show that soil samples taken from a popular shooting area had 48.45 ug of lead per gram of soil – over twice the average amount of lead found in other areas. Other samples taken in popular shooting areas confirmed the result. Although Maltese soils, being alkaline, tend to stop lead from dissolving into one of its salts, the use of fertilizers as well as the presence of organic matter in the soil may bring about an increased tendency towards mobilization of lead.[3] Lead in the form of a salt is a highly toxic material.

Vella,[4] using the *Trade Statistics* and other information, estimated that about 230 tons of lead shot are used each year and stated that lead shot is a potential pollutant because it falls on or gets lodged in produce. The possibility of lead ending up as a complex ion in the crops through roots, has not yet been investigated locally. Some butchers have informed me that grazing animals, such as goats and cows, are known to contain 'a handful of lead shot in their stomachs' when they are slaughtered. This lead shot is likely to originate from pellets which get lodged in fodder whilst it is still in the fields, rather than being picked up when grazing.

Working on the figures given by Vella, 7.1 million cartridges are loaded locally each year. To these one must add 2.5 million ready-made cartridges which are imported. This means that a total of about 10 million cartridges are used each year. If one million cartridges are used for clay pigeon shooting,[5] while the other 9 million are used for shooting birds, and if one assumes that a bird is killed for every three cartridges used, then a minimum of 3 million birds are shot each year.[6] To these one must add the number of birds which are trapped.

Tourism and hunting

The number of tourists who visit the Maltese Islands has increased dramatically over the past thirty years. The figure of 19,600 tourist arrivals recorded during the whole of 1960 is now surpassed by far in each month of the year. The total number of tourists in 1990 exceeded 871,000[7] earning the Maltese economy almost Lm160 million.[8] With over 7600 people directly employed in tourism,[9] the tourist industry can be considered as a major contributor to the Maltese economy.

The largest number of tourists come from the United Kingdom – almost half a million each year. German tourists are second in line with over 130,000 and 30,000 tourists come from Scandinavian countries.

The season peaks during summer, but the number of tourists who visit Malta in spring and autumn is steadily increasing and these are also the times when bird shooting and trapping are at their peak. The larger the number of tourists who visit Malta at these times of the year, the larger will be the number of complaints regarding shooting and trapping because more tourists are deeply disturbed by the daily massacre of birds. Incidentally, gross earnings from tourism on a per capita basis during the first and last quarter of the year are consistently higher than those during the high season. This is because low-season visitors are more likely to be up-market tourists.[10] Undoubtedly, more tourists of this type, who tend to seek cultural fulfilment, would visit Malta in the more pleasant times of the year, spring and autumn, were it not for the shooting and trapping of wild birds.

There is a lot more that Malta can offer besides sun, sea and sand, but official brochures normally include only the usual 'touristy' activities and visits to museums. Attempts to organise tours based on visits to the countryside and sites of natural and scenic interest ran aground as tourists were reluctant to spend their holiday seeing caged birds at trapping sites and wild birds being shot and trapped wherever they went.

Although many tourists still visit Malta mainly to enjoy the sun at the beaches, others come to take a break in a favourable climate amongst hospitable people. They are attracted by brochures advertising archaeological sites, the historical heritage and other places of scenic beauty. On their way to these places, they constantly come face to face with sights of finches hopping frustratedly in cages. These are the same tame birds tourists feed on their bird-tables back at home, but here they are netted. Those who see colourful birds disappearing from the sky in a puff of feathers, get very distressed, but feel helpless. They know that it is the birds they pay so dearly to warden and protect that are being shot and netted in the Maltese Islands.

A tourism consultant commissioned by the Government to make a report on the feasibility of green tourism in Malta noted the evidence of extensive shooting and trapping and stated that 'spring and autumn visitors and those arriving at the height of the shooting season, would have to be extremely insensitive not to come in contact with shooters and trappers or not to recognise the gunfire'.[11]

Those who come during the hot, dry summer months are still able to get a bitter taste of the customary slaughter. During a walk in the countryside early in the morning or late in the evening, one may well come across a shooter taking pot shots at sparrows or roaming the place for a late migrant or a summer visitor. A walk in the afternoon may well bring tourists face to face with a shooter or a small party of shooters shooting at swifts. If tourists are lucky enough not to come across any shooting scenes, they cannot fail to notice countless numbers of spent cartridges as the crunch of metal and plastic underfoot betrays their presence wherever one walks. In places such as Chadwick Lakes and Għajn Riħana, as well as other valleys with dams and large water reservoirs, one is very likely to come across the odd wing of a swift or a swallow – leftovers from target practice.

The large number of small rubble constructions and raised pillars of stone cannot fail to attract tourists' attention. Many do not know what they are, and when they ask they are shocked to learn that all those stone constructions are shooting and trapping hides and that the raised pillars are the places on which caged decoys will be laid out to attract other finches to the netting site.

Letters in the local and foreign press highlighting this ordeal are very frequent. Foreign journalists have often written whole articles describing their experiences in Malta. Some have gone as far as suggesting a tourist boycott of Malta until Malta aligns itself with the rest of Europe in nature conservation law and its enforcement.

A number of television programmes, vividly showing the incredible slaughter of migratory birds, have been made and screened in the UK, Germany, Denmark and Italy.

Tourists who come to Malta in spring and autumn are bound to wonder whether the phrase 'the crack of dawn' actually originated here! They feel cheated that the tourist brochures they saw back at home featured only idyllic scenes of the countryside and rural areas, but omitted the more recent standard feature of caged, agitated, wild birds fluttering and rubbing their foreheads raw in tiny cages around netting sites, which pervade the most scenic places, and the ubiquitous shooters in search of tired migrants.

In their quest for killing and trapping birds, shooters may well be killing the goose which lays Malta's golden eggs. It is significant to note that following just one article in *BBC Wildlife Magazine*,[12] over 400 letters were received by the Ministry of Tourism, yet the song of the caged birds remains the same, while the birds which are shot are silenced forever.

Shooters and trappers tend to dismiss the fact that bird shooting and trapping harms the tourist industry. Some constantly claim that tourists who complain about bird shooting in Malta should see what happens in their own countries. Blood sports such as foxhunting and bullfighting are often used to justify the killing of birds in Malta. Although I do not condone any blood sports, there is one difference between shooting in Malta and blood sports abroad. A tourist visiting Spain is not compelled to see a gory bullfight and a visitor to the British Isles is unlikely to ever come across a foxhunt. In Malta, it is impossible to go anywhere and not see shooting, trapping or caged wild birds.

Shooting and religion

Religion plays a role in bird shooting. Christianity is influenced by the theories of Aristotle, who claimed that man is supreme. He argued that just as the universe revolves around the world, whatever there is in the world revolves around man. Hence, all creations exist for the sake of man. St Thomas Aquinas, the greatest philosopher in western Christianity, was greatly influenced by Aristotelian theories. It was then claimed that since animals had no reason, they had no rights. This idea that God created all living creatures to serve man's needs is deeply ingrained in Judaeo-Christian religious philosophies and continues to provide one of the rationalisations with which many shooters justify the wholesale destruction of birds.

The Church in Malta plays a very passive role in environmental issues, and that of bird shooting is no exception. Apart from sporadic efforts by individual members of the clergy, one can say that the Church in Malta, through its silence, approves that which goes on in the name of hunting.

'I am sorry when I hear someone swearing on missing a bird' – Christianity at its best.

A clear example of the passive role played by the Church is that the Church authorities do not even condemn publicly the shooting which takes place at Malta's largest cemetery – the Maria Addolorata National Cemetery. During both spring and autumn migrations, shooters shoot even while funeral services are in progress. Yet, one never reads or hears a single word of disapproval by the Church authorities about the desecration of cemeteries by shooters.

On the contrary, in a number of instances, members of the clergy have taken an active role in favour of shooting. Apart from a very early morning mass, called the 'shooter's mass', which is still said at a number of villages, individual priests have held sermons for shooters where shotguns were blessed. At a meeting for shooters and trappers, a priest even blessed a number of stuffed birds.[13] During some village feasts, sparrows with coloured strings tied to their legs have been released.[14]

TIMES OF MALTA, SATURDAY, APRIL 24, 1976

MASS FOR GAME HUNTERS

Game hunters surround the temporary altar as Mgr. Sultana blesses firearms at Xaghra.

More than 100 game hunters turned up at the locality known as "Ta' Kaccaturi" near Xaghra for a religious service at the start of the shooting season. The service included open-air Mass by the Archpriest, Mgr. E. Sultana, and the blessing of shotguns. All the readings during the Mass were by game hunters. A gun, bullets and game were presented during the Offertory.

The celebrant explained that the Holy Scripture speaks of the right to kill and consume animals and birds. The Law also gave the people the right to hunt. But the Archpriest also explained the dangers inherent in game hunting as well as the damage that could be caused through inattention to third persons.

The game hunters fired shots in the air at the end of the service.

Religion too plays a role in hunting. The Archpriest Mgr. Sultana is seen blessing shotguns at Xaghra Gozo during a specially organised mass for hunters. The early morning shooters' mass is still said in many villages.

Of saints and legends

There is also a legend which is interpreted as associating religion with hunting. An apparition of the Virgin Mary to a hunter is said to have taken place before 1452, but the legend about it was written about 220 years later by Fr F. M. Azzopardo. The legend, which talks about a dream and not an apparition, is recorded in Azzopardo's manuscript of 1670, and goes:

> Two noble youths, who were also hunters, left their houses at Mdina and as usual went hunting. When they arrived at the place where the hallowed cave is found, they saw a rabbit, which they tried to hunt. The rabbit dodged the hunters and their dogs by going into a hole in the cave. Both hunters did their best to make the rabbit re-emerge, but with no success. One of the hunters gave up and left, while the other decided that he should catch the rabbit and went into the cave. As he was very tired, he lay down to rest. The other hunter waited for him at the usual place where they used to meet to go home together, but he waited in vain. He went looking for him at his parents' house, but he was not there. They were very worried and after he failed to return after three days, they thought that he had died.
>
> It so happened that after fifteen months, while the other shooter was passing in front of the cave, he saw his friend walking out of the cave. At first he thought it was a ghost or an illusion, but he soon realised that it was his friend he was seeing. He was surprised to hear him say that he had slept for a few hours when he knew he had been missing for fifteen months. He was even more surprised to hear that he had seen a noble-looking, well-dressed lady holding a child. And this vision made him feel certain sweet feelings and he could not but conclude that the lady was the Blessed Virgin Mary, mother of God.[15]

After the 'apparition', the Maltese placed an image of Our Lady in the crypt, and later the Dominicans decorated the walls with various paintings. The original paintings had been destroyed by dampness through time. The mosaic medallions which are in place include one of Our Lady and a sleeping hunter. They are the work of a Maltese artist and were made at the turn of this century.[16]

Like most legends, this legend raises some questions as to its credibility. It is doubtful how one can sleep for fifteen months without nourishment and remain alive. But if one were to attribute this to some divine intervention, one could still question the legend on other grounds. Why, for instance, did the relatives of the hunter conclude that he had died when he did not return home after three days? Is it possible that the other hunter did not return to look for him in the small cave in which they had been together? Furthermore, what makes it more suspect is the fact that the legend is without any message and, as mentioned before, the legend is about a dream, not an apparition.

There is no doubt that legends are legends and should be treated as such. Some shooters maintain that Our Lady of the Grotto is one of their patron saints because it is claimed that there was an apparition to a sleeping shooter. One can also argue that the shooter was made to sleep so that the rabbit could escape death at the hands of the hunter. In which case, one can also interpret the legend as one for the protection of nature!

The association between shooters and Our Lady of the Grotto started after a precedent was set in 1957, when the Dominican Fathers invited shooters to participate in a pilgrimage on the occasion of the coronation of the venerable statue of Our Lady of the Grotto. The Dominicans wished that shooters be united in their veneration of Our Lady of the Grotto as their protectress. They urged shooters to wear their shooting attire or at least their hunting belt with cartridges and their guns. Shooters in rows of four followed the Dominican Fathers and a large number of devotees walked behind the shooters. When the pilgrimage reached the Dominican Church, the shooters lined the churchyard and fired several volleys as a salute to Our Lady.[17] The shooters kept participating in the yearly pilgrimage until 1986, when, as Fr L. E. Attard, a Dominican Father, wrote: 'some shooters caused great trouble to the Dominican fathers when, against all orders, they shot at pigeons, sparrows, electric bulbs and loudspeakers'. From then on, shooters were no longer invited to participate in the feast.[18]

However, other parish priests had borrowed the habit. At St Julians, where the feast of the Belgian Saint Julian is celebrated, shooters fire blank cartridges from the roof of the church as the statue emerges from the main door. This has been going on since 1983. Some shooters claim that St Julian is their patron saint and Azzopardi[19] wrote that using guns in honour of saints is a tradition; however he gives no supporting evidence. His claim that muskets were used by the militia during feasts is unfounded. The use of guns for salute, known as *feu de joie*, is associated with military activities and has never had any traditional connections with church festivities or civilian functions. Their claim that muskets were used in honour of saints, hence the word *musketterija*, is unfounded. *Maskli*, small metal containers filled with gunpowder, were used to fire petards, not muskets, as alleged.[20]

In the mid-eighties, the habit also spread to Mellieħa where the feast of Our Lady of Victory is held on 8th September each year. At Mellieħa shooters fire a salute from the roof of the official residence of the parish priest. In both cases, the participation of shooters is an official part of the Church outdoor festivities.

The Church authorities are not only giving shooters an opportunity to appear as some sort of devout heroes, boosting their image in the process; but the guns, which are used to take the life of God's creations, and which flout so openly the laws of the country, are allowed to appear as paying tribute to saints.

At a time when His Holiness Pope John Paul II is speaking of 'genuine conversion in ways of thought and behaviour, where Church and religious bodies, non-governmental organisations, indeed, all members of society have a precise role to play in such education' and about 'ecological awareness, due respect for nature and respect for life',[21] it is anachronistic and highly condemnable that Church authorities allow shooters to use their guns in honour of saints. It is no surprise, and may have been acceptable when the Dominican fathers started it in 1957. It was a different mentality then, and they realised, although quite late in the day, that it was more than just profane but managed to stop it in 1986. Yet, other sections of the clergy seem to think otherwise and not only allow it to happen, but even encourage it.

Of saints and men

The calendar of saints is a calendar whereby people associated saints with certain days of the year. Shooters too had such dates and there are a number of dates which are linked with shooting and trapping. Aquilina[22] and Azzopardi[23] list a number of proverbs and sayings associating saints with birds and shooting. According to this calendar, it was believed that redwings appeared between 25th January and 10th February, feasts of St Paul. The feast of St Gregory on 12th March marked the start of quail shooting, while the nightjar appears on the 13th, feast of St Joseph. The feast of the Annunciation on the 25th saw the departure of the skylark and the arrival of the short-toed lark.

The first migration of turtle doves took place on 23rd April, feast of St George. The second migration took place on the feast of the Holy Cross on 3rd May, while the third migration took place on 12th May, the feast of St Philip. According to the Saints' calendar, turtle doves could still be seen until the *Imnarja* – the feast of St Peter and St Paul, celebrated on 29th June. It was said that in autumn, turtle dove migration started on 8th September, the feast of Our Lady of Victory, while our Lady of Sorrows on the 15th saw the departure of the short-toed lark and brought the skylark. Another saying went that on St Michael's day (29th September), the skylark appeared. According to the Saints' calendar, finch trapping started on 16th October, the feast of St Theresa and by St Leonard's day (6th November), it is difficult to trap chaffinches. All Saints' Day on 1st November brought thrushes, St Martin on the 11th marked the end of quail trapping, while St Catherine on the 25th marked the end of the season for woodcock. Christmas day marked the end of rabbit shooting.

In a study about bird catching in Italy, Bondietti[24] noted that the Italian shooters have a similar calendar in Italy too.

In the Maltese Islands, the shooter is also represented in the Christmas crib! In spite of the fact that gunpowder and firearms had not been invented until well over a thousand years after the birth of Christ, many Maltese cribs include a figurine of a shooter. A member of the MUSEUM, a local Catholic movement, informed me that he had stopped making shooter figurines as children were placing shooters in a position to shoot at white pigeons symbolising the Holy Ghost and at angels![25]

Shooters' arguments

Bird activity in the Maltese Islands centres mainly around spring and autumn migrations. Migration provides an excuse for the shooters. Shooters argue that migratory birds are not indigenous, that they come to Malta for a very short time. Thus, one has to kill as many as one can for, once missed, that bird will never be seen again. Another excuse which is frequently used to explain why protected birds are shot is that 'if I don't shoot it, someone else will, so I'd rather shoot it myself'.

Little do the shooters know, and little do they care, about the consequence of their shooting. Those who do know, do not care. Many shooters do not admit that bird shooting affects bird populations. For example, Maltese shooters refuse to admit that the reduction in the number of turtle doves has anything to do with their shooting. In typical fashion, Maltese shooters attribute the disappearance of the former flocks of turtle doves only to building development and to lights at night which, they contend, scare the birds away. They also blame the destruction of habitat and the use of pesticides abroad. Maltese shooters are not interested in searching for the truth. They accept as true only what they want to believe.

Another argument which is used is that bird shooting is also a means of pest control. This argument is used by the shooters who continuously contend that the closed-season in Malta does not make any sense and that the Spanish sparrow, which shooters conveniently label as a pest, should not be protected during the summer months. The real reason for all this concern about the 'damage' that is allegedly done to the crops is that shooters want to be able to shoot all year round and still be within the law, and not because they pity the farmers, whose fields they trample so often in order to try to flush or retrieve birds.

The labelling of the Spanish sparrow as a pest is arrived at without the collection or presentation of any scientific data. In any case, the shooters do not want to accept that even if it is a pest, the gun is not the means to control it. A more expensive, less efficient means of pest control is hard to imagine.

The political situation

Local politics are dominated by two major parties and shooters do their utmost to blackmail the politicians with their votes. This is coupled with the fact that 'no Maltese MP wants to lose his popularity for a cause he is not the least interested in'.[26]

The situation has grown worse in recent years, so much so that even politicians who were renowned for their sympathies towards nature conservation, were no longer willing to speak their mind where bird shooting was concerned. The late Dr Anton Buttigieg, at one time Minister of Justice, who later became President of the Republic, and who was also known as the poet of nature due to the large number of poems he wrote about the subject, once said 'I will not sacrifice my political future for a few birds'.[27] When it comes to deciding upon issues related to shooting, most politicians prefer to be non-committal rather than call a spade a spade.

It is common knowledge that some Members of Parliament from both sides of the house have often tried, as some still do, to defend the so-called 'rights' of shooters, either by interfering in the duties of the police when they apprehend shooters in bird sanctuaries, or by speaking in Parliament or writing in the press in favour of shooters and shooting. Attard mentions a case where 'one contesting candidate promised a special reduction in the sporting licence for farmers'.[28]

In a letter to the press, Mr J. R. Scicluna, then president of the Association of Shooters, Trappers and Conservationists, sums it all up: 'Considering that no party wins by more than a marginal and minimal majority in Maltese elections, and also bearing in mind that the hunters of Malta exceed in number this very narrow margin and that they have the sport embedded in their very hearts, it is surely prudent for politicians to be careful to look after the interest of the hunter'.[29]

The Socialist Government did its best to please the shooters before the general elections of 1987. In a string of subsequent events, the closed-season for bird-shooting was illegally shortened by the Prime Minister, as was declared by the First Hall of the Civil Court on 29th July 1988. This case is, however, pending appeal proceedings. Two large public afforestation areas were given over to the Shooters' Association for its members to shoot in. The lands in question were given without any title or written contracts[30]. In another vote-catching exercise before the elections of 1987, Mr Denis Sammut, then executive director of the Bank of Valletta, and a candidate for the Socialist Party, signed an agreement whereby the Bank of Valletta sponsored the Shooters' Association with a sum of Lm5000.[31]

On 16th March 1987, that is after the dissolution of Parliament prior to the elections of May 1987, the Hon. Wistin Abela, then Minister of Finance and Customs for the Socialist Government, authorised the payment of Lm6250 as financial assistance to the Shooters' Association. These monies represented 50 cents from every paid shooting licence. In spite of the fact that there was a change of Government following those elections, the Shooters' Association still receives these monies officially each and every year to the time of writing.

It is most unfortunate that the issue of bird shooting is not high on the agenda of local politicians, and whenever it is referred to, it is used as part of the political game. As soon as the shooting licence fees were increased at the end of 1989, a poster against the increase was displayed at one of the Socialist Party clubs in Mosta. There was no such sign on the same club when the shooting licence fees were raised under the Socialist administration. More unfortunate is the fact that the politicians are either unaware of what is going on with regard to bird shooting and trapping or, if they are aware, they try to tone things down.

To give just a few examples, the present Leader of the Socialist Party, Dr Karmenu Mifsud Bonnici, has, on more than one occasion, spoken in favour of shooting. He said that areas should be allocated for bird shooting, so that shooting can be conducted safely away from the general public,[32] and that a future Socialist Government would allocate parts of the Islands for shooters and trappers, as it had done in the past.[33] On other occasions he argued in favour of bird shooting and trapping as such 'hobbies' keep shooters and trappers 'away from vices such as drugs'.[34] On more than one occasion he visited shooters at l-Aħrax in Mellieħa during the spring shooting season, where he was greeted with a fusillade of shots in salute. One such activity held on 12th May 1991 was an official activity of the Malta Labour Party.

Dom Mintoff, who was the Prime Minister in the 1970s, wrote that 'the record of the present and past generations in the preservation of all forms of wildlife has been discouragingly poor. Year after year, hundreds of thousands of migratory birds have been ruthlessly shot or trapped'.[35]

Yet, Mr Mintoff does not believe that bird shooting is a problem. He thinks that shooting is self-defeating, in the sense that the more shooters shoot, the less there is to shoot in subsequent years.[36]

On the other hand, Dr Stanley Zammit, Parliamentary Secretary for the Environment, visited shooters at il-Miżieb, one of the afforestation projects which the Socialist Government had handed over verbally to the Shooters' Association. The Parliamentary Secretary assured shooters that the government did not intend to withdraw lands which were being used by the Shooters' Association, neither would the government reduce or stop the annual financial contribution it made to the association.[37] Such an assurance was given in spite of the fact that a honey buzzard, a protected bird of prey, was shot in front of his very eyes during his visit to Miżieb. Dr Edward Fenech Adami, leader of the Nationalist Party and current Prime Minister, stated that the question (not the problem) of bird shooting has to be discussed clearly and calmly by the parties concerned and the right balance should be found.[38] Another example of noncommittal behaviour.

More recently, in an interview published in the Nationalist Party weekly Il-Mument on 19 January 1991, the Prime Minister said that 'with regards to hunting, I believe that he who says that shooting should be abolished is only dreaming and I don't think that such a proposal is in itself good. Certainly hunting has to be controlled, more so if it involves a rare species – protection should be real and not simply on paper. But more important is the aspect of education.'[39]

This partitioning of shooters and the vociferous anti-shooting community is unfair and discriminatory in more ways than one. Firstly, there are many more people who oppose bird shooting than is apparent at first glance, but they are not so open about it. Secondly, shooting takes place in the country-side, the same place where non-shooters seek their recreation. The rights of people to live in and enjoy nature is not acknowledged in the partitioning which local politicians place between shooters and non-shooters. One can also argue that even wild birds have a right to live and that man has no right to kill for the sheer fun of killing.

No official action

In the past, wildlife has aroused little interest among the local general public. The interest it aroused was only in shooters. The lack of general interest meant that shooters had a free hand. This resulted in a lack of restraint and responsibility among shooters for both the number of species shot and the quantity of the bags.

In 1870, Wright remarked that in the Maltese Islands 'nearly everybody has a gun'.[40] The Superintendent of Police, in his report of 1907 wrote that 'the considerable yearly increase in the number of licences to carry firearms for sporting purposes is quite out of proportion to the area of these islands, and, for obvious reasons, deserves the serious consideration of Government'.[41] On the other hand, Despott emphasised that it is not enough to have a law which remains a law on paper, and which is not enforced 'like it often happens'.[42] Four years later, Despott remarked that there were 'hundreds of guns and nets ever ready for any migrant' and that 'war [is] waged against feathered creatures'.[43]

In two subsequent editorials, in 1931, the *Daily Malta Chronicle*[44] wrote that the 'Wild Birds Protection Act is practically a dead-letter in every line of its wording'.

Payn[45] wrote that 'all who have written on the ornithology of Malta have bewailed the frightful slaughter of small birds which takes place in our islands. . . . During the migration periods, every adult male on the island seems to be prowling the fields with gun and a capacious gamebag, and those who are not are watching the clapnets instead. Every field and fruitgarden has its armed watcher, every small grove of trees in which exhausted migrants might take refuge is beaten through ten and twenty times a day'. He also noted that the laws were 'observed mainly in the breach'.

In 1949, Gibb[46] noted that 'despite legislation to restrict it, birdcatching remains the popular pastime of the country people. There is a brisk market for all species that may be kept in captivity or in glass cases as ornaments, or, better still, committed to the pot'.

Roberts[47] echoed previous writers when in 1954 he wrote: 'Those birds which do interrupt their journeys are offered small inducement to remain here for long owing to the activities of the so-called sportsmen who run all over the island mercilessly slaughtering or maiming everything in feathers'. Brockman[48] wrote that 'it is a great shame that no official action seems possible to reduce the indiscriminate slaughter by gun and trap which goes on' and, 'there is, it is true, a local ordinance which lists the protected birds, but I have never heard of a prosecution under it'.

In 1967 Hogg[49] noted that the Maltese have 'a passion for shooting anything larger than a flea that can be taken on the wing' and that 'for the Maltese, hunting connotes the persistent, relentless, round-the-year shooting of anything that flies'.

The late A. Gauci, a shooter who was Secretary of the Shooters' and Trappers' Association, wrote a number of weekly articles in a column entitled *Shooting Topics* in *The Times of Malta* during the early 70s. In one of these articles, he wrote that 'indiscriminate shooting at almost anything that moves at all times of the year is the order of the day'.[50]

Turner[51] wrote that 'although this vast slaughter continues unchecked, the Government of Malta is not in itself unmindful of the problem. But the problems of solutions are, or appear to be, so immense that no one will take an initiative. Nor does the opposition have any better conservation policies'. On the other hand, Gauci[52] wrote that 'the problem on the whole is not such an abstruse or complicated one. It is, rather, a very puerile problem if the powers that be had a shred of will to act. A dozen mobile cops showing up one day at Buskett, another day at Ta' Qali or any other similar spot, would do quite a lot to stamp out lawlessness'.

In the early 80s, Gauci echoed his previous statement when he wrote 'in the vast majority our present-day shooters are nothing less than trigger-happy shooters who revel in their bang bang against anything flying'.[53]

Flagrant abuses

The *Protection of Birds and Wild Rabbits Regulations*, which are currently in force, were published in 1980.[54] It was a Socialist Government which had already been eight years in office that made such regulations. However, these regulations have hardly ever been enforced. To make matters worse, the present regulations have a loophole with regards to the closed-season. During the closed-season for bird shooting, wild rabbits can be hunted. Some shooters pay the licence to shoot rabbits as this enables them to shoot all year round.

From statistics published by the police for the years 1980 to 1983, only one person was charged with infringements of the bird protection regulations.[55] This does not imply that shooters are law-abiding citizens. Bird sanctuaries like Buskett and the Addolorata National Cemetery, which have been protected since 1932, are literally infested with shooters – especially from mid-April to mid-May and through the months of September until December when birds of prey, and later thrushes and woodcock, migrate over the Maltese Islands. Even during the short closed-season one has to be extremely lucky not to come across a shooter at Buskett. It is the police force which was, and is still, failing to do its duty in this respect.

A problem which is increasing from year to year is the shooting of birds from sea-craft. High-powered boats, speedboats and rubber dinghies with high-powered engines carrying two, sometimes three or four shooters in them, go out at sea and wait for migratory birds from close inshore to a few kilometres offshore. There they shoot anything from ducks, herons, gulls, terns and waders to birds of prey.

What survives the barrage at sea and comes to land finds the rest of the army of shooters in wait. Nothing is spared. Large and colourful protected birds are shot to be stuffed and mounted. Turtle doves, thrushes and woodcock are shot for the pot. Smaller birds like swifts and swallows are very often shot at simply as target practice.

One can safely say that the main cause of bird killing in Malta is to satisfy the hunting instinct that some macho men cannot control. There is a stiff competition during the shooting season and shooters are often heard boasting of their bag or bemoaning their luck of having failed to kill that large or colourful bird; which brings us to the second reason behind the killing – taxidermy.

Bird stuffing

Taxidermy started becoming popular in the post-war period. It is another result of the rise in standard of living. Freezers and deep freezers are a product of our times and they enable the storage of carcasses for whole months, if not years. Previously what was shot had to be stuffed or consumed almost immediately, now it can be frozen and stuffed at leisure.

The introduction of field guides for the identification of birds enabled shooters to identify the birds which they shot and more shooters started paying attention to rarer species. Field guides today are even better as they contain colour plates, making bird identification easier. These guides, combined with binoculars which many shooters now carry with them in the field, enable shooters to identify the birds they shoot. The number of collections of stuffed birds increased, as did the number of shooters and taxidermists. Mr Vincent Sammut, who was a keen collector before the 1960's, informed me that there were only five taxidermists at that time. Now there are well over fifty, not to mention the ever-increasing number of shooters who stuff and mount their own birds. A look at the totals of birds in Table 9, which were stuffed by Taxidermist A between the years 1958 and 1977, shows that the number of birds which he stuffed and mounted increased from a mere 45 specimens in 1958 to over 1000 in 1977.

Nowadays, most shooters have a collection consisting of, on average, about 100 stuffed mounted birds, but there are others whose collections run over the 250 mark. Most try to collect at least the male and the female of the species as well as the immature. If there are colour variations or different colour phases because of moult patterns, then they try to add these to their collection as well. However, as a general rule, with the exception of ducks which change their plumage before winter and are practically already in breeding plumage in winter, the birds in spring are usually preferred for stuffing purposes as they are often in full breeding plumage and more attractive. One can often hear shooters complaining that the bird they shot is not fully dressed and thus not suitable for their collection.

The records of the three taxidermists on pages 156–165, may shed some light about the extent of the problem. One of these taxidermists used to stuff and mount birds for four consecutive years starting in 1983. During this time, he stuffed a total of 2041 birds of 140 species, that is an average of 42.5 birds a month. During 1983 alone, for example, amongst other birds, he stuffed: 48 red-footed falcons, 19 hobbies, 24 marsh harriers, 10 montagu's harriers, 6 pallid harriers, 3 sparrowhawks, 23 honey buzzards, 22 kestrels, 2 lesser kestrels, 1 long-eared owl, 10 short-eared owls, 8 scops owls, 13 kingfishers, 4 rollers, 3 wrynecks, 39 golden orioles and 10 cuckoos.

As can be seen from the above figures and the tables, the number of birds which are stuffed is very high. This number, however, does not necessarily reflect the number of birds killed. Some birds may be wounded and manage to escape being retrieved. Others are killed and left to rot either because they were too badly mutilated when they were shot, or because the person who shot them would already have more than one example in his collection.

A typical example is the kestrel. One can often see three or four stuffed in different postures in a collection. After that, a shooter will not mount any more kestrels, but he would still shoot them whenever they fly within range. The same can be said for the other birds of various species which are shot and are not even picked up; like swifts, hirundines and small waders.

Shooters' excuses

The excuse which most shooters use to justify the killing of non-game birds is that there is hardly anything to shoot at and that they shoot only one for their collection. However this is nothing more than an attempt at self absolution, because when there were heavy influxes of certain species, each shooter bagged as many as he could, irrespective of the fact that the birds were non-game birds and protected by law. There have been many such instances: the unusually large influx of red-footed falcons which occured during the closed-season in May 1987 when thousands of red-footed falcons were shot on two consecutive days, is just one of them. Magistrate Mallia, himself a shooter, wrote that 'people shot at them from the roofs of their houses'.[56] One could hear shooters boasting of having shot 29 such falcons on just one morning. I was shown a picture of a dining-room table which was covered with carcasses of such birds.

Large numbers of harriers are shot each spring, both from land and from seacraft. On certain days in spring of 1989, many were the shooters on land who shot four to six harriers each. A particularly lucky shooter in Gozo managed to shoot 19 marsh harriers in just one afternoon. He was the talk of the town for days on end. Harriers, like all birds of prey, are protected by law. In spring of 1990, there were large influxes of hoopoes and golden orioles on a number of days and many shooters shot dozens of them each day. Shooters are indiscriminate even when there is plenty of 'game' to shoot – at the end of April, during a strong migration of turtle doves, shooters shot at golden orioles, cuckoos, little bitterns and birds of prey that were grounded by bad weather along with turtle doves.

Many shooters used to (and some still do) go to places in which Spanish sparrows are known to roost. There they stand in wait and shoot at sparrows as they come in to roost.

All birds, especially those the size of a skylark or larger, are heavily persecuted and large bags of birds like golden orioles, are taken each year. During the spring of 1986, a shooter from Attard, for example, shot, amongst other birds: 37 golden orioles, 29 cuckoos, 11 kestrels and 4 marsh harriers.

Sultana and Gauci estimated that over 100,000 turtle doves are shot each year.[57] A bag record published in the fourth issue of the newsletter of the Shooters' and Trappers' Association called *Id-Dura* states that the average bag, based on 32 shooters for 1988, was of 9 turtle doves per shooter.[58] Considering the fact that there were 14,972 licensed shooters during 1987, at least 135,000 turtle doves were killed during 1988 alone. The average bag of 9 turtle doves per shooter includes only those birds shot between sunrise and 10 am. One has to keep in mind that during the hunting season, shooting takes place all day long and to the number of licensed shooters one must add a considerable number of shooters who hunt without a licence.

The estimate that over 100,000 turtle doves are shot each year is, to say the least, a conservative one. When one considers the fact that on average, shooters shoot at least 10 turtle doves each, and that on good years, the average number of turtle doves per shooter is at least thirty, then the yearly toll of turtle doves ranges between 160,000 to half a million. One must also keep in mind the fact that there are a number of shooters who shoot much more than the average bags I have worked on. In an article about turtle dove shooting, a shooter stated that there was a year in which he shot 202 turtle doves, while in 1982 he shot 110. He stated that, for a number of years, he shot between 50 and 80 turtle doves each year.[59]

Bird trapping

As Bannerman and Vella Gaffiero noted, apart from shooting, there is 'a much more damaging netting system in operation'.[60] Although finches are not usually shot, they are systematically trapped. Over a million finches are trapped each year. Most trapping takes place in spring from February to April and in autumn between October and December. Some trappers also trap wintering finches by feeding them and then catching them with small nets. Although forbidden by law, mist nets, which can catch any type of bird, are increasingly being used by trappers. Mist nets are quite often illegally imported from Australia and have been seen on sale at the Valletta Sunday Market.

A recent introduction is the use of tape recordings of bird songs, which are sold in shops selling shooters' goods. These destructive luring devices are very efficient. Sold at around Lm70 when they first appeared on the market five years ago, they now sell for half that price.

Many people trap robins in winter and yellow wagtails in spring. Finches, as well as protected birds like short-toed larks, dunnocks, buntings and tree pipits, are openly sold on the market. Their prices depend on the numbers caught – hawfinches sell in the Lm14–Lm35 region; siskins may sell between Lm4 and Lm40; a male greenfinch may fetch anywhere between Lm2 to Lm20; a male goldfinch sells between Lm4–Lm15; male chaffinches sell between Lm2 and Lm6. Female finches cost less than males. At the same time that a male chaffinch fetches Lm2, one can easily buy a bag with 10 females for that price. Being more abundant, linnets and serins are perhaps the cheapest finches on the market. One can often buy female linnets for as little as 5 cents each.

The high prices which greenfinches and goldfinches fetch lead to both legal importation as well as smuggling – especially from Tunisia and Sicily. Quite often, customs officials find quantities of greenfinches and goldfinches hidden in suitcases or wrapped inside the linings of jackets or hidden in false bottoms of vehicles. On discovering such birds, the Customs confiscate them and the offenders are charged in court. The birds are destroyed as they are feared to be carriers of disease.

A not so different situation

The Maltese Islands have often been described as a black spot for migratory birds. I shall not enter into the arguments as to whether Malta is in or out of the main migration routes. But from the following chapters one can conclude whether Malta is a real black spot or not – at least for those birds which dare to choose our islands as a resting-place during their long flight to and from their breeding-grounds.

The record of our dealings with the birds is black indeed. But there are some shafts of light in view. During the past decade or so, more and more people have come to appreciate the living bird in its own living world. More people are becoming aware of the need to protect the environment. Belatedly we seem to be learning to like birds, not for their feathers or for their flesh. Perhaps we are beginning to narrow the abyss our recent predecessors opened between our species and the avian kind.

Indeed, today's situation is different from that at the turn of the century. To begin with, in spite of statements such as Wright's, who said that 'nearly everybody had a gun',[61] which make one think that the countryside was crawling with shooters, in 1914 there were less than a thousand shooters, and in 1934 there were 2,745 licensed shooters and less than 700 licensed trappers. The number increased greatly in the post-war period.

In 1987 there were 14,972 people who had a licence to hunt and another 1313 had a licence to trap birds; that is a density of about 59 shooters and trappers for every square kilometre of countryside – a conservative estimate, when one considers the fact that many people shoot or trap birds without a licence. And, as if in an effort to further crowd with shooters the little countryside which is left, the local Shooters' Association wants the age for obtaining a shooting licence to be reduced from 21 to 18.[62]

A mere 50 years ago, guns and ammunition were not as readily available. They were also relatively more expensive and less efficient. Low income as well as less free time made it impossible for people to shoot as they do now. Aldo Azzopardi, a keen shooter and author of *The Maltese Shooters' Handbook*, wrote that 'every shot from the old family muzzleloader had to provide something for the pot; he [the shooter] could not allow himself the pleasure of a 'sporting' shot'.[63] Taxidermy was neither popular, nor widely practised.

There were less roads and transport was a far cry from what it is today. Few people had cars and reliance on the horse-drawn cart meant shooters could not travel far from home and many areas were hardly ever visited. As a consequence, species which were keenly hunted, like golden plovers, could winter in certain areas without any disturbance at all. Quail used to breed regularly, while the stone curlew was a resident breeding bird. It was last recorded breeding in 1911.[64]

As the late Gauci, himself a shooter, wrote: 'The real curse came with the ever-increasing high standard of living which brought within reach of everyone gunpowder and guns before minds had evolved sufficiently with the necessary intelligence in the proper exercise of this sport. The joy of handling guns was not enough in itself, but was superseded by the crazy joy of the kill'[65] and 'The coming of the automobile brought an upheaval in the sport of shooting and brought it within the reach of almost everybody. Out of a sport which required perseverance and stamina it made a game for kids'.[66]

These statements were further reinforced by Sammy Borg, a renowned shooter and a keen collector of stuffed birds, who wrote '. . . automatic guns have degraded shooting to the point where one can no longer consider it a decent sport but an expensive and destructive hobby, eating up the common heritage of mankind – in other words, another horrid creation of the consumer society'.[67]

In the past, it was also unheard of for Maltese shooters to go and spend two or three weeks in Gozo during the spring migration, paying as much as Lm100 to rent a shooting butt. Gozo has today become a holiday island for Maltese shooters who invade the island in force each spring and autumn. Naturally, friction is now very evident between shooters resident in Gozo and visiting Maltese ones due to a conflict of interests.

But today's situation is different. The jackdaw (protected since 1932), the peregrine falcon and the barn owl (protected since 1980) have had to be deleted from the list of our breeding birds, due to intensive shooting. But one no longer hears or reads headlines which boast of large and/or rare birds, such as pelicans, eagles, cranes or storks, having been shot. One now hears and reads about such shooting in a manner of shame and disgust.

This conscience has not been created by any intervention from the authorities, but it has been formed thanks to a handful of people who voluntarily laboured in conservation movements, and who, over the past

9. NIXTIEQ!

"Twitt, twitt; twitt, twitt;" qalet alwetta tittajjar.

— X'ferħ tittajjar u tgħanni fil-beraħ. Nixtieq kont alwetta!

— Imma inti ma jonqsok xejn, għandek kulma trid u tixtieq qalbek.

— Uff, kif dejjaqni kollox. U le, aħjar mitt darba li kont flok dik l-alwetta, bla ħsieb ta' xejn u dejjem tiġġerra!

Fil-ħin sewwa jinstama': Bumm! u l-alwetta taqa' mejta fl-art. Kien il-kaċċatur li spara tir u qatel dik it-tajra!

18   19

The shooting mania may be a result of the lack of, or the wrong type of education. The above picture story is about a skylark which ended up shot. This story, as well as another one about a father who bought a linnet and a cage for his son, was part of a Maltese textbook studied in Primary Schools up to the early 70s. For children brought up with such education, there was no inconsistency between what they learnt and what they saw.

twenty years or so, have managed to raise an awareness of the need to protect the environment – of which birds and man are a part.

The myth of tradition

Those who shoot today claim that hunting is a tradition. Bird shooting cannot simply be called a tradition because some people have been killing birds for a long time. As the statistics of shooting licences show, shooting gained in popularity in the period following the second world war. Most of those who used to shoot were people from the upper classes of society who saw hunting as a prestigious pastime. The increase in the number of shooters has nothing traditional about it. Apart from all this, one cannot say that hunting is traditional when non-traditional means, such as breech-loading and repeater shotguns, efficient shotgun cartridges, electronic bird calls and plastic decoys as well as cars, rubber dinghies and fast motor-powered boats and other non-traditional paraphernalia are used.

Even if one were to accept that hunting is a tradition, traditions may well be wrong. The Romans, for instance, had a tradition of feeding Christians to the lions. It was a tradition which we have fortunately outlived.

Some shooters say that hunting is 'natural', that it is an 'instinct'. Cats and other predators such as wolves and weasels have many adaptations for hunting. They have speed for running down prey, sharp claws for catching and incisive canines for tearing flesh. These biological adaptations, as well as other physiological and morphological ones, are present in natural hunters but are absent in man.

Primitive man was never a hunter, but a hunter-gatherer and one cannot speak of a hunting 'instinct' with reference to man. The 'instinct' was to obtain food, and not to hunt. Thus the claim that hunting is an 'instinct' is unfounded.

Even if one were to agree that hunting was 'natural', being natural is not a good enough reason why it should be performed in our times. We often have natural desires to do a number of things, but some of them we have to control if we are to live in society.

Some argue that shooting is a 'sport', and in a romantic vein, they try to describe the thrill of the kill, having stalked the bird with a dog since the very first light of day. Such shooters usually indulge in saying that their fun arises not from killing the bird but in seeing their dog rushing, pointing and finally flushing a bird from thick cover. But, in all honesty, the real fun, the climax, is not when the bird is flushed and takes flight, but when it is shot. If the fun is really to see the dog stalk, point and flush and not to kill, then there would be no need to shoot the bird when it takes to the wing. Indeed, there would be no need for the shooters to carry a gun at all!

Others try to argue that shooting is an important source of revenue for the Government. A leading article in *Il-Passa* (a monthly paper for shooters and trappers) stated that in the five year period between 1985 and 1989, the sum of over Lm690,000 was paid as duty on items related to bird shooting, such as shotguns, loaded cartridges, cartridge cases, lead shot and gunpowder.[68] This implies that the Government has a revenue of less than Lm140,000 a year from material which is used primarily for killing birds. A very cheap price which does not in any way compensate for the lives of millions of birds which are shot and trapped each year. Neither does it compensate for the social costs which range from pollution resulting from lead shot to the accidents and the risks and inconvenience caused to the non-shooting sector of the public.

Among the excuses used to justify shooting, the commonest one heard is that shooting is something which takes place almost worldwide, as if everything that takes place worldwide is in itself something good. Even if it were so, hunting is not practised anywhere as it is in the Maltese Islands. Nowhere is bird shooting so uncontrolled. Nowhere in the world are birds killed for the thrill of the kill for no purpose other than machismo. Nowhere, that is, except in the Maltese Islands.

We are living in a country and in an age where no-one needs the protein from birds or animals that one shoots. Shooting is not a sport, it is a fanatical passion. Shooting is a pastime. It is done solely for fun. The pleasure is in the killing and killing can never be allowed to become a pleasure in a civilised world. Bird shooting and trapping should disappear gradually. This should be a natural step in the evolution of mankind.

Chapter 2

Hunting Practices in Malta

There is a debate whether the sling-stones, which date back to 4500 BC, are the earliest hunting weapons used in the Maltese Islands.[1] The fact that, so far, only two spear-heads were found, as well as the lack of pottery bearing incisions of birds, animals or hunting and the lack of finds of wild animal remains makes one conclude that hunting was not an important feature of daily life in prehistoric Malta.

Except for falconry, we have almost no information at all about hunting and hunting methods before the 14th century, but in all probability, cross-bows and slings were used. In the Court documents of the 1480s, one finds an account where a witness testified that it was the habit of the accused to carry a crossbow for shooting rock pigeons in the west of Gozo.[2]

Falconry

The use of trained falcons for hunting was a popular pastime of the nobility on the continent. It is not known when or by whom falconry was first introduced into the Maltese Islands. Azzopardi[3] suggests it was the Arabs, but provides no supporting evidence.

In 1239 Emperor Frederick II annexed Malta to Sicily. Documented records show that a year later he sent a team of eighteen falconers with horses and men under the leadership of falconer Guiljermo Ruffino to report back to him on the number of falcons that there were on the islands, how they were kept and how many were caught from the wild that season.[4]

In the early 1400s, falconers were considered to be important people and were exempted from carrying out night-watch duties.[5] Both Abela[6] and Ciantar[7] state that falcon trappers enjoyed many exemptions due to the privileges and provisions laid in their favour by the overlords and their ministers, particularly the Viceroy of Sicily. Such privileges were given in May 1492 and confirmed in 1493. They were kept in force by various Grandmasters as they are registered in the Chancellery of the Order.

Bresc noted that between 1428 and 1458, the falconer, one of the few officials of the mediaeval administration, was a Maltese. The administration had very limited expenses and 'the only significant expenditure was on the hunting, capture, feeding and shipment to Sicily of falcons for the king. Falcon hunting was a major royal prerogative on Malta, and partly explains the king's interest in the island'.[8]

The birds themselves came to be possessions of the greatest value and were looked upon as symbols of power and influence. They even made their appearance on crests and on coats of arms. In the 15th century falcons were being used for hunting even in Malta. Specific mention of the use of a falcon for hunting is found in an account dated 1499.[9] During those mediaeval times, kings and nobility used to keep falcons and the Maltese nobility had petitioned the king to be allowed to keep a number of royal falcons, which were considered to be property of the King, 'as in Malta there was nothing to do except to go hawking'[10] and to prevent them from becoming 'idle'.[11]

The Knights of St John, who were granted the Maltese Islands in fief, were obliged to pay the yearly nominal rent of a falcon or a hawk on All Saints' Day.[12] However it later became customary to send a number of falcons to the kings of France, Spain, Portugal and Naples.[13] The custom of sending falcons to kings existed before the Knights of St John were given Malta. Written documents dated 1446 indicate that falcons were already being sent to the King of France.[14] In the mid-1500s, falcons were trapped both in Malta and in Lampedusa, where the Grandmaster used to send falcon trappers during the migration period.[15]

The obligation to send falcons compelled the Order to create the rank of the Grand Falconer.[16] The duties of the falconer were to prepare these falcons, to issue hunting licences and determine the dates when the hunting season was to open and close. At the beginning of the hunting season he had to send game to all the Council members of the Order as well as to the Inquisitor. He also had to provide game for the Grandmaster's table. The falconer accompanied the Grandmaster on his hunting excursions and presented him the gun, which was loaded by the chief hunter and carried by the pages.[17]

Some of the Knights may have practised falconry and under Grandmaster Lascaris, one of the buildings in Valletta housed the falconry of the Order and was the falconer's official residence. The street where it was located was then called *Strada della Falconeria*. The falconer had some supporting staff which included the posts of *cacciatore* (probably a falcon trapper), *guardiano della caccia* (a game warden) and *capo caccia* (a supervisory rank).[18]

Grandmaster La Vallette was very fond of falconry and had received a gyrfalcon as a gift from the king of France.[19] This grandmaster died at an old age following sun-stroke after a day hunting partridges with his falcon.[20] During his reign, he had confirmed the exemption from night-watch duties and taxes to those who manned the *paragni*, which were the falcon trapping stations. At that time, there were about 20 falcon trappers.[21] When the falconer's regiment was formed in 1751, its soldiers, who numbered 20, were exempted from paying taxes.[22]

Both Abela[23] and Ciantar[24] mention the use of *paragni*, a set up of net and a domesticated falcon used as a lure, with which other falcons were caught. This they termed as an ingenious invention. In his description of

Gozo, Agius[25] gives a list of 13 places where 20 falcon traps were set and states that in some years, up to 50 falcons were trapped.

De Soldanis,[26] who wrote one of the earliest Maltese dictionaries in the mid-1750s, mentions the *mansab tal-bies*, that is the trapping site for falcons. De Caro[27] and Haskins[28] describe hunting methods using falcons and trained dogs, some of which may have been used by falconers in our islands.

Game hunting

Hunting was a popular pastime for some of the Knights. In an account of Count George Albert of Erbach, who visited Malta during the reign of Grandmaster Wignacourt (1601–1622), one reads that hawks, crossbows and light firearms were used for hunting.

One also finds a description of Buskett, which 'consisted not so much of forest trees as of thick shrubs of many different kinds and of stunted oaks'. The account goes on to say that at that time there were 'about 60 head of deer and roe deer, as well as some African gazelles and here and there stood feeding sheds where the Grandmaster liked to watch the game'. For the stock of game, the Grandmaster was indebted to the Viceroy of Naples.[29]

In Gozo, between 1738 and 1742, the Knights De Marbeuf and De Remiking, who were both avid hunters, reared a quantity of rabbits and partridges for shooting. However, these were practically annihilated by shooters, as had happened to a previous stock some thirty years before.[30]

Ciantar[31] wrote about the hunting of several species of birds. He also mentions migratory birds like thrushes, doves and birds of prey as well as beccafichi (i.e. garden warblers, whitethroats and blackcaps).

Firearms make an appearance

It is indeed difficult, if not impossible, to trace the exact date when the shooting of birds was introduced in the Maltese Islands. Through Count Erbach's account we know for sure that light firearms for hunting were already in use in the early 1600s. In June 1582, an edict, which specifically mentions the use of firearms for hunting purposes, was issued.[32] Regulations were then issued in the form of *Bandi*, which were decrees issued by the Grandmaster. Various *Bandi* made it compulsory for shooters to obtain a licence from the *Gran Falconiere*. However, a licence as we know it today, which has to be obtained from the police, was introduced in 1854.[33]

Ciantar[34] mentions the use of the arquebus for shooting, but we read nothing about how popular this was. Shooting started becoming more popular when firearms started becoming more readily available. In 1864 Wright spoke of 'crowds of native sportsmen who sally out during the shooting seasons',[35] and later wrote that 'nearly everybody has a gun'.[36]

All kinds of birds were shot. On golden orioles, Adams wrote, '. . . luckless is the advent of the few that seek a temporary resting place on Maltese soil, for no sooner is their attractive plumage noticed than a dozen guns are put in requisition, when, if not annihilated, they are at least expelled beyond the precincts of the islands.'[37]

In 1892 Cooke[38] wrote about the 'unjustifiable crusade which is carried on, in season and out of season, against birds of all kinds'. Twenty-five years later, Despott wrote about the 'great slaughter wrought by sportsmen both licensed and unlicensed ones'[39] and estimated the number of shooters at a thousand, 'perhaps twice as many if we count the unlicensed ones, and to these may also be added another army of netters'.[40]

Besides the fact that local shooters neither had the time nor the means, those who had a gun shot only for the pot.

The song remains the same

Old time shooters will readily confirm that they shot at and ate almost any bird. De Boisgelin[41] wrote that 'flights of birds of passage come to Malta and afford much amusement to sportsmen, who shoot them with great perseverance'. Wright[42] mentions specimens of birds of prey which he had in his collection which were shot in 1861 and later noted that 'all kinds of birds from an eagle to a nightingale, are sent to the market as "game" '.[43] Adams too noted that 'the poulterers' shelves are stocked with all manner of birds, great and small'.[44] Indeed, anything from a stork[45] to a hirundine[46] was shot and exposed for sale on the market.

In his 'Notes of a Naturalist in the Nile Valley and Malta' of 1870, Adams wrote: 'Nowhere are the feathered tribes more persecuted than in Malta. I believe that I shall be within the mark in stating, that about one-half of the migratory species are captured or shot.'[47]

Seddall wrote: 'Malta fails to convey any impression of its being in any sense an ornithological paradise. Yet, with all these detracting influences, a day occurs now and then on which neither could the sportsman desire better sport, nor the collector a greater variety in his bag. Such a day, I remember occurred on 17th April, 1854, when, having taken my station on the shores of Fort Manoel Island, near the bridge, I was fully occupied the whole day in observing and securing specimens of the flocks of sandpipers, herons, and other waders, which descended every few minutes. . . . The oyster catcher, the glossy ibis, stilt plover, besides many other treasures, found their way into my bag.'[48]

Despott's works continually refer to species having been either taken or shot. Shooters were as indiscriminate as they are today, the only difference being that most birds were eaten and not stuffed. Some shooters used to try and sell game which they shot in order to buy more gunpowder and lead shot. In the 1920s, a turtle dove was sold for one penny while a nightjar would fetch half a penny. At that time, a farmed rabbit fetched one shilling three pence, that is, fifteen times the price of a turtle dove and thirty times that of a nightjar.[49] Payn stated that in the late 1930s scops owls sold for two pence and nightjar for three pence each.[50] In late April 1968, turtle doves sold for around one shilling each at the open air market at Rabat.[51] Gauci stated that turtle doves were sold at thirty cents apiece in the early 70s,[52] that is a quarter of the price of farmed rabbits.

Birds at the market

Writing about the nightjar, Wright stated that 'as many as 130 have been shot in a day by one gun' and that country-people in Gozo used to catch nightjars with a noose at the end of a stick.[53] This was still practised at Wardija in Malta in the early 1900s.[54] The old folk in Gozo say that they used to catch nightjars 'bil-ħafura', that is using the stem of the wild oat grass (Avena sterilis).[55] Such a method of capture was also used at Baħrija.[56] When mentioning birds like the hoopoe, Despott states that 'great numbers are taken . . . and many are brought over into the market, where they are sold as an article of food'.[57]

Wright noted that 'it [the scops owl] is sold in great numbers, with nightjars and other birds for the table and is considered good eating by the natives'.[58] This was still common practice in Despott's times, who noted that thousands of nightjars were shot and many ended at the market together with large quantities of scops owls.[59] Despott wrote 'I have many times seen, in my visits to the Valletta Market, large heaps consisting of several hundreds of these birds'[60] – to give a few examples: 23 were noted on 7th April 1916, 277 were noted on 8th April while 75 were noted on 15th April. Shooters used to shoot scops owls in the carob trees during the day, when the birds were resting.[61]

When shooting scops owls, shooters used cartridges loaded with less lead shot and gunpowder. This was done both to economise on ammunition and because the birds were shot at very close range.

To give an idea of the large quantity of scops owls which used to be shot by individual shooters, it is enough to quote Despott, who wrote: 'Passing through Wied Zembak, I met a man who had killed 11 scops owls, and I learned from him that he had taken 28 of these birds the day before'.[62]

According to Despott, practically any species of bird was sold on the market in Valletta. His records of 27th March 1916 read: 'The birds noted at the market to-day were the following: 126 hoopoes, 32 wheaters, 79 wrynecks, 288 rock-thrushes, 6 larks, 3 redshanks, 3 marsh harriers, 5 montagu's harriers, 4 moorhens, 4 spotted crakes, 1 short-eared owl, 8 scops owl, 1 bittern, 1 purple heron, 17 Spanish sparrows, 75 quails, 12 song thrushes, 2 ringed plovers, 2 stone curlews, 2 kestrels, and 1 lesser kestrel'.[63]

Nets known as bat-nets or regna, though illegal, were widely used both for finch trapping[64] as well as for other birds like nightingales, which went for the pot.[65] The licence for bird trappers was introduced in 1932. In 1936, the number of licensed trappers stood at 700.

Laws were openly defied and birds which were then protected such as warblers, nightingales, starlings and golden orioles, were often sold on the market sometimes with their feathers plucked to make their identification more difficult.[66,67] Payn wrote that from his personal observation, laws were 'observed mainly in the breach'.[68]

Shoot less to kill more

Small birds which were considered as game were hardly ever shot on the wing. Despott talks about the shooting of wagtails while they were roosting, 'amongst which great havoc was wrought both by fowlers and the so-called sportsmen. One of these killed 34 of them in a single shot, from the canes at the bottom of Wied Zembak. . .'.[69] Writing about bee-eaters, Wright stated: 'Towards the evening, they settle to roost on carob trees, and nestle so close to one another that I have known as many as twenty or thirty to be brought down with one shot'.[70] Azzopardi remarks, 'It was carefully drummed into the young mind not to waste a cartridge on a single lark but to wait until a number of them could be had in one shot as they lay close together on the ground.'[71]

The same can be said for other species, which today are frequently shot on the wing like swallows, martins and thrushes. Swallows were often shot at while they were resting on wires so that as large a number as possible were killed with a single shot.[72] In the case of thrushes, old shooters have told me how they used to rig a small milk tin with some stones in it in carob trees. When a thrush settled in the tree, rather than flushing it by throwing a stone at the other end of the tree to shoot the bird when it flew out, they used to pull gently at the string attached to the tin which made a faint rustling noise. This made the thrush emerge from the thick cover and sit on an outer branch, where it was more easily shot – to economise on cartridges.[73] This method of using rigged tins to flush birds is still sometimes used and I have seen such tins rigged up in the middle of a small eucalyptus plantation on the outskirts of Qormi close to the airport. A similar method of flushing birds is also known to be used in Italy.[74]

Shooters shot at harriers and used to lure them with quail-call.[75] This method is still practised today. Schembri[76] and Gulia[77] wrote that the fat of harriers was used as a balm for treating wounds, ulcers and glandular blockages. Sultana and Gauci state that in the past, breast feathers of herons were placed on wounds instead of ointment.[78]

The shooting of raptors remained a common practice and Despott wrote: 'We had a plentiful passage of several harriers and hawks, amongst which great havoc was made by sportsmen'.[79] Although some birds were stuffed and mounted, very few shooters had collections – the practice of taxidermy has only gained popularity in recent times. For instance Despott wrote that there were a number of small collections and mentioned only 11 collections, including his own.[80]

Needless to say, there were those few who could afford to shoot and who shot solely for sport. General Sir Frederick Ponsonby, who governed Malta between 1827–36, had a shooting resort at Marfa and certain people, especially guests of the Government or distinguished people, were invited to accompany the Governor on shooting expeditions. In one of his letters from Malta, Disraeli wrote that he had accompanied the Governor on a shooting expedition.[81] Schembri recorded that General Ponsonby shot two extremely rare birds – a demoiselle crane[82] near Corradino and in 1835 he shot a great bustard[83] at Marfa.

Baden Powell, who was in Malta in the early 1900s, used to shoot woodcock at the Governor's country palace at Buskett – of which he was in charge. Powell wrote: 'I arranged with the head gardener that when any woodcock were seen, he was to hoist a yellow flag on the tower. This was visible to me from my office eight miles away in Valletta. When I saw the flag flying, I would jump into my cart and drive out to Verdala, and the gardener in the meantime would have called together a few beaters, and we would proceed to get the cock.'[84]

Despott wrote about the indiscriminate shooting of shearwaters, especially in summer. He wrote that during summer time, boat loads of shooters, often without a licence, used to go out of the bays of Marsascala and Marsaxlokk towards sunset and cause a real massacre of shearwaters. The birds were not used for anything but simply shot for fun though fishermen used to pluck their underwing feathers for use as bait.[85]

Trap shooting

The fact that, earlier last century, there were people who could afford to shoot, could be borne out by the fact that a gun club existed. The Malta Gun Club was already in existence in 1827.[86] Shooting competitions using live and clay pigeons, as well as turtle doves, were frequently organised. Turtle doves were considered to be better sport as they were more agile.[87] In the case of pigeons, sometimes two birds were released simultaneously from different traps.[88] Pigeon shoots were held in winter while turtle dove shooting competitions were held in May and June – during and immediately after the spring migration. Trapped turtle doves were usually sold for shooting matches.

Competitions were held on the grounds of the Gun Club (sometimes referred to as the Malta Garrison Gun Club) at Tigne and they were often organised for a prize. The competitors were mostly locally stationed British servicemen and visiting ones as well as members of high society. The oldest published result is that of a pigeon shooting match which took place on 5th September 1832 between servicemen of the army and navy.[89]

The club met with difficulties finding a new premises in November 1888, and a site close to Manoel Island was identified,[90] but one does not read any more of the club until 1907, when Muscat's, then leading agents for sporting and other goods, set up a shooting school and a shooting ground at Marsa, where all kinds of shooting – including clay-pigeon shooting – could be practised. The grounds could be hired for private practice and matches.[91] Ground charges were three pence for an afternoon while clay pigeons and cartridges cost a penny each. Guns were hired for one shilling per afternoon.[92]

The Malta Shooting Club was formed soon after with a club premises at Valletta. Several sporting firms in England offered silver cups and other prizes to the nascent club. The subscription fee for membership was £1 4s and the first registration was 10s.[93] The fees indicate that membership was restricted to the upper classes. Shooting competitions were held first at Marsa, and later at the club's shooting ground at Attard.[94] One comes across regular adverts and results of shoots until 1915.[95]

A typical advert reads:

> MALTA SHOOTING CLUB turtle doves shooting sweepstake competition will be held on Sunday 23rd instant at 3 pm. Friends and members are cordially invited. They may also take part at the said competitions, under the usual conditions.[96]

The prizes for trap shooting competitions were often sponsored by Muscat's, who were agents for sporting goods, as well as for guns and ammunition. During such competitions, only their cartridges could be used.

Competitors had to be members of the Malta Shooting Club or their friends and had to pay the entrance fee for the competition. This depended on the prize and varied between 1s 6d and 10s. Non-members used to place themselves around the shooting range to shoot at the birds which the competitors failed to kill.[97]

The club probably encountered difficulties as after the shoot of 3rd June 1915 the next advert for a shoot is that of June 1923.[98] It then probably disbanded, for in 1937 one reads of the formation of a new shooting club. Clay-pigeon shoots were then being held at the Mile End ground at Hamrun and later at Attard.[99] In 1972, the Attard range closed down and the range moved to Bidnija. At the same time, the Malta Shooting Club became the Malta Shooting Federation.[100]

Live bird trap shooting was made illegal in 1935,[101] legalised again in 1955[102] and abolished again in 1980,[103] but it still takes place and shooting competitions using both live as well as clay pigeons and sparrows are often organised.

Although they are illegal, groups of shooters frequently organise such shoots. Sparrows are usually trapped at water-holes by the shooters themselves, or by their children, who watch or 'start' the birds during the shoot. Sometimes the birds are bought from others who trap them specially for that purpose. The Maltese weekly *It-Torċa* reported that sparrows were being bought at 2 cents each. In the same story it was reported that often large quantities of birds were shot and that carcasses of birds were gathered in small heaps and burned.[104]

When trap shooting of Spanish sparrows takes place, it is carried out by placing the birds singly on a platform in a closed box. There are two main types of boxes from which birds are released. One has a spring which tosses the bird into the air, while the other is a closed box except for a wire-mesh front. The birds are inserted through a small hole and the box is placed facing away from the shooters. The bird flies when a string which raises the front is pulled.

The spring-operated box has a platform which compresses a spring which is kept compressed by a lever. When the string which is attached to the lever is pulled, the spring hurls the bird in the air to be shot at. With pigeons, they are either placed singly on the ground under a box, from where they fly when the box is pulled over by a string, or else they are tossed in the air by hand. During competitions at the shooting club, there used to be three boxes and the shooter did not know from which box the turtle dove was going to be released. Someone used to throw dice and signal to another official which string to pull.

Some cheating, resulting in cruel practices, takes place during these competitions. Sometimes the person responsible for releasing the birds to be shot is also entrusted with loading the traps. If he wants a certain shooter to have a better chance, he squeezes the bird before he places it in the box. When the bird is flung in the air, it is hardly able to fly and thus provides a very easy target. If, on the other hand, the 'starter' wants to act against a certain competitor, one of the birds' claws is pulled or broken. This makes the bird fly more rapidly because of acute pain.[105]

BOX USED FOR TRAP SHOOTING

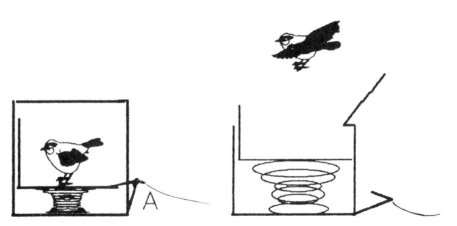

When the lever A is pulled, the compressed spring is released and the bird is hurled in the air, only to be shot at.

Shooting for the pot

Although, as stated earlier, all kinds of birds are shot and shooting takes place primarily for fun, some of the birds which are shot are eaten by the shooters themselves or are given to people, usually the elderly, who like them.

The main game birds in spring are turtle doves and quails. Trained dogs are used for quail shooting and the shooters in search of quail walk to and fro, following their dogs in fields or other open areas. If the dog is a trained one, when it picks up the scent of a quail, it stops and awaits the signal from its master before flushing the quail. In this way, the shooter has some time in which to prepare himself before the bird takes flight and is shot. If the dog is not a trained one, it will flush the bird as soon as it tracks it, and the chances of the shooter killing the bird are reduced.

Turtle doves migrate singly, in pairs or in flocks and shooters await them in shooting butts. Early in the morning, shooters position themselves in their hides before dawn breaks. Turtle doves which would have landed at night, thus known as 'ta' bil-lejl', are the first ones to get shot. These birds are usually flushed by the shooters while walking to their shooting butts early in the morning.

When the echoes of shots before dawn subside, the shooters wait for the very first light of day and the migrating birds that come with it. Turtle doves are usually shot on the wing and some shooters use decoys to draw migrating birds within shooting range. Very often, turtle doves alight close to the decoy where they are shot while sitting – and an effort is made to kill more than one with a single shot.

Turtle doves were cooked in different ways, but the most popular country way was to make a broth and the cooked meat was then used in pies. Today, turtle doves are still cooked in this way, but with the advent of better cookers some are also grilled, roasted or dressed in a variety of ways.

Ruffs are mostly shot in spring and summer while nightjars are shot in spring as well as in autumn. Nightjars are usually shot late in the evening or before the break of dawn. Shooters usually stay out late in September to shoot them. Nightjars used to be considered a delicacy and some are still eaten today.

Dottorel, thrushes, stone curlews, woodcock, snipe and golden plover are the main game species which are hunted from October until April or May. Lapwings, which appear late in winter, are also shot.

Practically all shooters shoot thrushes. They appear in large numbers and are considered good targets. They are lured by cassettes, calls or, less commonly, by live caged decoy. Thrushes are usually shot on the wing but, with the exception of song thrushes, many are stuffed rather than eaten.

Woodcock are eagerly sought by many shooters and some almost specialize in their shooting. Woodcock are shot at dawn and dusk, when the birds usually fly around. During daytime shooters often use trained dogs to flush them from thick cover along valley beds.

Those who shoot golden plovers imitate their call using locally-made reed-pipe whistles. Some older shooters are renowned for their ability in luring plover with such calls, but today their whistles are ineffective when compared to the recorded call of the live birds played from the bird song devices.

Duck shooting is very popular and many duck are shot from sea-craft. Formerly, duck were shot only at the salt-pans, at places along the coast or in inland valleys and on water reservoirs in wintertime. Along the coast, especially in bays or inlets, one can frequently see clusters of plastic duck decoys, which attract migrating duck to settle down with the decoys, where they are shot. Calls are also used to lure duck within shooting range. Duck are shot mostly between November and March. Some shooters go out at night and scan water reservoirs with powerful battery-operated lights in order to shoot duck which would have managed to settle there during the night.

Spanish sparrows were also considered as game birds and many were shot in the summer months. Shooters used to shoot, as some still do, sparrows while these are flying to their roosting sites. Large numbers of sparrows were also trapped over water-holes in the summer months. Such trapping used to take place when the young were fledged, and sparrow pie was quite common to country folk up to twenty years ago. Sparrows are still shot all year round. Their shooting intensifies during the summer months and before the migration seasons.

Skylarks, which used to be shot in much larger numbers, ended in pies. Skylarks are still shot today, but more for the fun of it than for the pot.

The real shooters

As has been stated earlier, and as one shall read later, a negligible number of shooters shoot only at game birds. In 1974, when the situation was not as bad as it is now – with shooters numbering less than half of what they do today – the keen shooter Gauci wrote:

> In the simple days the shooter took comfort from the enjoyment of the countryside, the occasional thrill of the chase, the healthy sun and air, as well as the friendly chat with the farmers. The few and far between examples of such sportsmen today constitute the laughing-stock of the multitude armed to the teeth with tons of expensive ammunition, chrome-plated guns and all the paraphernalia which the trade offers for sale.[106]

Not all shooters shoot at any bird in sight. Not all the shooters shoot swifts, swallows and martins; but a large number of shooters, especially the younger ones, do. The great majority of shooters who do not shoot passerines shoot at birds of prey, large birds or colourful ones, irrespective of whether these are protected or not.

In March, most shooters go out specifically to shoot harriers in the afternoon, while, in autumn, they go out to shoot honey buzzards and other migrating raptors. During both these times, migration of unprotected birds is rather poor and shooters go out specifically to shoot birds of prey, and not game birds. I recall seeing at Buskett a turtle dove and a lesser kestrel flying past a shooter from different directions. While ignoring the turtle dove which was closer, he shot and killed the lesser kestrel. This goes to prove that some shooters prefer to shoot a bird of prey, rather than a 'game' bird.

Tables 4A and 4B, which contain observations of birds at Buskett, show that in September more birds of prey migrate and are killed than game birds.

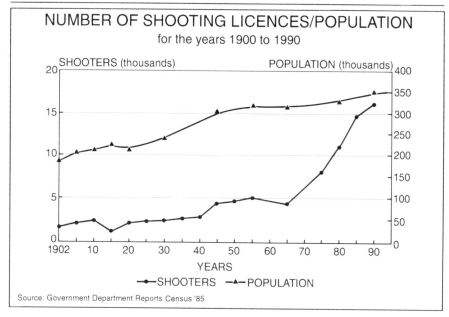

NUMBER OF SHOOTING LICENCES/POPULATION
for the years 1900 to 1990

Source: Government Department Reports Census '85

Note the increase in the number of shooting licences from 1,709 in 1902 to 4,716 in 1950. The increase in the number of licences started in the 1970s when the standard of living started improving.

TABLE 1

Proportion of shooters and trappers to the size and population of the Islands

Year	1957	1967	1985	1987	1990
Population	292019	302218	340907	343334	352430
Number of shooters			14629	14972	16760
Number of trappers			1440	1313	1528
% of population who own a licence to shoot			4.29	4.36	4.75
% of population who own a licence to trap			0.422	0.38	0.43
Area of Maltese Islands (km^2)	315.5	315.5	315.5	315.5	315.5
Density of shooters/km^2		13.53	46.38	47.46	53.12
Built-up areas (km^2)*	11.1	14.6	39.3	40.5^x	42.3^x
Unbuilt area (km^2)	304.4	300.9	276.2		273.2
Density of licensed shooters/km^2 of unbuilt land		14.19	52.97	54.44	61.35

* This figure includes only urban development and does not include roads and other developments which lie outside the building schemes.

^{x} ca 3000 building permits for new houses, each measuring about 200 m^3, are issued each year. This means that about 0.6 km^2 are built each year. Hence about 1.2 km^2 were built up between 1985–87 and 3 km^2 between 1985–90.

Sources: Structure Plan Brief – Town Planning Division, Parliamentary Questions 12242 sitting 194, 28508 sitting 544, 29328 sitting 553. Times of Malta 28.11.89.

TABLE 2

DISTRIBUTION OF SHOOTERS IN THE MALTESE ISLANDS (1990 FIGURES)

Locality	Total population	Male population	Number of licensed shooters	Licensed Shooters as a % of male population	as a % of village population
Attard	6045	2970	200	6.73	3.31
Balzan	4816	2367	150	6.34	3.12
B'Buġia	5979	2983	301	10.10	5.03
B'Kara	21218	10546	453	4.30	2.13
Cospicua	7895	3936	89	2.26	1.13
Dingli	2157	1109	235	21.19	10.89
Fgura	9070	4554	280	6.15	3.09
Floriana	3220	1575	15	0.95	0.47
Għaghur	2390	1216	257	21.13	10.75
Għaxaq	3843	1914	204	10.66	5.31
Gudja	2335	1127	140	12.42	5.99
Gżira/Ta' Xbiex	10454	5150	136	2.64	1.30
G'Mangia/Pieta	4460	2230	76	3.41	1.70
Hamrun	13697	6627	233	3.52	1.70
Kalkara	2126	1057	72	6.81	3.39
Kirkop	1744	884	97	10.97	5.60
Lija	3207	1568	181	11.54	5.64
Luqa	5633	2788	660	23.67	11.72
Marsa	7994	3991	187	4.68	2.34
Marsascala	2159	1107	101	9.12	4.68
Marsaxlokk	2539	1280	138	10.78	5.44
Mdina	414	189	15	7.94	3.62
Mellieha	4640	2334	276	11.83	5.95
Mġarr	2336	1196	254	21.24	10.87
Mosta	12812	6299	990	15.72	7.73
Mqabba	2349	1170	127	10.85	5.41
Msida	6136	2975	219	7.36	3.57
Naxxar	6823	3479	486	13.97	7.12
Paola	11912	5777	339	5.87	2.85
Qormi	19330	9611	462	4.81	2.39
Qrendi	2319	1151	143	12.42	6.16
Rabat	13192	6449	1446	22.42	10.96
Safi	1381	658	235	35.71	17.01
San Ġwann	8516	4364	274	6.28	3.22
Senglea	4224	2080	18	0.86	0.43
Siġġiewi	6212	3063	460	15.01	7.41
Sliema	13542	6416	117	1.82	0.86
St Lucia	3348	1728	99	5.73	2.96
St Julians	10285	5145	289	5.62	2.81
St Paul's Bay	4717	2365	241	10.19	5.11
St Venera	8101	3931	154	3.91	1.90
Tarxien	7088	3516	150	4.27	2.12
Valletta	9199	4368	26	0.59	0.28
Vittoriosa	3542	1791	26	1.45	0.73
Żabbar	13735	6972	680	9.75	4.96
Żebbuġ	10325	5088	589	11.58	5.70
Żejtun	11952	5937	467	7.87	3.91
Żurrieq	8435	4142	281	6.78	3.33

GOZO

Locality	Total population	Male population	Number of licensed shooters	Licensed Shooters	
				as a % of male population	as a % of village population
Għajnsielem	1790	888	211	23.76	11.79
Għarb	967	457	197	43.11	20.37
Għasri	342	157	63	40.13	18.42
Kercem	1442	725	220	30.35	15.27
Munxar	531	253	72	28.46	13.56
Nadur	3402	1614	767	47.52	22.55
Qala	1272	580	274	47.24	21.54
San Lawrenz	517	246	99	40.24	19.15
Sannat	1372	687	193	28.09	14.06
Victoria	6932	3320	600	18.07	8.66
Xagħra	3209	1575	577	36.63	17.98
Xewkija	2819	1360	360	26.47	12.77
Żebbuġ	1180	583	185	31.73	15.77

Sources: Demographic Review of the Maltese Islands: Parliamentary Question 28508 sitting 544, Parliamentary Question 29328 sitting 553.

TABLE 3

Number of paid trappers' licences

Years	1983	1985	1987	1990
Trapping licences	2529	1440	1313	1528

Source: Parliamentary Questions 12242 sitting 194, 28509, sitting 544.

TABLE 4a

A page from my log-book of observations of bird migration over Buskett. Observations were carried out on 18th September 1981 between 12.30 and 20.00 hours. The wind was southerly and cloud cover was of about ¼ to ½. It will be noted that the later it gets, the more birds of prey are shot. This is due to the fact that thermals start disappearing as the afternoon progresses and birds of prey lose height. One will also note that relatively few other birds are observed, except birds of prey, and consequently, more birds of prey are shot than any other species. (Note: re-seen means that the birds had already been seen that same afternoon. The term broadwing is used for any broad-winged large bird which is not identified).

Time	Birds observed	Comments
1230	13 Honey buzzards	
1235	2 Honey buzzards	
1245	1 Turtle dove	shot
1250	3 Turtle doves	2 shot
1255	1 Alpine swift	shot
1300	1 Marsh harrier	
1302	1 Falco species	
1304	2 broadwings	
1305	1 Cuckoo	shot
1315	1 Hobby	shot
1316	4 broadwings	
1356	1 Osprey	
1358	2 Honey buzzards	
1405	1 Eleonora's falcon	shot
1412	2 broadwings	
1416	2 Golden orioles	shot
1420	1 Honey buzzard	
1421	1 Hobby	
1423	1 Honey buzzard	
1425	1 Golden oriole	shot
1426	1 Honey buzzard	
1427	1 Lesser kestrel	
1430	3 Honey buzzards, 2 Kestrel sp.	
1440	1 Honey buzzard	shot
1440	2 Honey buzzards, 1 Kestrel	
1442	21 broadwings	
1448	4 Honey buzzards, 1 Kestrel	shot
1453	5 broadwings	
1455	1 Honey buzzard	
1500	1 Kestrel sp.	
1507	1 broadwing	
1510	1 Honey buzzard	shot
1511	2 Honey buzzards, 1 Kestrel sp.	
1515	1 Black stork	shot
1518	1 Honey buzzard	
1525	1 Honey buzzard	shot
1529	16 Honey buzzards	
1539	1 Lesser kestrel	
1541	4 Honey buzzards	2 shot
1546	10 Honey buzzards	
1552	6 Honey buzzards	
1556	2 Honey buzzards (re-seen)	shot
1602	1 Marsh harrier	
1603	2 Turtle doves	shot

TABLE 4a *(contd.)*

Time	Birds observed	Comments
1607	1 Marsh harrier, 1 Kestrel	shot
1609	1 Marsh Harrier	
1612	1 Falco sp.	
1620	1 Honey buzzard, 4 broadwings	
1631	2 Honey buzzards	shot
1634	8 Honey buzzards, 1 broadwing	
1635	14 Honey buzzards	
1640	2 Kestrels	1 shot
1656	1 Honey buzzard	shot
1658	1 Honey buzzard, 1 Kestrel	both shot
1659	4 Honey buzzards, 1 Marsh harrier	
1700	4 Honey buzzards	shot
1701	18 Honey buzzards (re-seen)	
1705	4 Honey buzzards, 1 Kestrel	(1 kestrel shot)
1720	4 Honey buzzards, 1 Black kite, 1 Hobby	
1727	1 Marsh harrier, 1 Falco sp.	
1730	2 Honey buzzards	shot
1732	7 Honey buzzards, 1 Marsh harrier (re-seen)	
1747	2 Honey buzzards	shot
1758	1 Sparrowhawk shot	
1800	4 Honey buzzards	
1802	1 Marsh harrier	shot
1815	2 Honey buzzards	shot
1816	13 Honey buzzards, 1 Marsh harrier (re-seen)	
1818	2 Honey buzzards	shot
1819	1 Honey buzzard	shot
1820	2 Marsh harriers, 4 Kestrels, 1 broadwing	
1822	1 Honey buzzard	shot
1825	1 Kestrel	shot
1827	2 Honey buzzards	shot
1830	4 Honey buzzards, 2 Marsh harriers	
1835	5 Honey buzzards (re-seen)	shot
1850	2 Honey buzzards, 1 Marsh harrier	
1853	2 Honey buzzards	shot
1900	1 Falco species	shot
1905	4 Honey buzzards	shot
1903	1 Lesser kestrel, 2 Kestrels	shot
1904	1 Eleonora's falcon (dk phase)	shot
1906	2 Honey buzzards (re-seen)	
1915	1 Falco sp.	shot
1916	1 Hobby	shot
1920	4 Lesser kestrels	2 shot
1935	1 Honey buzzard (re-seen)	shot
1940	3 Honey buzzards (re-seen)	shot
1945	11 Marsh harriers	
1947	2 Marsh harriers	shot
1950	4 Marsh harriers	1 shot
1953	1 Honey buzzard (re-seen)	shot
1955	1 Honey buzzard, 1 Falco species	shot
1957	1 Marsh harrier, 1 broadwing	shot
2000	1 Nightjar	shot

TABLE 4b
(Totals of Table 4a)

Species	Total seen	Total shot	Percentage shot
Black stork	1	1	100
Black kite	1	—	—
Honey buzzard	144	41	28.5
Marsh harrier	30	5	16.6
Sparrowhawk	1	1	100
Osprey	1	—	—
Broadwings	42	1	2.4
Lesser kestrel	7	3	42.8
Kestrel	14	8	57.2
Kestrel Sp.	4	—	—
Hobby	4	2	50
Eleonora's falcon	2	2	100
Falco sp.	6	3	50
Turtle dove	6	5	83
Cuckoo	1	1	100
Nightjar	1	1	100
Alpine swift	1	1	100
Golden oriole	3	3	100
Totals	269	78	29

TABLE 5
Percentage of birds of prey shot at Buskett

September 1981 Date	Total birds of prey seen	Total birds of prey shot	Percentage shot
13	12	1	8.3
14	56	5	8.9
16	89	29	32.6
17	265	44	16.6
18	255	66	25.9
19	171	35	20.5
20	71	16	22.5
26	23	6	26.1
Totals	942	202	21.4

The average of birds of prey shot per day is 20.2% of the birds seen.

Chapter 3

Changes in Shooting Paraphernalia

Early firearms and hunting

The first documented record of bird-shooting with guns in the Maltese Islands is that given by Ciantar,[1] who mentions the use of the arquebus, which was a type of match-lock musket. Match-lock muskets had a slow-burning fuse, which was brought to touch the powder through a touch hole when the trigger was pulled, thus causing it to fire.

Later, wheel-lock muskets, in which a key was used to wind a coil spring in a serrated wheel, came on the scene. When the trigger was pulled, the released spring revolved the wheel against iron pyrites, producing sparks which ignited the powder in the primary pan. It was this flame which touched off the powder in the barrel, thus firing the gun.

During the first half of the 16th century, flint-locks were already on the scene and match-lock muskets, wheel-lock muskets and flint-lock muskets were undoubtedly used for game shooting by the Knights of St John and by locals who could afford them. This is confirmed by the *Bando* of June 1582,[2] which prohibited hunting with the *scopetta*, that is, a muzzle-loader and other implements during the closed-season.

The urge to shoot made some locals use home-made versions of the match-lock musket for hunting. Ganni Borg, from St Paul's Bay, recounts how, during the early 1900s, he himself had made a gun using a short piece of water pipe, blocked at one end and tied to a piece of wood which made do for a stock. The gun was loaded from the muzzle and had a hole, into which the head of a matchstick was inserted. Whenever he wanted to shoot, he had to strike the head of the match against the match-box, thus igniting the powder and discharging the gun. A later modified model which he made and used was similar to the arquebus.

Breech-loading guns appear

The percussion cap muzzle-loader, locally called *xkubetta* was the next weapon to be used for hunting. These weapons were quite popular until the first breech-loading shotguns, in which the ammunition is inserted in the rear end of the barrel rather than in the muzzle, were introduced. The next improvement came with the introduction of centre-firing cartridges, from which word *senter*, meaning shotgun, was introduced into

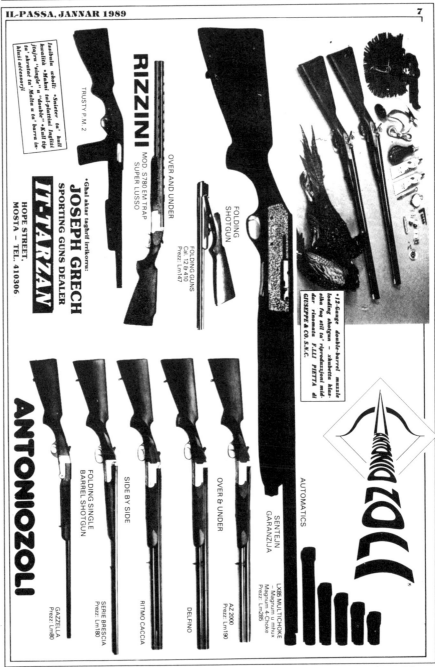

A typical advert advertising shotguns. Note the aesthetic military connection of the normal automatic shotgun. Even more macho is the TRUSTY P.M.2 MODEL. A variety of chokes, which control shot pattern and range are shown in this advert.

the Maltese language. Hammer guns, locally termed *senter tal-grillijiet*, came into use and indeed one might still come across an old farmer or a young boy wielding one of these museum-pieces. They are usually 16-bore, and their cartridges have smaller diameter and thus less lead shot, yet some are still in use along with many of today's 12-bore repeaters.

Following the introduction of centre-firing cartridges, a lot of changes in shotguns and other accessories related to shooting started taking place especially after the mid-1950s, when the five-shot repeater shotguns made their first appearance on the local market. Plastic cartridge shells gradually replaced cardboard ones. Primers, gunpowder, wads and guns have been changed time and time again, each time with significant improvements.

Changes in guns

Apart from afore-mentioned changes, screw-on chokes were one of the most significant improvements. Chokes reduce the barrel-diameter and control the shot pattern and ranges. These give the shot increased power and range and are quite fashionable, especially with the younger shooters.

Magnum shotguns were an innovation which reached our shores in the early 70s. These guns have a barrel which is about 80 cms in length – some 20 cms longer than normal shotguns. They use 75 mm (3 inch) long cartridges which contain 50 grams of lead shot. Because they have at least 20 extra grams of lead, when compared to normal cartridges, they have a longer shot-string, thus giving a denser pattern of lead shot, making them more effective at longer ranges. Old cartridges used to contain 30 grams (one ounce) of lead shot but today, besides the Magnum, which are normally used for Magnum guns only, one finds a range of cartridges which contain between 32 and 42 grams of lead shot as a standard load.

Better gunpowder

The gunpowder manufacturers improved on their products by stabilising them and by making them more powerful. Different types of gunpowder ranging from slow- to fast-burning are now available. The type used depends on the length of the barrel. Slow-burning powder is used with long barrels, since the length of the barrel allows all the powder to burn progressively, but still developing the desired velocity of the shot. With shorter barrels, fast-burning powder is preferred to give the desired velocities since all the powder needs to burn before the shot leaves the barrel. Powder burning outside the barrel is lost energy since it neither effects the range nor the velocity of the shotcharge.

Most of the gunpowders in use today are waterproof and practically all gunpowder is unaffected by winds. Old-timers will readily recall the 'white powder' which they had to use, which used to fail to ignite in damp conditions. It was slow to burn or failed to ignite when winds were southerly and damp.

In fact, most shooters who used to load their own cartridges loaded only when the winds were northerly and thus dry. Shells, wads and gunpowder were often left 'to dry' in the hot scorching sun. Often, different brands of powders were mixed and primers were primed with black powders in an effort to counter the effect of the winds. Loaded cartridges were frequently left out in the sun to prevent them from becoming humid.

During the war shotgun cartridges were rationed,[3] but this did not discourage shooters who frequently used cordite – the gunpowder used in rifle cartridges – for their guns. Cordite was extracted from rifle cartridges or anti-aircraft shells and ground in coffee-mills or rubbed on cheese graters. It was used in small doses and sometimes mixed with the black powder which was used for fireworks. Because of the high pressure which cordite exerted, many muzzle-loaders were ruptured.[4]

My grandfather recalls that even the primers of rifle cartridges were extracted. The cartridge was filled with water after the powder was extracted, and the bullet was placed in its original position. The bullet was hit by a hammer and the pressure created by the water forced out the primer. Due to the fact that rifles had a stronger firing-pin than shotguns, their primers were substantially harder. So, not to damage the shotgun firing-pins, primers were filed while they were still wet, and then dried in the sun before being placed in cartridges.[5] Shotgun cartridge primers were also often re-used after they were filled with a mixture of nitrate, while primers for muzzle-loaders were made from the tops of milk bottles, which were duly shaped and filled with a small amount of explosive.[6]

Plastic wads

Wads which separate the powder from the shot were made of different materials, depending on how well-off the shooter was. Country folk made use of scraps of paper, or bits of rags. A fisherman from St. Paul's Bay, who was also a shooter, used to load his own cartridges using bits of old fishing nets as wads.[7] Wads were later made of felt, cork, fibres, or *Boraggio chimico* – a mixture of sawdust, cork and paraffinated rubber which sticks together when worked between fingers or when pressed in the cartridge.

Today, plastic wads in the form of cups are widely in use. They are significantly better in that they give less recoil because they are lighter, since the heavier the wad, the greater the recoil. The cup protects the lead shot both from abrasion from the barrel and prevents the welding of the lead shot by the hot gases produced by the burnt gunpowder. The skirt-like washer at the end of the wad expands with the heat on shooting and the hot gases are thus effectively sealed off. This sealing of the gases gives better velocities to the shot since the gases which propel the shotcharge are kept behind the shot column.

Long before the introduction of plastic wads, both Fiocchi, an Italian firm, and Winchester, an American firm, used to load cartridges with a shot-protecting collar in order to protect shot from abrasion and welding. In a 1963 catalogue of Manufrance of St. Etienne, France, one can see cardboard versions of shot-protecting collars which are also advertised as increasing the range of the shot.

To solve the problem of shot welding, old-time shooters used to dip the wads in molten wax.[8] Such treated wads sealed off the gases better, but also gave them a bigger recoil due to increased weight of the wad. The legs of the plastic cup are designed to cushion the recoil. Another advantage of the plastic cup wad is the effective increase in range since the shot is kept concentrated over a larger distance.

The use of plastic shells has eliminated the risk of damp gunpowder, since they are less prone to absorb moisture than cardboard shells. Also, better powders give today's cartridges an incredible speed. Some locally manufactured cartridges match foreign ones in quality. Punch and Pattern cartridges, which are manufactured locally, are frequently advertised as having velocities in the range of 387 to 407 metres per second.[9]

A type of gunpowder available only recently on the local market gives heavy loads of over 36 grams of shot the same velocities as light ones used in trap shooting. High velocity cartridges help shooters as they can shoot directly at a bird rather than having to calculate where the bird will be when they shoot.

Special cartridges

Other developments in the field of cartridges came with spreader cartridges. These are mostly used very early in the morning when birds usually fly at a very close range and, as their name implies, they scatter the shot over a wide area in a very short distance. Old-time shooters tried to achieve this effect either by mixing lead shot of different sizes or by flattening some lead shot and loading it on top of the wad separating the gunpowder from the shot, the rest of the shot being placed immediately on the flattened lead shot. Another method, which some shooters who load their own cartridges still use, is to divide the shot into three equal parts and to separate each measure of shot in the cartridge by a thin cardboard wad. Some shooters prefer to use different sizes of lead shot between each wad in such loads.

Nowadays spreader cartridges have either a cardboard cruciform separator which separates the shot into four equal parts or a plastic wad with a plastic cruciform separator. These separators spin in the barrel and are slightly crushed at the narrower end of the barrel. This causes the shot to scatter over a short distance. Some shooters load cartridges with home-made cruciform separators made out of thick cardboard, since this causes the shot to scatter more at very short distances. Shooters generally use such cartridges for quail shooting, since quails are flushed and shot at a very close range.

In other types of spreader cartridges, both locally loaded as well as French-loaded ones, one finds a plastic wad with fins around a circular container in its middle. This type of wad divides the lead shot into five equal parts and, while spreading that part of the shot which lies alongside the fins, it sends, without dispersing it, the middle part of the shot. Thus it spreads the shot less than a normal spreader but more than a normal cartridge.

RC, an Italian firm producing cartridges which are used in the Maltese Islands, produces a spreader load called *Dispersante* which are loaded with flat lead shot, also giving a spreader effect. A number of French firms

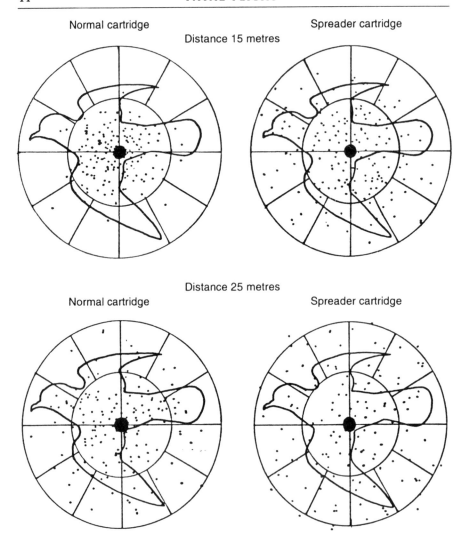

Shot patterns. Note that with normal cartridges, the shot is still concentrated at
25 metres; thus one has to shoot very accurately to kill. With spreader cartridges,
the shot is scattered and thus one does not need to shoot as accurately to kill.

produce spreader cartridges which are loaded with cube-shaped shot. These
cartridges are sometimes available locally, but they are not very popular as
they are perceived as too erratic and dangerous by most shooters.

One cannot fail to mention that today's lead shot is significantly better in
the sense that it is rounder and harder and thus more stable. It was common
to come across lead shot which is not spherical in cartridges loaded say 15
years ago. Such shot is rather erratic in its pattern.

Cartridges which were imported from abroad were rather too expensive for most shooters. Thus, relatives who had emigrated to countries like Canada and America frequently sent, or brought over with them, that 'priceless' box of factory-manufactured cartridges as a gift. The rising standard of living gave people money to spend. The cost of raw material made home-loaded cartridges almost as expensive as factory-loaded ones, which were also better. Thus more shooters started using foreign cartridges and achieving better results, especially when shooting birds at longer ranges.

Locally-made cartridges

Today, there is a small manufacturing industry which produces cartridges for the ever-increasing local market. One can find a number of brand names, and at least 4 million cartridges are loaded by local manufacturers each year. Franwin and Pelican are the two leading brand names each loading an average of 2 million cartridges per year. Besides Franwin and Pelican, there are at least ten other brand names of locally-made cartridges.

Locally-made cartridges are nowadays significantly cheaper than foreign cartridges but match them in quality. In an article about one of the local companies, it was stated that it started off as a small business concern where cartridges were hand-loaded. Then it developed into a factory where a machine which loaded 800 cartridges an hour was bought in 1973. A bigger machine had to be bought four years later to meet the demand.[10] Machines in use today are capable of loading 3500 cartridges per hour.

In 1974, it was estimated that about 80 per cent of local shooters loaded their own cartridges.[11] By the amount of factory-loaded spent shells, which one sees littering our countryside, one concludes that the figure must now be only a fraction of what it was in 1974.

The home-loaded variety are usually heavy calibre ones. These are used for birds of prey and other large birds which may be out of the range of a normal cartridge. Since the sale and use of lead shot which is larger than 3.2mm is illegal, cartridges with large size lead shot are not easily available; however they can be bought on the black market. Cartridges containing only nine pellets, hence their Maltese name *tad-disa' ċombiet*, are frequently used and by the roundness of the pellets it is evident that the lead shot is being manufactured professionally and is not homemade.

Heavy gauges

The urge to kill at longer ranges and higher altitudes made shooters experiment and develop special loads. At one time, chained pellets were commonly used for shooting large birds which were out of range. Manufactured in Ancona, Italy, they were designed for ranges between 100 and 150 metres. In 1972 the keeping, sale and use of such cartridges was made illegal. The .22 rifle was commonly used to shoot large birds between the 1960s and the mid-70s.[12] They are still used today.

Some shooters make large-size lead shot themselves; others load a single slug in the shape of a bullet. The use of heavy-gauge ball-bearings instead of lead shot is still a common practice. Both Azzopardi[13] and Gauci,[14] advised against it as it is dangerous to the shooter. In spite of the dangers, they are still being produced and are commonly used in places like Buskett where hundreds of raptors are killed each year.

Another method which is commonly used to increase the range is that of cutting the cartridge at various places around the wad which separates the powder from the shot, before the cartridge is placed in the magazine. This weakens the shell so that when the gun is fired the shell of the cartridge breaks and the uppermost half of the cartridge which contains the lead shot comes out as a whole. The shot, kept together like a bullet, is carried over incredible distances. It is however rather erratic and very dangerous.

The pouring of molten wax over the shot before the cartridge is closed and wrapping the shot in tin foil are other ways to increase range. Some shooters fill the plastic cup wads with heavy gauge lead shot and lubricating grease as they believe that the range of the shot is increased in this way.

Calls and decoys

De Boisgelin wrote that 'the Maltese are remarkable for imitating the notes of different birds, and catch them with surprising skill'.[15] Scicluna wrote that the local shooter has to 'be able to use lures and bird-calls in a professional fashion'.[16] The bird trapper had to rely only on song birds which he placed around the trapping sites. Many shooters today still use calls and whistles to attract birds, and a locally manufactured whistle made of great reed is used to attract golden plover, dottorel, stone curlew and curlew. Some shooters also use such a whistle to imitate the call of the widgeon.

There are a number of people well-known for making reed-pipe whistles. They now cost between Lm1.50 and Lm3, depending on their quality. Calls made out of bamboo cost Lm8. Higher prices are paid for whistles which are considered to be exceptional. In the 1930s, a very good plover call cost 2s 6d – which was equivalent to a day's pay.[17]

Golden plover whistles were often decorated. Many had a silver mouthpiece, while others had a silver jacket around the upper part of the whistle. I have seen a whistle with a gold mouthpiece, for which two gold rings had been melted. Occasionally, one comes across plover whistles which have some engraving or which are made of bone, instead of reed. Keen old time plover shooters used two whistles when calling plover. They used one with a lower frequency when the plover they were calling was still far off, while a smaller whistle with a higher frequency was used when the bird was getting nearer.[18]

The call of lapwings is imitated by a pencil-like whistle which has a slit in which a piece of stretched elastic vibrates when the whistle is blown. Some shooters make these calls themselves using two thin pieces of reed and a piece of a palm frond. Some shooters are able to imitate the lapwing call by blowing a piece of grass held tightly between their fingers.[19]

Calls for ducks are imported from Italy and the United States. These cost around Lm4.50 and shooters also use them to lure herons.

A special type of call, called *kwaljarin* (colloquially called *kirjolin*) is used for attracting quail. This call is Italian in origin, and the Maltese name has been derived from the *quagliere*, which was described by Franceschi.[20] It is made of a piece of leather which is sown in the form of a tube, or a piece of rubber tubing, which is wrapped around a whistle. The whistle is most commonly made of reed. Local shooters often made them from pieces of bone, bits of metal or hard plastic pipe, which were sealed at one end or spent rifle cartridges in which a slit was carved. When the call was too harsh, a small hole was drilled to make the call softer.[21]

The call of the female quail is copied by holding the whistle between the fingers of one hand while tapping on those fingers with the other hand. Thus the air in the rubber tubing is compressed and released through the whistle, which gives out the right sound. Both lapwing and quail calls can be bought for about Lm1 each.

The call of the male quail was imitated by a locally-made whistle carved out of stone, or stamped out of lead and later, aluminium. The call was a flat piece of stone or metal, into which a shaft was carved, with a small hole running through it. It was small enough to fit into one's mouth and the air blown through it produced the call. Such calls were an innovation in the 1930s; before then, only the call of the female could be imitated.[22]

Whistles to lure song thrush and skylark are imported from Italy. Song thrush calls cost around 50 cents each and are made of a piece of collapsible tubing, into which the whistle is inserted. Shooters hit the collapsible part of the whistle against their chest and the compressed air which flows through the whistle gives out the flight call of the song thrush. The call for song thrush is sometimes called '*tal-mea culpa*', because its method of operation entails the beating on one's chest which is similar to the symbolic gestures one makes in the act of contrition.[23]

Shooters, who were better-off financially 30 years ago, were able to afford clockwork versions of song thrush calls. These calls had a clockwork mechanism which, when wound, started giving off the call repeatedly. Measuring about 17×17 cm, these Italian-made gadgets were a little bit bulky and were mostly used by car owners and who did not have to walk long distances to their shooting-places.[24] Some ten years ago, Italian-made battery-operated calls which imitated the calls of song thrush and blackbird, became available, but these were even more cumbersome than the clockwork versions. Nevertheless they were, and are still, used by some shooters for luring song thrushes.

The call to lure the skylark is either produced by mouth or by a small round button-like metal whistle. Calls to attract meadow pipits and yellow wagtails are similar to those of skylarks, except that they are smaller. Such calls are imported from Italy, but some are also made by local tinsmiths and cost some 10 cents each. Franceschi describes these calls in his work about Italy, and states that they were made of brass, silver or bone.[25] In Malta, many shooters are able to imitate the calls of skylarks, song thrush, meadow pipits and wagtails without using any whistles.

Live song thrushes are sometimes used by shooters to lure migrating song thrushes – as are golden plovers. They are usually placed in a cage, which is hidden among some stones or in trees, to prevent them from being frightened and fluttering.

The shooting equipment manufactured by Manufrance of St. Etienne, France, was very popular amongst shooters who could afford to buy their products.[26] One can see in their pre- and post-war catalogues a number of gadgets like clockwork decoys and a large variety of whistles and calls for cuckoos, larks and various waders, which some local well-off shooters used.

Use of tape recordings

Today tape recordings are slowly but steadily replacing whistles. They are very commonly used both by bird trappers as well as by shooters on land and at sea. Such devices, which are small enough to fit inside the palm of a hand, are advertised and sold from many shops. There are a number of models which range from Lm35 to Lm50. Their cassettes cost Lm5 each. The ones I have seen advertised had three cassettes: one with calls of golden plover, lapwing, stone curlew, song thrush, dottorel, godwit, quail and turtle dove; tape two had calls of hawfinch, linnet, siskin, goldfinch, greenfinch, serin, chaffinch and ortolan bunting, while the third cassette was advertised as having calls of grey heron, purple heron, egret, night heron and other birds. New cassettes with calls of more species are released from time to time.

These calls are professionally recorded bird songs. In an article entitled 'the cassettes revolution', published in the shooters' paper, these bird song devices were praised for their remarkable efficiency in luring birds. It was stated that such gadgets improved places which were otherwise not so good for shooting and trapping – especially those found inland and in the heart of built-up areas. Song thrushes and skylarks were reported to keep flying in search of the caller in spite of the fact that they were continuously being shot at. Lapwings were reported to settle a few meters away from the speaker emitting their call. Even starlings, which are considered to be difficult to deceive, were being lured by such calls.[27] Such calls are also being used to lure bee-eaters and crakes. According to this article, these cassettes are being manufactured by the company Bird Sing which is run by Dottor Umberto Cecchi of Italy.

Other decoys

Gulia[28] noted that during both migrations, shooters prepared the *alwettiera* for luring skylarks. This decoy is probably French in origin, but Franceschi[29] mentions it in his work related to Italy. The decoy consisted of a pair of wooden wings on which small mirrors were stuck. There were some variations in these decoys: some had two pairs of wings stuck at right angles beneath each other; some had a pair of glass eyes or pieces of coloured glass. There were both factory-made clockwork models, as well as manually operated ones, the latter being more common. The decoy was made to revolve by means of a string which was wrapped around its shaft. The string was let loose when it was pulled so that it was automatically wound again and, when pulled, it revolved in the opposite direction. The light falling on the mirrors is reflected in many directions as the gadget turned clockwise and anti-clockwise. Shooters often made these decoys themselves and I was shown a clockwork home-made version which adapted the mechanism of a clock. In December 1989 I saw two plastic versions of *alwettiera* in a shop at Rabat. They were both battery-operated and one had a pair of wings, while the other had two pairs. They were priced at Lm17 and Lm21 respectively.

It is not really clear why skylarks are attracted by the decoy when it revolves. Old timers who used it informed me that other birds such as meadow pipits, golden plover and even kestrels were attracted to it. Some shooters say that it gives the impression of a fluttering owl while Gauci[30] states that some local shooters, though having used it widely, erroneously believed that the revolving mirrors mesmerised skylarks. Some believed it gave the impression of sparkling water.

The *alwettiera* was mostly used to attract wintering skylarks, which are considered to be more cunning since they are used to calls and shooting. According to old-timers who used it, it seems that it was much more effective when used on dry land, away from pools of water, seeming that birds could have mistaken it for water. Sultana and Gauci[31] also gave this explanation as to why skylarks are attracted to it and stated that its use was more effective during winters with low rain falls. Although I have seen it for sale, I have never seen anyone using it in the field, firstly because today very few skylarks are given the chance to winter, and secondly because skylarks are much more easily and effortlessly attracted by the tape recordings described earlier.

In the past, duck decoys used to be made of wood, while for certain species like golden plover, when decoys were needed, stuffed specimens were used. Today plastic decoys have replaced wooden ones. Plastic decoys of many species of duck, small waders, golden plover, lapwing, gulls, curlews, herons, egrets and even turtle doves and thrushes can be bought. They are very effective and relatively cheap. Wader plastic decoys cost around Lm1.50 while duck decoys cost Lm4. Duck decoys of most species can be found in the market. At a glance, one can hardly tell them from live birds especially at a certain distance. Shelduck decoys cannot be bought since shelduck are protected in Europe. Local shooters make their decoys themselves by painting other duck decoys as shelduck.

The use of live decoy birds has been a common practice for quite a long time. Falcons were lured to nets by live decoys. It seems that live decoys were also used to lure other migratory birds, since a number of subsequent edicts prohibited those hunting with nets from moving their birds when a falcon was sighted during the period in which licensed people were catching falcons.[32]

The fluttering decoy, locally known as *ġoga*, is still used for finch trapping and for turtle dove shooting and trapping. Turtle dove fluttering decoys are blindfolded by a leather hood placed on the bird's head. The bird is also tied by leather straps around its legs. It is then placed on a small platform at the end of or on top of a stick which is tossed up by means of a hinge or pulley action when a string is pulled. When the string is released, the *goga* falls down and the decoy bird flutters gently as if it has just alighted, thus attracting and drawing closer the birds that are flying within sight.

Earlier this century, finches used to be tied by their legs[33] while pipits were tied through their nose.[34] More detailed information about live decoys is given in the chapter about trapping.

Chapter 4

Shooting from Sea-craft

It is generally thought that the first people to carry guns at sea were fishermen. However, in 1772, Ciantar wrote about the shooting of rock pigeons from boats during the months of June and July. The author describes how shooters sailed along the coastal cliffs where the pigeons were known to breed and, by the sounding of drums and other noises, they frightened the pigeons out of their nests and shot them with arquebuses.[1]

This method of shooting rock pigeons along the southern parts of the islands was also noted by Wright, who wrote about 'sportsmen amusing themselves by pursuing them [rock pigeons] in boats'.[2]

Shearwater shooting

Wright's 1863 account of a visit to the Islet of Filfla, relates how on their way back to Malta, they amused themselves by using their remaining powder to shoot at the shearwaters, which appeared in considerable numbers. He also noted that on Filfla they came across several nets stretched on canes, with several live and dead shearwaters in these nets, adding that they were informed that the nets were set by fishermen, who used the feathers and flesh as fishing bait.[3]

Both Schembri[4] and Gulia[5] wrote that fishermen used the meat of both the cory's and manx shearwaters as bait in their fish-traps. Gulia noted that their axillary feathers were used as bait.

Despott wrote that, previously, shearwaters were caught alive with nets, and were released after having some of their underwing feathers plucked. These feathers were sold commercially and often exported to the East. Despott expressed his indignation about the massacre of shearwaters both by fishermen who shot shearwaters for their underwing feathers and by shooters, who shot them just for fun. Despott remarked that, due to the intensive shooting, shearwaters were decreasing in number adding that while ten years previously a shooter used to earn between £10 and £15 from selling such feathers, in 1913 shooters were not able to get more than 10 shillings worth.[6]

In spite of the fact that shearwaters have been protected since 1980, it is sad to note that they are still shot especially during the closed-season in summer while the birds would have their young in the nest. One often hears of 'sackfuls' of shearwaters being shot during the summer months. The only difference today is that some of those who shoot shearwaters collect the

51

dead birds and take them home to throw away, or else sink them at sea in a bag which they weight with stones, thus avoiding leaving evidence of their crime. In one instance recently, a fisherman gave a boat-load of shearwaters to a pig-breeder to feed to his pigs.[7]

Fishermen who used to carry shotguns, claimed, as they still do, that they used them to kill any large fish which they might catch. But there is no doubt that those who carry guns do so both to shoot at birds, and for protection in case they have any disputes with other fishermen – mainly Sicilian, who are frequently found fishing in Maltese territorial waters. It was through these fishermen/shooters that shooters on land used to hear the news of large flocks of birds passing out at sea.

The current trend

Gauci stated that it was during the mid-70s that 'shooters were taking their sea-craft in the attempt to have a shot at wild fowl resting on the calm seas'.[8] The pioneers of this new mania were two shooters who in the early 1970s started using a small dinghy to cross to Tas-Safra, which is a rock formation situated off the coast at Baħar iċ-ċagħaq. From these rocks they used to shoot at ducks and other seabirds. Then they started crossing over to St Paul's Islands and to Comino.

Two shooters from Rabat followed suit. They bought a larger rubber dinghy than that used by the other shooters and started to venture out further than their colleagues, from whom they borrowed the idea. They soon discovered that flocks of wildfowl used to rest off Ta' Ċenċ cliffs in Gozo and they started landing large catches of ducks and other birds that were not often shot on land.

Other shooters started following their example and, following some successful bags, many shooters bought rubber dinghies, or made them out of fibreglass. Others who had speed-boats or other sea-craft started going out to hunt at sea as well.

Most shooting from sea-craft takes place from February until April and from October to December, though there are shooters who go out practically all year round. Plastic duck decoys are often used at sea, and these, coupled with the use of duck call whistles and tape recordings, are very effective with most species of duck and some waders. A shooter from Rabat used to take a live mallard as a decoy.

Bags at sea are rather large and shooters who go out on dinghies proudly talk about their large catches. To mention a few bags which I know of, 18 ferruginous ducks were shot from a flock of 35 by 2 shooters from Rabat; a bag of 21 birds including a turtle dove, three glossy ibis, one grey heron, several other heron species and several garganeys were shot by a shooter from Rabat on 6th April 1980.[9] Il-Passa, the monthly paper for shooters, carried picture stories of bags of 55 duck.[10] In a caption story in March, one can see five dead shelduck together with three other duck,[11] while in a feature article about shooting from seacraft, 21 dead birds can be counted.[12]

In spring of 1989 when harriers migrated in considerable numbers, shooters on dinghies and other sea-craft shot dozens of harriers each during the afternoons. On 22nd April 1990, I saw four shooters on two dinghies off the northern coast of Gozo shoot 70 harriers in under ten hours, while I was informed by a trapper that he saw over 50 being shot from sea-craft the previous day.

The following are bag records from a single dinghy with three shooters. These records of 14 days in September and October of 1990 clearly illustrate the magnitude of the problem:

Species	September									October				
	3	4	5	8	17	21	22	23	24	1	7	19	20	25
Grey heron	–	–	–	–	–	–	–	4	–	–	1	–	1	–
Little egret	2	1	–	–	–	–	–	–	–	–	–	–	1	–
Eleonora's falcon	–	–	–	1	–	–	–	–	–	–	–	–	–	–
Honey buzzard	–	–	–	–	–	2	3	–	–	–	–	–	–	–
Osprey	–	–	–	–	–	–	2	–	–	–	–	–	–	–
Marsh harrier	–	–	–	–	–	–	6	4	1	–	–	–	–	–
Kestrel	–	–	–	–	–	–	–	2	–	–	–	–	–	–
Short-eared owl	–	–	–	–	–	–	–	–	–	–	–	1	–	–
Nightjar	–	–	–	–	–	–	–	–	–	1	–	–	–	–
Black terns	–	2	–	–	–	–	4	2	–	–	–	–	–	–
Herring gull	–	–	–	–	–	–	–	–	–	–	–	–	–	2
Black-headed gull	–	–	–	–	–	–	–	–	–	–	–	–	–	4
Sandwich tern	–	2	–	–	1	–	–	–	–	–	–	–	–	–

Although it is illegal to hunt at sea within 3 km from any foreshore, more shooters are investing in rubber dinghies and powerful outboard motors. In late February through to March, one can often count over 40 such dinghies in the channel between Malta and Gozo. A shooter who goes out frequently from November until March, and who has a powerful outboard engine, spends up to Lm400 in petrol and ammunition during this period.[13] I was told by someone who used to go shooting at sea, using a smaller dinghy, that he used around Lm7 of fuel on each excursion.

One can often see two or three shooters on such dinghies, in which they wait for migratory birds a few kilometres offshore. At sea, shooters usually use Magnum repeater shotguns which use 7.5 cm long cartridges having 50–54 grams of lead shot instead of the 32 or 34 gram ones that are normally used on land. Magnum shotguns have a longer effective range because of the design of their barrel and the greater density of lead shot. All this combined with the manoeuvrability of the rubber dinghy, has proven itself a deadly trap for birds.

Nothing is spared

Needless to say, all kinds of birds are shot. Bags at sea may include anything from cranes to nightjars and hoopoes. In spring and autumn, duck, herons, egrets, cormorants, grebes, waders and large birds of prey such as the honey buzzard, short-eared owl and harriers, are very commonly shot from such sea-craft. During summer months, cory's shearwaters, which

are breeding during that time, are shot for fun both by some fishermen
as well as by shooters from dinghies. Waders such as oystercatcher, grey
plover, avocet and curlew, are often shot from sea-craft during the summer
months.

In autumn, considerable numbers of honey buzzards, harriers and other
birds of prey are shot at sea. Birds of prey fly low over the sea because of
the absence of thermals, and thus present very easy targets. Besides, these
rubber dinghies are very fast and can easily outpace most species.

In winter, ducks, gulls, terns, grebes as well as cormorants which try to
winter along our shores, are shot. Gannets are frequently shot, especially
on windy days. I know of a shooter from Rabat who bagged nine gannets
in a single winter.

Gannets are often lured by a silver-painted glass bottle which is tied by a
thin rope and thrown into the sea. The dinghy is driven at a speed at which
the bottle skims the surface of the water. The gannet mistakes it for a fish
and as the bottle is drawn nearer to the dinghy, the gannet is lured within
shooting range.

Birds like black-necked grebes, some of which winter with us, suffer
greatly at the hands of such shooters since they are very tame and tend to
swim and dive, rather than fly away. I have, on more than one occasion,
witnessed massacres of parties of such grebes in bays such as Mellieħa Bay
and Marsaxlokk Bay. I recall a dinghy landing nine great crested grebes
at Mellieħa Bay in the winter of 1980. Larger birds such as flamingos,
spoonbills, cranes, storks and ibises are shot more frequently at sea than
on land.

The last pair of peregrine falcons breeding at Ta' Ċenc in Gozo, were
shot from such dinghies. The same can be said for a pair of short-eared
owls which were breeding on Comino, the male of which was shot at sea
in mid-March just off Comino.[14]

Inadequate legislation

Although the bird-protection regulations prohibit shooting within 3 km off
any coast, such shooting still takes place and it is indeed rare to hear of
anyone being arraigned in court for having infringed such regulations.
When, occasionally, a shooter is brought to court because he is found
hunting at sea within 3 km offshore, he is usually acquitted on technical
grounds. The law states that no-one can *discharge* a firearm within the 3 km
limit, and unless a person is actually seen shooting – unlikely when the
police or army patrol boat is around – a person is not found guilty of having
infringed the regulations, not even if in possession of a gun, ammunition
and dead protected birds.

The following article has been translated from *Il-Passa*.[15] It is a statement
taken from the horse's mouth, and may shed some more light on the problem of shooting from sea-craft. The article tries to give the impression that
shooting from sea-craft is something which is really difficult; whilst in fact
it is rather easy and very productive in terms of the number of birds killed
– and hence popular.

IL-PASSA Jannar 1984

Jissogra ħajtu biex jaqbad papra (jew 55)!

IL-BOROK "... L-ISBAĦ KAĊĊA"

•Minn pagna 4

borok, dejjem skond fejn ikun qed jonfoħ ir-riħ, huwa jitfa' l-mazzra u jorbot id-decoys – papri tal-plastik li huma mportanti biex jiġbdu l-borok lejhom.

Joe qal li kultant jir-nexxilek tiġbed xi qata' borok lejn id-direzzjoni tiegħek, dejjem wara li tgħajtilhom bis-suffara, u dawn jintefgħu gozz ħdejn il-papri tal-plastik. Darba minnhom qata' kbira ta' borok

snieter u l-affarijiet l-oħra kollha taz-żewġ kaċċaturi, baqgħu fil-qiegħ.

Joe qal li l-periklu li ghad-dew minnu dawk it-tnejn minn nies jista' jgħaddi minnu kull min joħroġ fuq il-bahar b'dinghy.

Hawnhekk lil Joe Agius ghamilnilu mistoqsija ta' l-aħħar: F'April x'jagħmel, johroġ għall-gamiem jew imur bid-dinghy? Huwa

Joe Agius (lemin) flimkien ma' siehbu Michael Falzon iżommu l-hamsa u hamsin papra li qabdu fit-8 ta' Marzu, 1982.

The shooters' paper Il-Passa reported: 'He risks his life to shoot a duck . . . (or 55)!'
The two shooters can be seen holding the 55 duck they shot on 8 March 1982.

HE RISKS HIS LIFE TO SHOOT A DUCK (OR 55)

Nowadays, everyone knows that Maltese and Gozitan shooters are getting crazy about duck shooting. To shoot at such a bird from land is almost impossible – thus, many shooters are setting up to go and shoot at sea. For the first edition of this paper, *Il-Passa*, we went to Rabat to talk to Joe Agius who, if not the best, is amongst the best duck shooters.

To go out at sea is risky . . . to go out in bad weather is dangerous, but to risk your life and go out on a rubber dinghy when you cannot swim is sheer madness. But Joe Agius, a 33-year-old shooter from Rabat, known as 'Joe of Rabat', does so because he is very keen on, or rather he has a craze for duck shooting; the passion of shooting at sea overwhelms him and Joe is even ready to risk his life to shoot a duck or two.

Joe, father of two, goes out at sea almost every day, especially around March when more duck migrate close to the Maltese Islands.

But what makes this shooter go out at sea. Why does he prefer a duck to a turtle dove, a quail or a woodcock? What does his family say when, in spite of bad weather, he grabs his gun and goes out at sea on his dinghy?

Joe replied to these questions when we met him a couple of weeks ago at a time when duck migration, although a bit poor, was at its peak. Joe told what made his craze grow for duck, which he now calls his 'children'.

Joe, a well-built man, has a small shop full of stuffed duck, where the shooters from the area meet every evening. He started going out at sea to shoot duck from a small boat, which although sea-worthy, was not fast enough to outpace a bird as strong and as agile as a duck.

After the small boat, Joe bought a Zodiac dinghy and, to play safe, he fitted it with two outboard motors, so that if one breaks down, he would still be able to make it ashore using the other motor. The dinghy, its motors, and other useful equipment like anchor, life-jacket, flares and binoculars cost him about Lm3000; a hefty sum of money when one considers that one needs to buy these things if one wants to hunt at sea.

But these are not the only things that one needs. One needs shotguns, cartridges which are not cheap, as well as fuel which is also expensive.

Joe told us that he has fourteen shotguns, but his favourite, which he always takes with him out at sea is a Breda magnum, a shotgun which uses heavy 3-inch cartridges and has a longer range. Most of the cartridges which Joe uses he loads himself at his shop, which was what he was doing when we went to visit him.

Joe told us what he had been through during these past years shooting at sea. The day he remembers best is 8th March 1982 when there was a strong duck migration. On that day, together with his friend Michael Falzon of St Julian's, he succeeded in shooting 55 duck. The day had dawned with a mild south-westerly wind and they saw flock upon flock of duck.

'I will never forget that day,' said Joe showing us a photograph of himself and his friend holding as best as they could, that day's bag. 'In fact, during March 1982 we had seen an unusual number of duck passing close to our shores.' During that year Joe said he had shot 143 duck, a record year which is hard to better.

Joe said that he goes out on his dinghy early in the morning after choosing the best place – which depends on the wind direction. He then anchors and lays out his duck decoys – important to lure migrating duck.

Joe said that, at times, one is successful in luring a flock of duck and, on calling them, they alight near the decoys. Once he recalls a large flock alighting near his decoys close to his dinghy and, after he moved a little bit closer, he shot at them while they were still sitting on the water killing 20 – another record number of birds shot at the same time for him.

But was he ever in danger? Joe told us that apart from that day with a lot of duck, he remembers two unpleasant incidents.

On one occasion a few years ago he was going out near L-Ahrax in Mellieha. A strong north-westerly wind was blowing and all of a sudden a large wave lifted the front of the dinghy and almost overturned it. Luckily the dinghy righted itself before Joe, his gun and all ended up in the sea.

In another incident Joe said that last March, together with his cousin Arthur Agius, he saved two shooters who had found themselves in difficulty after their dinghy had overturned in heavy seas between Malta and Gozo.

It was about 6 pm, a north-westerly wind was blowing, when, while heading towards the shore, they saw something floating in the sea. Suspecting something was wrong, they investigated and, to their surprise, saw an over-turned dinghy and two drenched people sitting on it. After taking the two shooters aboard, the four of them managed to turn the other dinghy back and towed it ashore. But the shotguns and the other accessories had been lost.

Joe said that this is a risk that faces anyone who goes to shoot at sea.

To a final question, whether during April he shoots turtle doves or duck, Joe replied that duck are the best game, and so he prefers them to turtle doves. 'It is better for me to shoot one duck than five turtle doves. To shoot duck you have to be lucky, but you have to be good to move close to a flock which has alighted at sea. Above all, a duck is a beautiful bird, that is why I go out to shoot duck all year round.'

And what do you do during the closed-season? 'I go out fishing,' Joe replied.

Chapter 5

Taxidermy

In order to remind shooters of the fun derived from the kill, many birds are mounted as trophies. Practically all shooters have a collection of stuffed birds. Labelled as 'a flourishing art' by Bannerman and Vella Gaffiero,[1] taxidermy is one of the main causes for most bird shooting.

Apart from the killing of birds, cruel practices are frequently employed by some taxidermists. In 1933, *The Daily Malta Chronicle* noted that large birds were often starved to facilitate the work of the taxidermist. This was done to diminish the amount of fat reserves that a bird usually has.[2] This cruel practice is still used by some taxidermists.

A story about an alleged record of taxidermy, published in the Maltese daily *l-Orizzont* in 1967, stated that: 'Joe Camilleri, of Luqa, has every right to be proud of the number of birds and small animals which he has mounted over the past 14 years – over 5000, which is thought to be a record. Camilleri, who is over 50 years old, estimates that he mounted over 500 birds just this year. The most common bird that is taken to Joe for stuffing is the hawk [presumably the kestrel], a bird which hunts itself [note the connotation between hunted and hunter!] and which has a wingspan of 18 inches [45cm]'.[3]

Mr Charles Coles, then Consultant Director to the Game Conservancy, after he came to Malta in 1982, wrote 'whatever the bag, it is the species that comprise the quarry that shocks and saddens. Egrets! nightjars! golden orioles! and so on'.[4]

In a report entitled *'An assessment of illegal shooting and catching of birds in Malta'*, Magnin stated: 'There are 40-50 taxidermists in Malta. In spite of the new regulations, all species of birds obtained are stuffed and mounted'.[5]

In an unpublished, undated paper entitled *'Comments on the ICBP Study report on the shooting and catching of birds in Malta'*, which was sent to the Federation of Hunting Associations of the EC (FACE), Mr J. R. Scicluna, President of The Shooters' and Trappers' Association wrote:

> Perhaps it should be pointed out that the 40 to 50 taxidermists mentioned in the report are, without a single exception, part-timers or retired individuals; no person in Malta could possibly earn a living from taxidermy alone.
>
> Stuffed birds fall into the following categories.
>
> (i) Serious collectors who treat their collections as an aid to their studies in common with several noted ornithologists and custodians of Natural History Museums in every country.

(ii) The big-game hunter mounts buffalo heads, and displays tiger skin rugs – the Maltese shooter on a far more humble note, keeps a stuffed Mallard or Woodcock on show on top of his gun cabinet as a hunting trophy.

(iii) Stuffed birds kept for their sentimental value – the bedraggled marsh harrier bagged by Grandfather when he was a boy (years before that bird was protected).

(iv) A small number of protected birds that are illegally shot, and just as illegally stuffed.[6]

Currently there are two licensed taxidermists and it is known that a returned immigrant is a full-time taxidermist in Nadur, Gozo, while there is another full-time taxidermist in Qormi, Malta. Both have a shop from which they sell ammunition, but their income is derived mainly from bird stuffing. The fact that the Shooters' Asociation confirmed that there are 40 to 50 part-time taxidermists, to which one must add the considerable number of shooters who themselves stuff the birds which they shoot, and considering the tables which show the quantity of birds which such part-timers handle, one immediately realises how grave the problem of taxidermy is in the Maltese Islands; and how misleading is the statement by Mr Scicluna that only a small number of protected birds are shot.

The claim that serious collectors treat their collections as an aid to their studies is misleading too. In Malta all collections of stuffed birds are mere collections. The fact that a few collectors label each species with its scientific name and date and place of capture, does not make a collection a serious or a scientific one.

Types of collections

Mounted stuffed bird collections can be divided into three categories:

First there are those very large, elaborate collections. These are the keen collectors who want to build as large a collection as possible. They buy and, in some cases, even import skins and their collection will include anything from raptors to small passerines. Each mounted specimen in such collections will have a label with the name of the bird, (often the scientific, English and Maltese names) as well as the locality and the date showing when and where the bird was shot. These collections resemble a sort of mini-museum. However, few, if any, can be classified as being scientific because they are simply collections and are not used for any specific studies but just serve as showpieces. This was the same in the time of Despott, who wrote that there was a 'pretty good number of collections' adding that 'some may have little or no scientific merit'.[7]

Secondly there are those who collect the specimens they themselves shoot as well as those which they acquire through exchange or purchase. These collections are perhaps the commonest type, and usually contain between 100 and 200 birds of about 100 species. As time passes, unless the collector loses interest in the collection, such collections may grow big enough to fall into the previous category.

Then there are others who mount only birds which are large, colourful or rare. Particular attention is given to larger raptors of which they try to mount as many different species as possible. Such collections usually contain between 70 and 100 birds and usually contain only the commoner large species. Some mount several of the same species, especially if they vary in colour. A typical case is the honey buzzard, which is very variable in plumage, of which in 1991 I have counted as many as ten in a collection of 88 birds. In this collection there were also an osprey, a buzzard, five marsh harriers, a pallid harrier, an eleonora's falcon, a hobby, a merlin, three red-footed falcons, three kestrels, a lesser kestrel, two short-eared owls and a scops owl. The shooter who owned this collection informed me that he had another ten birds at the taxidermist as well as 'about another ten in the freezer, as the taxidermist was too busy as he had two deep freezers full of birds'. The fact that a part-time taxidermist skins, stuffs and mounts an average of three or four birds per day and the fact that a bird shot in autumn is not stuffed and mounted before the following spring may shed some light on the large volume of work that taxidermists handle.

Some collections are passed on within the same family. Where the father is a shooter who collects stuffed birds, his sons add to it and usually inherit it.

Common throughout all types of collections is the fact that the rarer the bird, the more prized it is in the collection. Bannerman and Vella Gaffiero wrote: 'We can imagine that in an island bristling with nets, guns and private collectors, few, if any, rosy starlings arriving in adult plumage would escape attention'.[8] Birds which are ringed or which have special features such as being isabelline or birds which are melanistic or albinistic, are considered as being special, and thus more worth collecting.

Birds of prey may often be seen stuffed with some sort of prey, usually a colourful bird such as a hoopoe, an oriole or a passerine or a stuffed or plastic snake. Stuffed skinks, bats, weasels and rabbits may also be seen forming part of collections.

Most collections are usually kept in a showcase (or showcases, depending on their size), at the entrance of the house or in a room where people are bound to see them. Stuffed birds are often exhibited in public exhibitions which are held as part of the activities marking special occasions.

Although one cannot speak of significant trade, whole collections are often sold and considerable sums of money are paid for particular species. A collector who had an upland sandpiper, which was the only local record of this species, was offered £300 for the stuffed bird in the early 1960s. The same person had two cranes in his collection. These he had bought individually as carcasses for £7 from a taxidermist.[9] The sum of Lm1900 was offered to a shooter who shot a griffon vulture in October 1991, yet the shooter refused to sell it,[10] while an Egyptian vulture shot a few weeks before was sold for Lm200.

Skins imported from abroad usually fetch about Lm25. Commoner species shot locally are often sold at cheap prices. I know of a taxidermist who used to sell a number of stuffed birds which his brother shot. These were mainly the commoner birds of prey like kestrels and marsh harriers and colourful birds such as the golden oriole, of which large numbers are shot each year. In 1985,

THE TIMES, SATURDAY, JUNE 25, 1983

HOTEL'S STAFF EXHIBITION

The committee of the Excelsior Sports and Social Club of the Grand Hotel Excelsior recently held its annual hobbies exhibition at the hotel.

It included oil and pencil paintings and photography, flower arrangements, stamp and key chain collections, crochet work and stuffed birds of prey (below), all made by the hotel's staff.

The exhibition was opened by Mrs. Maureen Zarb Mizzi.

MALTA NEWS — Thursday, November 24, 1977

□ GHAXAQ, Wednesday. — Minister for Works and Sports, Mr Lorry Sant, yesterday night officially opened an exhibition of hobbies and work undertaken by the Socialist Government. The exhibition is being organised by the Ghaxaq Section of the Ghaqda Zghazagh Socjalisti as part of a week of activities.

After a welcome speech by the section's president, Mr Twanny Agius, Minister Sant congratulated the members of the section for organising a week of activities and wished them success for the future.

Stuffed birds are often exhibited as part of bigger exhibitions marking special occasions.

TIMES OF MALTA, MONDAY, SEPTEMBER 23, 1968

The taxidermist, Mr. A. Sammut and his wife Mrs. Sammut, holding the short towed eagle.

Eagle shot down at Siggiewi

BY A STAFF REPORTER

While at "Is-Saiib tal-Gholja", limits of Siggiewi, on Saturday afternoon, Mr. Norbert Abela of Birkirkara, spotted and shot down a short towed eagle. Mr. Abela said that the eagle was flying at an approximate height of 90 feet. The bird's wing span is about six feet.

Mr. Abela, winner of the Malta Official Trap Shooting Championship, used high calibre cartridges to shoot down the bird, which was hit in one of its wings.

The short towed eagle is a rare visitor to Malta. Records show that since 1857, only two such eagles, one in August 1857 and another in October 1914, were caught over the Maltese Islands.

At present the eagle is being embalmed by the taxidermist, Mr Aurelio Sammut, of Balzan.

TIMES ✠ MALTA

FOUNDED ... ...August 7, 1935

MALTA OFFICE	LONDON OFFICE
Strickland House	Orbit House
341, St. Paul Street	9, New Fetter Lane
Valetta	E.C. 4
TELEPHONES: CENTRAL 24031 (6 lines)	CABLES: BERQA MALTA

THURSDAY SEPTEMBER 26, 1968

LETTERS TO THE EDITOR

SHOT DOWN

Sir. — I would like to congratulate Mr. Norbert Abela on shooting down the eagle. A magnificent effort!

Yours truly,

Msierah.   G.C. BRIDGLAND

A short-toed eagle shot in 1968 featured prominently as a news item of The Times of Malta and was also shown on the 8 o'clock news on television. Unlike the pelicans, this bird, being somewhat more difficult to 'catch', was 'shot down'. Note also a letter congratulating the shooter who shot the eagle.

this taxidermist used to sell stuffed kestrels at Lm2, marsh harriers for Lm5 each, while a pair of golden orioles stuffed and mounted side by side on the same perch were sold at Lm1.50. Stuffed mounted birds are often sold from shops which sell shooters' goods or directly from taxidermists.

Colourful birds and occasionally herons and birds of prey, are often found in houses of non-shooters as a piece of decorative furniture. These would either have been as a gift from relatives who shoot or else bought. Up to about 40 years ago, stuffed birds were occasionally given as wedding gifts. It is quite common to come across small collections of stuffed birds and individual birds in shops, especially bars and restaurants frequented by shooters or whose owners are shooters.

Members of Parliament, priests, doctors, lawyers and other professional people were frequently given stuffed birds as gifts. A shooter from Żebbuġ, Malta, told me that he once shot a booted eagle, which he stuffed and gave to a Member of Parliament as he wanted to return a favour. A priest who lives at Rabat has a collection of 149 specimens which were all given to him by different shooters (see Table 6). Generally speaking, however, the birds which are usually given have no particular value, except for the fact that they would have been shot by the person who gave them. They usually involve the commoner species such as kestrels, honey buzzards, marsh harriers and night herons.

Old and worn or badly mounted stuffed birds, such as birds of prey and herons, are sometimes used as bird-scarers in an attempt to keep sparrows away from crops and fruit.

A considerable number of birds are shot each year for these collections and it is a known practice that skins are also imported both legally and illegally. The collecting of stuffed birds as well as their importation have been going on since the end of last century.

Early collections

Attard wrote that Ardoino, who lived between 1817 and 1903, was one of the first to practise taxidermy in Malta.[11] Some of the stuffed birds in the university's Natural History Museum dated from 1840.[12] Despott listed 11 collections, including the university collection as well as his own. He also stated that his private collection contained over 250 species and nearly 1000 specimens. Further to this, Despott added, 'In addition to these collections [the 11 he mentioned] there are those of local bird-stuffers; these are, of course, continually fluctuating in number and, moreover, exotic species are very often introduced'.[13]

Both Wright and Despott, listed a number of species which they knew or suspected as having been imported. Commenting about the catalogue of the collection of birds at the museum compiled by Leach, Despott wrote: 'Some species, however, are included, which, though existing in the museum, bear neither date nor locality and are probably imported specimens'.[14] Wright mentions specimens of red-backed shrikes received from Athens[15] as well as of flamingos which he shot in March 1859 on the lagoon of Tunis, 'using a heavy charge of powder and pistol bullets'.[16] He also mentions a specimen of a sandgrouse which had been imported from Tunisia[17] and six purple gallinules, two of which ended up in the university museum and were claimed to have been taken in Malta whilst in fact it resulted that they 'had been brought over by a seaman from Syracuse'.[18]

Despott gives records of magpies and wrote that 'these birds are at times imported from Sicily and sold to local bird-fanciers'.[19] He also states that several Algerian chaffinches were imported from the north coast of Africa in the summer of 1911.[20] Despott also gives a record of an Algerian grey shrike which he suspects as having been an imported bird.[21] He also ascertains that four specimens of Algerian red-necked nightjar were imported from north Africa in 1908[22] while pin-tailed sand grouse were imported 'on several occasions'.[23]

Importation of bird-skins – the current situation

One can find a quantity of birds which are imported, some of which do not occur in the Maltese Islands. I have personally seen an eagle in Hamrun which was brought to Malta by a returned emigrant from Australia. During the 70s, an exchange of skins with a collector in the UK was taking place. A number of British sea-birds, ducks and even birds of prey and individual tits have found themselves in local collections.[24]

Sultana and Gauci list a number of species which are not recorded in the Maltese Islands but which they have seen in local collections. They also state that skins of vagrant species 'have been imported from various countries and claimed to have been taken in Malta to fetch more money from collectors'.[25] They mention, amongst others, imported specimens of long-tailed duck, eider, Senegal coucal, snowy owl and tawny owl. Specimens of these species, which are not recorded in the Maltese Islands, exist in local collections.

Table 11 shows a list of species which were imported and stuffed by Taxidermist C. Most of these birds do not occur in the Maltese Islands and those which do are rare. These were marked in the log book and the taxidermist confirmed that they were imported from the United Kingdom and Libya.

It is a known fact that Maltese working in Libya frequently bring skins of desert birds like larks and moussier's redstart. It is known that an active exchange of skins is taking place between local and foreign collectors. It is also known that Maltese collectors frequently obtain skins of specimens which do not occur in Malta through their relatives residing abroad. Some shooters go through a considerable hassle to import skins of birds illegally. I know of a person who in the late 80s imported the skin of a mute swan he killed while on holiday in the UK. To smuggle it into Malta, he hid the skin in dirty baby diapers.

More recently, tour operators have been operating hunting tours to Egypt and Maltese shooters who go on such tours are allowed to import skins of species which are not protected in the Maltese Islands. However, this restriction was enforced only lately. Shooters on the first two tours imported into Malta their whole bag, irrespective of whether the birds were protected or not.[26] Among them were an Egyptian goose, a quantity of cattle egrets, purple gallinules, spur-winged plovers, little owls, Senegal coucals, painted snipes, little green- and blue-cheeked bee-eaters, black-shouldered kites and at least 2000 palm doves – most of which have found their way into local collections. I have personally seen a painted snipe, 2 black-shouldered kites, a hooded crow, a palm dove, a cattle egret, a spur-winged plover, and a little owl in a local collection. In this collection, there were also a garganey, a greenshank and a redshank, a stone curlew, a black headed gull and a cormorant which were all shot in Egypt.

Sultana and Gauci advised that 'present and future compilers of records of accidental or rare species to Malta have to be very cautious about specimens found in collections, especially when dealing with mounted specimens claimed to have been taken in Malta during the years 1976 to 1981'.[27]

It is a fact that considerable numbers of birds or bird skins have been discreetly imported since the early 70s. Locally unprotected species are now being imported on a more regular basis. Since it is a known fact that some collectors claim that stuffed specimens which have been imported were taken locally, it is best not to accept any records from stuffed specimens as this can create a confusion in ornithological records as well as encourage the killing of birds both locally and abroad.

Bird stuffing today

The birds listed in Tables 9, 10, and 11 (pages 156–165) were stuffed by three taxidermists who stuffed birds on a part-time basis. One of the taxidermists who gave me the records of Table 10 stated that he knew of at least another 20 taxidermists during the time in which he used to stuff birds and who, on average, handled the same numbers of birds as he.

Table 9 covers the years 1958–77, Table 10 covers the years 1976–1986 while Table 11 covers the years 1983–86. The tables were compiled from log books which the taxidermists used to keep.

Taxidermist A kept only a list of birds taken to him but did not note the names of the shooters who shot them. There were between 700–1000 shooters in his area. Taxidermist B stuffed birds for an average of 35 shooters from three villages, in which over 1000 shooters lived while Taxidermist C stuffed birds for an average of 30 shooters while there were over 1300 shooters living in the areas he catered for.

From Table 10, out of a total of 2519 birds which were stuffed and mounted by Taxidermist B, only 846 (33%) were not protected species. If one were to add other species which cannot be considered as real game, such as herons, crakes, some waders and thrushes, which are not yet protected locally, then 88% of the birds stuffed were non-game species.

Also from Table 10, out of the total of 2041 birds which were mounted by Taxidermist C, only 618 could have been shot and/or trapped, the remaining 1423 were protected species. This table shows that 70% of the birds which were stuffed, were protected species. If one were to add to the

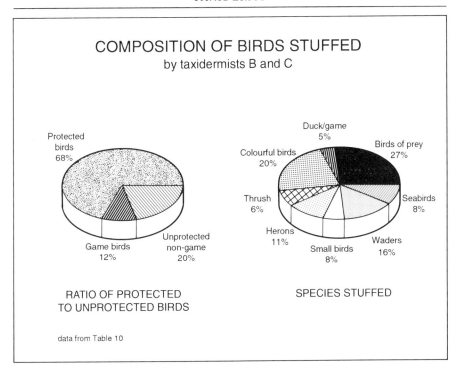

COMPOSITION OF BIRDS STUFFED
by taxidermists B and C

Protected birds 68%

Game birds 12%

Unprotected non-game 20%

RATIO OF PROTECTED
TO UNPROTECTED BIRDS

Duck/game 5%

Birds of prey 27%

Colourful birds 20%

Thrush 6%

Seabirds 8%

Herons 11%

Waders 16%

Small birds 8%

SPECIES STUFFED

data from Table 10

list of protected species, those birds which cannot be considered as game, then 87% of the birds stuffed were non-game or protected species. These figures give a clear indication of the seriousness of the problem of illegal shooting of protected birds.

From Table 10, one can deduce that during the eleven years between 1976 and 1986, a total of 1238 birds of prey were stuffed by two part-time taxidermists. Birds of prey accounted for 27% of the birds handled by taxidermists. During these years, the worst hit were the kestrel (274), marsh harrier (186), honey buzzard (186), red-footed falcon (169), short-eared owl (125), hobby (91) and montagu's harrier (49).

As shown in the table with the estimated number of birds which are shot, it is obvious that these figures do not reflect the actual number of raptors killed, as the birds that are shot for fun, those which are too badly mutilated, as well as those which are shot or wounded and not retrieved, never show up at taxidermists' shops.

One must also bear in mind that there are at least two full-time taxidermists who stuff larger quantities of birds, and that a considerable number of shooters stuff their own birds, and these are not included in the number of part-timers mentioned above.

Certain species which appear in the aforementioned tables are rare or threatened both on a national as well as on an international level. Undoubtedly, Maltese shooters can affect the status of particular species due to their intensive shooting both locally and abroad. One of those shooters who went to Egypt, shot, amongst many other species, 10 black-shouldered kites in five days.

Certain sharp increases in Table 9 are worth pointing out. The average number of night herons which were stuffed during the first 5 years was of 6.4 night herons each year. During the last five years, that is a mere 15 years later, the average rose to 65.5 birds per year. The same can be said for other species like the purple heron, whose average rose from 6.2 to 44. The average of honey buzzards rose from 4.2 to 27.4, that of kestrels increased from 18.6 to 59.4 while the average number of the hobby rose from 1.8 to 20.8 birds per year. These increases can be explained partly by the increase in the number of shooters but is more likely to be due to the increase in the popularity of bird stuffing.

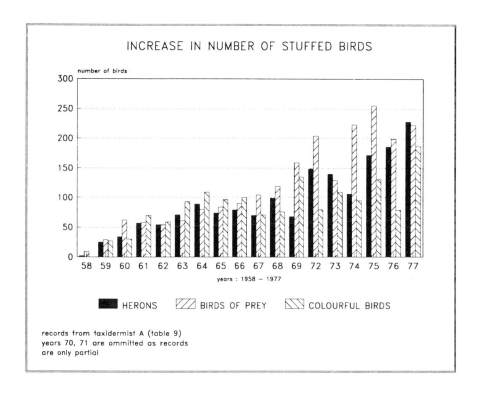

INCREASE IN NUMBER OF STUFFED BIRDS

number of birds

■ HERONS   ▨ BIRDS OF PREY   ◺ COLOURFUL BIRDS

years : 1958 – 1977

records from taxidermist A (table 9)
years 70, 71 are ommitted as records
are only partial

The various conclusions from Tables 9 and 10 show that there is an immediate need to curb taxidermy, which is the main reason for the killing of these birds in the Maltese Islands. They also show that the picture depicted by the President of the Shooters' Association in his report to FACE[28] is indeed a cover-up for the massacre of birds which takes place under the guise of hunting.

TABLE 6

A list of birds in some private collections. Collection A is at L-Iklin; B, E and H at B'Kara; D at Rabat; E, F and I at Attard; C and G at Paola; J, K and M at Mosta and L at St Paul's Bay.

Collection year collection started	A ?	B 80	C ?	D ?	E ?	F 80	G 80	H 85	I ?	J 68–75	K ?	L ?	M 74–82
Little grebe	1	1	–	1	1	–	–	–	–	–	–	–	–
Great crested grebe	2	1	–	1	1	1	3	1	–	–	–	1	–
Black-necked grebe	1	3	1	1	–	2	–	2	–	–	1	–	–
Cory's shearwater	1	1	1	1	–	1	–	–	–	–	–	–	–
Sooty shearwater	–	–	–	–	–	–	–	1	–	–	–	–	–
Manx shearwater	1	2	–	1	1	–	–	1	–	–	–	–	–
Storm petrel	1	1	2	–	–	1	1	1	–	–	–	–	1
Gannet	2	2	1	–	1	–	–	–	–	–	–	–	–
Cormorant	1	–	–	1	1	–	–	1	2	1	–	–	–
Bittern	2	–	–	1	1	–	–	–	–	–	–	–	–
Little bittern	3	1	3	1	2	1	2	–	2	–	–	1	–
Night heron *	2	2	1	3	1	2	–	4	2	1	2	1	3
Squacco heron *	1	2	1	1	2	1	1	–	1	–	–	–	–
Little egret *	1	1	2	1	1	1	–	1	1	1	–	–	–
Cattle egret	–	–	1	–	–	–	–	–	–	–	–	–	–
Grey heron *	2	1	2	1	2	1	1	–	1	–	1	–	–
Purple heron *	4	1	–	2	1	2	1	–	1	1	–	–	1
Glossy ibis	1	1	1	1	1	–	–	1	1	–	–	–	–
Black stork	–	–	–	–	1	–	–	–	–	–	–	–	–
Spoonbill	1	–	–	–	–	–	–	–	–	–	–	–	–
Flamingo	–	–	–	–	–	–	–	–	1	–	–	–	–
Shelduck *	2	1	2	1	2	1	–	1	–	–	1	1	–
Widgeon *	2	3	1	1	3	1	1	1	2	1	1	–	–
Teal *	1	1	1	3	1	4	–	–	1	2	1	1	–
Mallard *	1	2	1	1	–	2	1	–	1	–	–	–	–
Pintail *	2	3	–	3	2	1	–	2	–	–	–	–	–
Garganey *	2	3	2	2	2	–	1	1	1	1	2	–	2
Shoveler *	2	1	1	–	3	–	–	–	1	–	–	1	–
Pochard *	–	1	1	–	–	–	–	–	–	–	–	–	–
Ferruginous duck *	1	2	–	–	1	–	–	3	1	–	–	–	–
Tufted duck +	1	2	–	–	–	–	–	1	–	–	–	–	–
Red-breasted merganser	1	1	1	1	1	1	–	–	–	–	–	–	–
Goosander	1	–	–	–	–	–	–	–	–	–	–	–	–
Honey buzzard	4	5	1	5	9	1	1	5	10	5	4	1	2
Black kite	1	2	–	1	–	–	–	–	–	–	–	–	–
Short-toed eagle	–	–	–	–	–	–	–	–	–	–	–	–	1
Marsh harrier	2	4	2	5	2	3	2	1	5	6	2	1	1
Hen harrier	1	–	–	–	–	–	–	–	–	–	–	–	–
Montagu's harrier	2	4	–	1	1	1	–	3	–	1	2	1	–
Pallid harrier	1	3	–	–	–	–	–	1	1	1	–	–	–
Sparrowhawk	2	1	–	1	–	–	–	–	–	–	2	–	–
Buzzard	1	2	–	–	–	–	–	1	1	–	–	–	–
Osprey	1	–	–	1	–	–	–	–	1	1	1	–	1
Lesser kestrel	2	3	1	–	2	2	–	1	1	–	–	–	–
Kestrel	2	3	5	4	2	2	–	2	3	3	3	1	1
Red-footed falcon	3	4	–	6	8	4	1	3	3	10	3	–	–
Merlin	1	2	–	–	1	–	–	–	1	–	1	–	–
Hobby	1	3	3	1	2	2	2	1	1	3	2	–	1
Eleonora's falcon	2	3	–	1	–	–	–	–	1	–	–	–	–

TABLE 6 (contd.)

Collection	A	B	C	D	E	F	G	H	I	J	K	L	M
Peregrine falcon	–	–	1	–	–	–	–	–	–	–	1	–	–
Lanner falcon	1	–	–	–	–	–	–	–	–	–	–	–	–
Saker falcon	1	–	–	–	–	–	–	–	–	–	–	–	–
Bobwhite +	–	–	–	–	–	–	–	–	–	1	–	–	–
Quail *	2	1	1	1	–	2	1	1	–	1	1	–	–
Water rail *	1	1	–	2	–	1	1	1	–	1	1	–	–
Spotted crake *	1	–	–	1	–	–	2	–	1	1	1	–	1
Little crake *	1	–	–	2	–	–	1	–	–	–	–	–	–
Baillon's crake *	1	–	–	–	–	–	–	–	–	–	–	–	–
Corncrake *	1	–	1	2	–	1	1	–	–	–	–	–	–
Moorhen *	2	1	1	1	1	1	–	–	1	1	1	1	1
Coot *	1	1	1	1	1	1	1	–	1	–	–	–	–
Crane	2	–	–	–	–	–	–	–	–	–	–	2	–
Oystercatcher	1	1	–	1	–	–	–	1	–	–	–	–	–
Black-winged stilt	1	1	–	1	1	2	1	–	2	–	–	–	–
Avocet	2	1	–	–	–	2	–	1	–	1	–	–	–
Stone curlew	1	1	–	1	2	1	–	1	1	1	–	1	–
Cream-coloured courser	2	–	1	1	–	–	–	–	–	–	–	–	–
Pratincole	2	–	1	–	1	–	–	–	–	–	–	–	–
Little ringed plover	1	–	–	1	–	–	1	1	–	–	–	–	–
Ringed plover	1	1	–	1	–	–	–	–	–	–	1	–	–
Kentish plover	–	–	–	1	–	–	–	–	–	–	–	–	–
Dottorel *	1	–	–	2	1	1	–	–	–	1	–	2	–
Golden plover *	3	1	3	2	3	3	1	–	1	3	1	2	2
Grey plover	1	1	–	–	1	1	–	–	1	1	–	–	–
Lapwing *	3	3	1	1	2	2	1	1	1	1	–	2	2
Sanderling	1	1	–	–	–	–	–	–	–	–	–	–	–
Little stint	1	1	1	1	–	–	2	–	–	–	–	–	–
Temminck's stint	1	–	–	–	–	–	–	–	–	–	–	–	–
Curlew sandpiper	4	1	–	–	–	1	1	–	–	–	–	–	–
Dunlin	1	–	–	1	–	–	1	2	1	–	–	–	–
Buff-breasted sandpiper	1	–	–	–	–	–	–	–	–	–	–	–	–
Ruff	2	2	1	1	3	2	–	2	2	–	2	1	–
Jack snipe *	1	2	1	1	1	1	–	–	1	1	1	1	–
Snipe *	1	2	2	1	2	3	1	2	1	4	2	–	–
Great snipe *	2	–	1	1	1	1	4	–	–	–	–	–	–
Woodcock *	2	3	1	1	1	1	2	1	1	3	1	2	3
Black-tailed godwit	1	–	–	–	–	–	–	–	–	–	1	–	–
Bar-tailed godwit	–	1	–	–	–	–	–	–	–	–	–	–	–
Whimbrel	1	1	–	1	–	–	–	–	–	–	–	–	–
Slender-billed curlew	1	–	–	–	–	–	–	–	–	–	–	–	–
Curlew *	–	–	1	2	–	–	–	–	1	–	–	–	1
Upland sandpiper	1	–	–	–	–	–	–	–	–	–	–	–	–
Spotted redshank	1	1	–	–	–	–	–	–	–	–	–	–	–
Redshank	1	2	1	–	–	–	–	1	–	–	–	–	–
Marsh sandpiper	2	1	1	–	–	–	–	–	–	–	–	–	–
Greenshank	3	1	2	1	3	–	–	3	1	–	–	–	–
Green sandpiper	1	–	–	–	–	1	–	–	–	–	–	–	–
Wood sandpiper	1	–	1	1	–	1	2	–	–	–	–	–	–
Common sandpiper	1	1	1	–	1	5	2	–	–	1	–	1	–
Turnstone	1	1	–	1	–	–	–	1	–	–	–	–	–
Pomarine skua	1	2	–	–	–	–	–	1	–	–	–	–	–
Mediterranean gull	2	2	–	2	1	1	–	1	–	–	–	–	–
Little gull	–	1	–	1	2	1	–	–	–	–	–	–	–
Black-headed gull	1	2	1	2	1	2	–	–	1	1	–	–	–

TABLE 6 (contd.)

Collection	A	B	C	D	E	F	G	H	I	J	K	L	M
Slender-billed gull	1	1	–	–	–	–	1	–	1	–	–	–	–
Audouin's gull	–	1	–	–	–	–	–	–	–	–	–	–	–
Herring gull	1	1	1	1	1	1	4	1	1	–	1	–	1
Sandwich tern	1	2	–	2	1	1	–	–	1	–	–	–	–
Little tern	–	1	–	–	–	–	–	–	–	–	–	–	–
Whiskered tern	–	–	–	1	–	1	2	–	–	–	–	–	–
Black tern	1	–	1	1	–	–	–	–	–	–	1	–	–
White-winged black tern	1	1	–	1	–	–	–	–	–	–	–	–	–
Wood-pigeon	1	1	1	–	–	–	–	1	–	–	1	–	–
Collared dove	1	1	–	–	–	1	–	–	–	–	–	–	–
Turtle dove *	2	2	1	1	1	2	3	2	2	2	1	1	–
Palm dove +	–	–	1	–	1	–	1	–	–	–	–	–	–
Great spotted cuckoo	1	–	–	1	–	–	–	–	–	–	–	–	–
Cuckoo	2	1	2	3	1	3	2	2	2	2	2	2	1
Barn owl	3	–	–	1	–	–	–	–	–	–	–	–	–
Scops owl	2	3	2	1	1	1	1	2	1	1	1	1	–
Long-eared owl	2	2	–	2	–	–	–	–	–	–	1	–	–
Short-eared owl	2	1	1	2	2	2	2	1	–	2	2	–	3
Nightjar *	2	1	1	1	1	1	–	1	1	1	1	2	–
Egyptian nightjar	–	–	–	–	1	–	–	–	–	–	–	–	–
Swift	1	–	3	1	–	1	–	–	–	–	1	–	–
Alpine swift	1	–	–	1	1	1	–	–	–	1	1	1	–
Kingfisher	1	–	1	1	1	1	1	1	–	1	–	1	1
Bee-eater	2	–	1	1	1	1	2	1	1	1	1	1	2
Roller	2	2	2	2	1	1	–	1	–	1	1	–	2
Hoopoe	2	1	4	2	2	3	2	1	1	1	1	1	2
Wryneck	1	1	–	1	–	1	2	1	–	–	1	1	–
Desert lark +	–	1	–	–	–	–	–	–	–	–	–	–	–
Short-toed lark	2	–	1	–	–	–	–	–	–	–	–	–	–
Woodlark	2	1	–	1	–	–	–	–	–	–	–	–	–
Skylark *	1	2	2	–	–	1	–	–	–	–	–	–	–
Sand martin	1	–	–	–	–	–	–	–	–	–	–	–	–
Swallow	1	1	–	–	–	1	–	–	–	–	–	–	–
Red-rumped swallow	1	–	–	–	1	–	–	–	–	–	–	–	–
House martin	1	–	1	–	–	–	–	–	–	–	–	–	–
Tawny pipit	1	1	1	–	–	–	2	–	–	–	–	–	–
Tree pipit	1	2	1	–	–	–	1	–	–	–	–	–	–
Richards pipit	–	–	1	–	–	–	–	–	–	–	–	–	–
Yellow wagtail	3	–	5	–	1	–	–	–	–	–	–	–	–
Grey wagtail	1	–	1	–	–	–	–	–	–	–	–	–	–
White wagtail	2	2	1	–	–	1	–	–	–	–	–	–	–
Waxwing	1	–	–	–	–	–	–	–	–	–	–	–	–
Alpine accentor	–	–	–	1	–	–	–	–	–	–	–	–	–
Dunnock	1	–	–	–	–	–	–	–	–	–	–	–	–
Rufous-bush chat	1	1	–	1	–	–	–	–	–	–	–	–	–
Robin	2	1	2	–	–	1	–	–	–	–	–	–	–
Thrush nightingale	1	–	–	–	–	–	–	–	–	–	–	–	–
Nightingale	1	1	1	–	–	–	–	–	–	–	–	–	–
Black redstart	1	2	–	–	–	1	–	–	–	–	–	–	–
Redstart	1	2	2	1	–	1	1	–	–	–	1	–	–
Moussier's redstart+	–	1	–	–	–	–	–	–	–	–	–	–	–
Winchat	1	–	2	–	–	–	–	–	–	–	–	–	–
Stonechat	1	–	3	1	–	–	–	–	–	–	–	–	–
Rock thrush *	1	3	–	2	1	–	2	2	1	–	1	1	1

TABLE 6 (contd.)

Collection	A	B	C	D	E	F	G	H	I	J	K	L	M
Blue rock thrush	2	2	–	–	1	–	2	–	1	–	–	1	–
Ring ouzel *	2	1	–	1	–	1	1	2	1	–	1	1	–
Blackbird *	2	2	–	3	1	1	2	–	2	–	1	–	1
Fieldfare *	2	2	1	1	1	1	–	1	1	–	1	2	–
Song thrush *	2	1	3	–	–	1	2	1	–	–	1	1	–
Redwing *	2	1	1	2	–	1	2	–	1	–	1	–	–
Mistle thrush *	2	–	–	–	1	–	2	–	1	2	–	–	–
Cetti's warbler	–	2	–	–	–	–	–	1	–	–	–	–	–
Fan-tailed warbler	1	1	1	–	–	–	–	–	–	–	–	–	–
Reed warbler	1	1	–	–	–	–	–	–	–	–	–	–	–
Great reed warbler	1	2	–	1	–	1	–	–	–	–	–	–	–
Icterine warbler	–	2	–	–	–	–	–	–	–	–	–	–	–
Sardinian warbler	2	2	1	1	–	–	–	–	–	–	–	–	–
Subalpine warbler	1	–	1	–	–	–	–	–	–	–	–	–	–
Garden warbler	–	2	1	–	–	–	–	–	–	–	–	–	–
Blackcap	1	1	1	–	–	–	–	–	–	–	–	–	–
Wood warbler	1	1	–	–	–	–	–	–	–	–	–	–	–
Willow warbler	1	1	–	–	–	–	–	–	–	–	–	–	–
Goldcrest	–	1	–	–	–	–	1	–	1	–	–	–	–
Spotted flycatcher	1	–	–	–	–	–	–	–	–	–	–	–	–
Red-breasted flycatcher	1	–	–	–	–	–	–	–	–	–	–	–	–
Pied flycatcher	1	1	1	–	–	–	–	–	–	–	–	–	–
Collared flycatcher	1	–	1	–	–	–	–	–	–	–	–	–	–
Golden oriole	2	1	7	1	2	3	3	3	1	1	2	1	–
Red-backed shrike	1	–	–	1	–	–	–	1	–	–	–	–	–
Lesser grey shrike	1	–	–	–	–	–	–	–	–	–	–	–	–
Woodchat shrike	1	1	3	1	1	1	1	1	–	–	1	2	–
Starling *	2	3	1	1	–	1	1	2	1	–	1	1	–
Rose-coloured starling	1	1	–	–	–	–	–	–	–	–	–	–	–
Spanish sparrow	2	–	1	–	–	–	–	–	–	–	–	1	–
Tree sparrow	1	–	–	–	–	–	1	–	–	–	–	–	–
Chaffinch *	2	2	1	–	–	1	–	–	–	–	2	–	–
Brambling	1	1	–	–	–	–	–	–	–	–	–	–	–
Serin *	2	1	1	–	–	–	1	–	–	–	–	–	–
Greenfinch *	2	3	1	–	–	1	–	1	–	–	–	–	–
Goldfinch *	1	1	1	1	–	1	–	–	–	–	–	1	–
Siskin *	–	–	–	–	–	1	–	–	–	–	–	–	–
Linnet *	4	2	3	–	–	–	–	–	–	–	–	1	–
Redpoll	1	–	–	–	–	–	–	–	–	–	–	–	–
Crossbill	2	–	–	1	–	–	–	–	–	–	–	–	–
Trumpeter finch	1	–	–	–	–	–	–	–	–	–	–	–	–
Ortolan bunting *	–	–	–	1	–	–	–	–	–	–	–	–	–
Reed bunting	2	2	–	–	–	–	–	–	–	–	–	–	–
Corn bunting	1	2	1	–	–	–	3	–	–	–	–	–	–
Number of birds	258	219	141	141	117	113	95	93	88	69	67	55	38
Number of species	177	131	106	97	72	78	61	63	62	38	49	46	25

NOTE: the symbols following the name of a bird signify:
* A species that is not protected by the regulations of 1980
⁺ Denotes that the species is known to have been imported in some of the collections.

Origins and numbers of Birds of Prey ringed abroad and recovered in the Maltese Islands

Osprey   ————
Black Kite   — ·— ·—

Honey Buzzard   ————
Buzzard   — — — —

Short-eared owl   ————
Marsh harrier   — — — —
Pallid harrier   — — — —
Montagu's harrier ··········

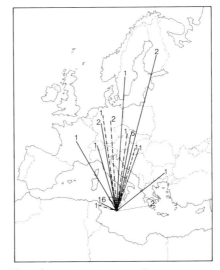

Kestrel   ————
Hobby   — — — —
Red-footed falcon — — — —
Eleonora's falcon   ··········

TABLE 7

Estimated numbers of some species of birds killed annually

	Woldhek	Sultana & Gauci	Magnin	Average number stuffed annually
Black-necked grebe	—	—	—	1100
Grebes (all sp.)	—	—	100–200	1400
Cory's shearwater	—	—	—	1000
Shearwaters (all sp.)	1000–2000	2000+	1000–2000	1900
Little bittern	—	—	500	2000
Night heron	1000–2000	—	1000–2500	5600
Squacco heron	—	—	500	1500
Little egret	—	—	1000	2100
Grey heron	—	—	500–1000	1600
Purple heron	—	—	400–800	2400
Herons & egrets	2000–3000	5000	1900–5800	13200
Garganey	—	—	—	2300
Ducks (all sp.)	1000–1500	1000–1500	1500–3000	5000
Honey buzzard	—	500–1000	500–1000	3200
Marsh harrier	—	—	400–800	6400

TABLE 7

Estimated number shot/trapped* annually	Comments
2300	Less than half the number of black-necked grebes shot are actually stuffed. Those shooting from sea-craft shoot large quantities of grebes.
2500	This figure includes the black-necked, little and great crested grebes. Most of the latter two species end up at taxidermists'.
10,000	Large quantities of shearwaters are shot at sea and remain uncollected. Those which end up at taxidermists' are individual carcasses which are collected and given to others to stuff or which are shot by shooters who had the opportunity to go and shoot from a friend's boat. More cory's shearwaters are shot due to their behaviour of staying in rafts and also because they fly close to any sea-craft.
13,000	See above comments.
2500	I have added a factor of 25% to the numbers stuffed to compensate for those which are shot but do not show up at taxidermists'. Bag records show that a shooter in every five shoots a little bittern each year.
12,000–16,000	At least 75 to 100% of all licensed shooters shoot a night heron annually.
2000–2500	Most squacco herons are shot from sea-craft and around the coast. A considerable number are shot and do not show up at taxidermists'. Bag records show that a shooter in every eight shoots one such heron each year.
5500	At least two and a half times the numbers stuffed, are shot. Bag records show that, on average, a shooter in every three shoots a little egret each year.
2100	A large percentage of grey herons and purple herons which are shot, end up stuffed. As with all heron species, many are shot from sea-craft and such shooters throw away considerable numbers. Bag records show that on average, a shooter in every eight shoots a grey heron.
3000	Purple herons are more frequently shot inland than grey herons. A shooter in every six shoots a purple heron each year.
16,000–32,000	The total was reached from records which show that each shooter shoots 2 herons of any species annually.
10,000	Most garganeys are shot from sea-craft. Bags of over thirty birds a day are common. In some years there are large influxes and larger numbers are shot inland as well as at sea.
12,000	Except for garganeys, most of the ducks which are shot end up stuffed.
3500	I have added a factor of 10% to the numbers stuffed to compensate for those which are shot and not stuffed. Bag records show that, on average, a shooter in every three shoots a honey buzzard each year.
9700	The total of 9700 was concluded from bag records, which indicate that every five shooters bag an average of three marsh harriers between them. Since the past four years, the number of shot harriers has increased dramatically. The figure of 12,000 harriers shot each year may be nearer to the real number which are shot currently. My impression is that during the past years, the number of marsh harriers shot equalled that of kestrels. Many are also shot from sea-craft.

	Woldhek	Sultana & Gauci	Magnin	Average number stuffed annually
Montagu's harrier	—	—	—	1800
Pallid / hen harrier (Circus sp.)	—	—	10–100	700
Harriers (all sp.)	—	200–400	—	8900
Kestrel	—	500–1000	750–1300	7700
Red-footed falcon	—	150–300	150–300	5900
Hobby	—	400–600	500–1000	3200
Other raptors	—	—	—	3000
Total raptors	1000–4500	2700–5000	—	34,000
Quail	1000–5000	4000–5000	1500–3000	1000
Moorhen	—	—	750–1000	2300
Rails/crakes/coot	500–200	1000–2000	450–800	1600
Black-winged stilt	—	—	50–100	1100
Dottorel	—	—	500	1100
Golden plover	—	—	1000–1500	1700
Lapwing	—	—	500–1000	1200
Ruff	—	—	500	1500

Estimated number shot/trapped* annually	Comments
4,000	In the records I had available 75% of the montagu's harriers stuffed were males. One has to multiply the number of males by three since, at least as many females and immatures are shot along with the males. While most of the latter get stuffed, females and immatures are not. Bag records show that a shooter in every four shoots a montagu's harrier each year.
2100	Bag records show that a shooter in 25 shoots a pallid harrier each year. All pallid harriers stuffed were males. At least as many females and immatures are shot, but many shooters mistake them for the commoner montagu's harrier.
15,800	See the comments for individual harrier species.
16,000–32,000	Each shooter shoots at least one to two kestrels each year.
6000–18,000	In good years, each shooter shoots literally dozens of such falcons. From data available, I have concluded that in poor years, a shooter in every three shoots a single bird, while in good years shooters shoot at least one bird each.
6500	Bag records show that 50% of what is shot, does not end up at taxidermists. On average, two hobbies are shot for every five shooters, each year.
3000	This includes the scarcer raptors such as osprey, black kite, some of the falcons, etc. of which considerable numbers are shot. Practically all those shot end up stuffed. Bag records indicate that some 250 black kites are shot each year.
64,000–96,000	Bag records show that, on average, each shooter bags a minimum of 5 raptors annually.
16,000–32,000	Practically every shooter shoots at least one to two quails per year.
8000	Most moorhens and crakes are shot by shooters who use pointer dogs. While the shooter who does not have a dog hardly ever shoots a crake, those who specialise in their shooting may kill over 50 birds in a season. Bag records show that practically every other shooter shoots a moorhen each year.
2800	Bag records show that a water rail is shot for every 21 shooters, while a coot is killed for every eight shooters.
1100	All the birds shot, end up stuffed, except those which are too badly mutilated.
1200	A dottorel is killed for every fourteen shooters. The number of birds killed can be much higher. Some are eaten.
4000–6000	Golden plovers and lapwings are shot by those shooters who shoot regularly in winter. Although much larger numbers used to be shot in former years, the number of shot plovers is likely to increase due to the introduction of tape-recorded bird songs. A large percentage of the birds shot end up in the pot and do not show up at taxidermists'. Bag records show that on average, a shooter in every three shoots a golden plover each year. To these one must add a few hundred which are trapped.
3000–5000	A shooter in every five shoots a lapwing.
6000	Most of the ruffs which are shot do not show up at taxidermists'. Bag records indicate that two ruffs are shot for every five shooters.

	Woldhek	Sultana & Gauci	Magnin	Average number stuffed annually
Woodcock	1000–10,000	3000	2000–3000	2000
Snipes	200–1000	8000	500–1500	2700
Common sandpiper	—	—	1000	1600
Other waders	—	—	—	7700
Waders (all sp.)	—	—	—	19,500
Black-headed gull	—	—	—	1800
Herring gull	—	—	—	1400
Gulls (all sp.)	—	—	1000	5300
Terns	—	—	100–300	1800
Turtle dove	20,000–200,000	100–200,000	100–200,000	1800
Cuckoo	—	ca2600	500–1000	5100
Scops owl	—	—	—	2100
Long-eared owl	—	—	—	300
Short-eared owl	—	—	—	4300
Owls	—	500–1000	500–1000	6700
Nightjar	2000–10,000	5000–8000	2000–3000	1600
Alpine swift	—	—	50–150	1000

Estimated number shot/trapped* annually	*Comments*
10,000–32,000	Woodcocks are shot mainly by shooters who specialise in their shooting. Most of the birds shot end up in the pot and do not show up at taxidermists'. Bag records show that ten shooters shoot eight woodcocks between them, each year.
16,000–32,000	One to two snipe are shot by each shooter annually.
12,000	Bag records show that every ten shooters shoot over seven common sandpipers between them, each year.
8000	The bag records show that over 1000 greenshanks and over 600 redshanks are shot each year. The figure for 'Other waders' includes the rarer waders, most of which end up stuffed.
78,000–195,000	On average, each shooter shoots four to ten waders of any species each year.
14,000	Bag records show that almost all shooters shoot a black-headed gull each year.
2000	The number of shot herring gulls may have decreased in recent years due to heavy persecution by those who shoot from seacraft. The breeding population has been drastically reduced. Bag records indicate that a shooter in every nine shoots a herring gull each year.
16,000–20,000	On average, shooters shoot more than one gull each year.
2,200	Most of the terns which are shot end up stuffed. Bag records show that 1400 sandwich terns and 800 marsh terns are shot each year. Many terns are being shot from sea-craft.
160,000–480,000	Ten turtle doves per shooter per year to 30 doves per shooter per year in good years. Bag records show that shooters shoot an average of fifteen turtle doves annually.
55,000	Bag records show that shooters bag over three cuckoos each, per year.
6300	At least three times the number of scops owls which are stuffed, are shot. In other words, one shooter in every three, shoots one such owl. In some years, the number of scops owls shot may be much higher.
300–350	Practically all of the long-eared owls which are shot, end up stuffed. In some years larger influxes occur and many more are shot.
4800	I have added a factor of 12% to the numbers stuffed to compensate for those which are shot and stuffed. In some years, the number shot may be over three times the one given. Bag records show that one third of all shooters shoot a short-eared owl annually.
11,500	See comments made for individual species of owls. Bag records show that shooters shoot two owls of any species each year. The figure of 20,000 owls shot annually may be a more realistic one.
32,000	Bag records show that, on average, shooters bag two nightjars each.
3600	Bag records show that each year a shooter in every four shoots an alpine swift.

	Woldhek	Sultana & Gauci	Magnin	Average number stuffed annually
Swift	—	—	5–15,000	—
Kingfisher	—	—	100–200	1700
Bee-eater	2500	ca2600	250–500	4300
Hoopoe	2500	ca2600	1500–2500	6500
Wryneck	—	—	—	900
Skylarks	10–80,000	20–50,000	50–100,000	—
Swallows and martins	—	40,000	30,000+	—
Robin*	40–500,000	50–100,000	20–50,000	—
Rock thrush	—	—	—	2100
Blackbird	—	—	25–50	1300
Fieldfare	—	—	—	1000
Redwing	—	—	—	700
Thrushes (all sp.)	11–300,000	2–300,000	2–300,000	8400
Golden oriole	5000	5000–8000	4000–7000	7800
Woodchat shrike	—	—	ca100–300	2300
Finches*	several 1000s	ca 1.5 million	3 million	—

Note that (all sp.) means all species of that particular family which occur locally.
* Denotes that this species is trapped.

Estimated number shot/trapped* annually	Comments
80,000–240,000	Five to fifteen birds per shooter per year is a conservative estimate. This number includes only those shot during migration periods when shooters shoot at Swifts only when there are no other birds in sight. Much larger numbers are shot during summer months by those who go out specifically to shoot them.
1700–2000	Bag records show that one kingfisher is shot for every nine shooters.
5000	Bag records show that, at least, one shooter in every three shoots one bee-eater each year.
16,000–48,000	Shooters shoot between one and three hoopoes each, each year. Bag records show that on average, shooters shoot over two hoopoes each, each year.
1000	Most wrynecks which are shot are stuffed.
200,000	An average of 10,000 shooters (i.e. the diehards who go out to shoot all year round) shoot an average of twenty skylarks each.
160,000–430,000	Ten to thirty swallows per shooter per year.
89,000–133,500	25% of the males aged 10–16 (i.e. 5077) + 10% of those aged 17–24 (2000) + 2% of the males aged between 25–64 (i.e. 1825 men) trap 10 to 15 robins each year.
2300	Most of the rock thrushes which are shot end up stuffed.
10,500	Many of the blackbirds which are shot end up in the pot, especially the females and immatures. Bag records show that on average, every other shooter shoots a blackbird each year.
4500	Fieldfares appear regularly at taxidermists'. In some years they are very common, which explains why not so many are stuffed. Bag records indicate that a shooter in every three shoots a fieldfare each year.
1000	A high percentage of the redwings which are shot, are later stuffed. A few end up in the pot.
240,000–550,000	Ten to thirty thrushes per shooter per year. Bag records indicate that shooters bag an average of 33 song thrushes and another thrush of any species, each year.
80,000	Bag records show that each shooter bags five orioles each year.
2500	The figure of woodchat shrikes may be much higher. Being very conspicuous when perching on exposed branches, it is very likely to attract the attention of trigger-happy shooters.
1–2.8 million	From field studies, I have concluded that trapping sites are used for an average of six weeks in spring and another six weeks in autumn. The number of finches trapped was reached by concluding that trappers trap an average of two to six birds per day, with a peak of ten birds on a single day in each migration. i.e. (42 days with 2 birds × 5309 trapping sites = 499,046 birds; plus 1 day with 10 birds × 5309 trapping sites = 139,058 birds. The results are multiplied by two to cover both spring and autumn migrations. The results are underestimations since trappers often catch large quantities in a single day, and because a large number of trappers start using their trapping sites on October 1st, and keep trapping birds until late April. Yet the figures suffice to show the gravity of the problem.

Woldhek[a] (1980), Sultana[b] and Gauci[c] (1982) and Magnin[d] (1986) published lists with estimates of the number of birds which are killed annually.
Woldhek's estimates were based on information given by Vella Gaffiero[e]
and Gauci, who estimated the number of shot birds from their knowledge
of a number of shooters and their yearly catch. The estimates by Sultana
and Gauci were based on their personal experience. They stated that the
estimates can be higher or lower than those they gave. Magnin's estimates
were based on a survey carried out with 14 Maltese bird-watchers.

a. S. Woldhek was the Chairman of the European Committee for the Prevention of Mass
   destruction of Migratory Birds.
b. J. Sultana was the President of the Malta Ornithological Society.
c. C. Gauci was the ringing Secretary of the Malta Ornithological Society.
d. G. Magnin collected data in Malta during October and November 1985.
e. J. Vella Gaffiero was the acting curator of the Natural History Museum and a practising
   shooter.

Method used to work out the data of the average number of birds stuffed and shot

The average number of birds stuffed per year was obtained by dividing the
total number of birds stuffed during that year by the number of shooters
which the taxidermist catered for. That is, for each species, the total for
each year was divided by 35 for the years 1976–82 and by 30 for the years
1983–86. The result for each year was then multiplied by the number of
licensed shooters for that year. The results for all years were added and the
gross total was divided by 11, which is the total number of years for which
data on the number of birds stuffed is available.

The total number of birds stuffed per year (T) was obtained using the
formula:

$$T = S\left(\frac{x}{n}\right)$$

Where x is the number of birds taken to the taxidermist in each particular
year, n is the number of shooters which the taxidermists catered for, and s
is the number of shooters during the year in which the total x was shot.

The mean number of birds stuffed was then obtained using the formula:

$$\frac{(T_1 + T_2 + T_3 + T_4 + T_5 + T_6 + T_7 + T_8 + T_9 + T_{10} + T_{11})}{11}$$

Where T_1 denotes the total number of birds stuffed during 1976, T_2 denotes
those stuffed during 1977 and so on. The number 11 is the total number of
years in which the grand total was shot.

example: Little bittern

year	number of birds stuffed	total T [ie $S\left(\frac{x}{n}\right)$]
1976	5	1148.786
1977	6	1378.543

1978	3	689.2714
1979	3	689.2714
1980	3	689.2714
1981	3	938.8286
1982	3	1063.886
1983	14	6473.133
1984	6	2850
1985	5	2438.167
1986	7	3453.45
total		21812.61
average		1982.964
to nearest 100		2000

Since the exact number of shooters between the years 1968 and 1981 is unknown, I worked out an average of 8041.5, which is the average of 5130 (the number of shooters in 1968) and 10,953 (the number of shooters in 1981).

The number of shooters I worked on was as follows:

Year	number of licensed shooters		
1976	8041.5	1982	12412 1
1977	8041.5	1983	13871 *
1978	8041.5	1984	14250 2
1979	8041.5	1985	14629 *
1980	8041.5	1986	14800 3
1981	10953	1987	14972 *

1. the total is an average of the years 1981-83
2. the total is an average of the years 1983-85
3. the total is an average of the years 1985-87
*. Number of shooting licences as published in *The Times* 28.11.89

The average number of stuffed birds was compiled from Table 10 for the reason that they were the only records which had the names of the shooters who shot the birds. Only those species whose yearly total or whose average over the eleven year period was equal to or exceeded 3 birds each year were counted. This was done to obtain a reasonable estimate. For the other species which were irregular at taxidermists, or whose yearly total did not average three birds per year, I thought that it would be better to make an estimate using both the data available as well as my personal experience.

There are a number of reasons why the estimates given are under-estimations. There are a large number of variables which I will now summarize, which affect the total of birds which are shot.

Not all birds that are shot end up at taxidermists'. Many birds are shot and thrown away because they are too badly mutilated to be stuffed, or because the shooters who shoot them already have them in their collections. Birds whose plumage is not in a good condition or which are not as colourful as can be, are not usually stuffed. A case in point is the golden oriole, which was a common bird at both taxidermists'. From the data I had available, 90% of the golden orioles which were stuffed, were males. At least as many females and immatures are shot each year, but most of them do not show up at taxidermists'. Thus if one assumes that all males are stuffed, which is a clear over-estimate, the number of orioles killed is at least 3 times higher. In reality, the number of orioles shot is much higher; as, like some other birds, many end up in the pot, either for consumption by the shooters themselves or by their dogs or are thrown away or not even picked up when shot.

Comparatively few specimens of turtle dove, woodcock, snipe, golden plover and thrushes reach taxidermists' shops. Many are shot and consumed. Shearwaters, small waders, hirundines and other small birds which are usually shot for the fun of shooting and do not show up at taxidermists' as they are not even retrieved when shot.

To these, one must add the number of birds which are shot and not found, and those which are shot, wounded and kept alive by shooters. One must also add those which are wounded and not retrieved, such as honey buzzards. Although many of these end up at taxidermists', many are shot at while flying at high altitudes, where they are wounded. In spite of the fact that they keep flying, they are unable to make the sea-crossing from Malta to the closest shores of North Africa in autumn or Sicily in spring.

Another factor which renders my result an underestimation is the number of shooters, which I have worked on, which is the number of licensed shooters. Although not necessarily all of those who pay a hunting licence actually go out to shoot birds, there are many who shoot without a licence. Usually, the latter are even more indiscriminate than licensed shooters because they are more trigger-happy. Since the number of unlicensed shooters is unknown, I had to multiply the number of birds shot with the number of licensed shooters, which is not the actual number of shooters.

I have also assumed that the shooters for whom the birds were stuffed, were licensed shooters. If some were unlicensed, then the fact that I am multiplying only by the number of licensed shooters, renders my result an underestimation. If, on the other hand, all shooters were licensed ones, my result would still be an underestimation because no allowance was made for the number of unlicensed ones.

The taxidermists whose records I had at my disposal are only typical of small part-timers. These taxidermists used to stuff birds for a small number of shooters from their villages. Taxidermist A stuffed birds for about thirty-five shooters from three villages, in which over a thousand licensed shooters lived. Taxidermist B stuffed birds for thirty shooters where there were over one thousand three hundred licensed shooters in the villages he catered for. There are a number of part-time taxidermists and at least two full-timers who handle a much larger quantity of birds than the two whose records I had at my disposal.

The species of birds shot depends on the particular quarry which the shooters look for. The area where they shoot makes a great difference. Shooters who shoot water birds prefer to frequent the coast, while those shooting in wooded areas are bound to shoot more golden orioles than water birds, for example.

Another factor which one must keep in mind is that the number of birds which migrate over the Maltese Islands varies from year to year, from species to species and from place to place. It so happens that in some years, species that are usually scarce appear in large numbers and many more are thus shot, and vice-versa. Both taxidermists, who were also keen shooters themselves, have told me that on more than one occasion they were out to shoot birds and saw no birds at all; and as soon as they returned home, other shooters came with birds they had shot. Migration would have been poor at the place where the taxidermists were, while the place where the other shooters had been was evidently better on that particular day.

Average number of birds shot and trapped

The average numbers shot was compiled from the bag records of ten shooters over a collective fifty-three year period. The total number of birds of each species was calculated for each shooter and the average bag per year was found. The averages of all shooters were then summed up and the collective average found. This was then multiplied by 16,000, the number of licensed shooters.

It resulted that on average, a shooter bags two herons, a duck, four birds of prey, a quail, five waders, a gull, sixteen turtle doves, three cuckoos, two owls, two nightjars, two hoopoes, thirty-four thrushes, ten starlings and five golden orioles each year. However, this does not include a number of species which are shot regularly, such as sparrows, wheatears, pipits, wagtails, swifts and hirundines, but which do not appear in bag records, and inevitably had to be omitted.

Neither do these figures include the number of finches trapped, given in Table 7. It is also worth noting that the figure of trapped finches does not include species such as tree pipits, short-toed larks and wagtails, which are trapped in considerable numbers by some trappers. It is indeed difficult to estimate the numbers of these birds which are regularly trapped.

It is equally difficult to estimate the number of other passerines which are frequently shot to be stuffed, as these too were omitted from the bag records I had available.

Chapter 6

Metaphors of Superiority, Masculinity, Virility and Machismo

A symbol of status

From the middle ages up to the early 1900s, hunting was a status symbol of the aristocracy; it was an assertion of social superiority. When hunting became a pastime of a wider stratum of society, social superiority was retained through *riservatos* – areas which are rented by or which belong to shooters. In such areas, only the tenants of the land or their guests are allowed to shoot. The rising standard of living enabled the average-income shooter to rent small tracts of riservatos and social superiority is now retained through the location, size and type of the riservato a shooter has. The best areas for shooting and the largest riservatos are usually in the hands of those who can afford to pay most.

The number of guns a shooter has, their type and make, are also signs of social superiority. Rich people usually have more expensive guns which are often engraved by hand. Such shooters usually use foreign-loaded cartridges, which are slightly more expensive than locally-loaded ones. The use of foreign-loaded cartridges is no longer a prerogative of the noble classes – shooters from all strata of society can now afford them – but affluent people have been using them for a very long time and they could afford to buy them when the average shooter could not. In fact, many old-time shooters will readily tell how much they treasured those single foreign-loaded cartridges which they used to obtain from other shooters in exchange for some dead rare bird or following some other favour. Farmers looked up at prominent people, such as the family doctor or the village lawyer, and they frequently allowed them to shoot on their land. The favour was returned by giving the farmer that box or two of foreign-loaded cartridges, and farmers would not accept other kinds of payment.

Social factors

In the past, men had little to fill their time with and little to do for recreation. Their imagination and means did not carry them beyond loading cartridges and shooting birds, providing something for the pot in the process. In the evenings, after work, there was little to do and few places to go to besides the village bar. Shooting provided them with a routine which was both manly and easy to follow. It became a part of their lives and they became obsessed by it.

Thus, one can easily link the growth in popularity of bird shooting and trapping with a certain lack of education on how to use one's free time. A keen shooter himself, Gauci wrote: 'It is indeed astonishing how even unto our day and age, so many thousands of otherwise sensible people from all walks of life, skilled and unskilled workers, professionals and priests included, low and high, young and old, fair and dark, simply toss off behind their shoulders their very livelihood, renounce their normal family life, just to dedicate themselves entirely to the craze of game'.[1]

The fact that there is such a craze is undeniable. The shooting fraternity does its best to perpetuate the shooting mania. Gauci wrote: 'We see youngsters, hardly out of their cot, showing unmistakable signs of things to come. They prop their left hand out as if pointing a gun at some target and with their pouting lips they try to imitate the popping of guns. They follow their imaginary quarry round the room swinging their left arm and banging with their lips still wet of their mother's milk. They are the shooters of tomorrow'.[2] Such behaviour is encouraged in houses where the father, or elder brother, is a shooter. I have on many occasions seen and heard parents of young children pointing at a sparrow or pigeon in the street or at a caged bird and asking the child 'What do we do to the birdie?' The child that says 'Bumm' is encouraged and shown clear signs of approval.

Shooters often take their young children with them when they go out to shoot birds. Children who grow up in such an atmosphere, in a house where stuffed birds stare from above every piece of furniture and who are taken on shooting excursions, soon develop the desire to shoot. Many children are introduced to shooting using catapults and air rifles, with which they kill lizards, geckos and small birds.

For families who have shooters, family outings are seldom without guns. Thus, from a tender age children not only play with their own toy gun, see stuffed birds and accompany their father on shooting excursions, but even learn to perceive shooting as a family affair. Such activities help shape the child's mind into the shooting routine of the adults around him.

A day in the life of a shooter

A shooter's life revolves around the migration of different species of birds, and there is a routine which is followed before, during and after each migration. But there are other aspects around which the shooter's life centres. The village bar is the focal point where they meet to talk about their favourite pastime – shooting. Envy and greed stimulate them and with raving minds they recount tales, joke, argue, quarrel, mock and console each other about it.

Besides the talk about who shot what, where and how, there is the concept of beating their own bag record of the previous year. One can also mention the walking and training of the retriever dog; the dusting of the stuffed birds in their home collection, the time spent looking at bird guides to see what they would like to shoot next, or to see how rare the bird they shot is and in which posture they would ask the taxidermist to stuff and mount it; the wish to shoot that elusive big or rare bird, for which they might already have a chosen stone or branch to mount it on and the chat with the taxidermist; meeting shooters they do not usually meet while seeing the birds that have been shot by other shooters. As the migration season approaches, the shooter who uses live, fluttering decoys has to prepare them. They see that their plumage is in immaculate condition and any worn or broken wing or tail feathers are plucked so that new ones grow in time for migration. At this time shooters would inevitably go to the place where they shoot to re-build or arrange their hide. There they would daub a number of stones with white paint and write RTO on prominent places: clear signals to other shooters that the land is reserved for shooting and that they are unwelcome.

Before the first migrants arrive, shooters would also start buying and trying out new cartridges. Some practise by shooting sparrows and other passerines such as pipits and shooters enjoy filling their time in the process of getting prepared for the next shooting season. For shooters, the first swallow or any other hirundine is a sign of spring, and the fever starts running high.

At the shop which sells shooters' goods, shooters may spend hours of masculine activity looking at guns and cartridges while chatting about bird shooting. The shooter scrutinizes the new guns and in his mind's eye, he sees himself in the field with that gun. He toys with new cartridges while discussing their performance with the shopkeeper, usually a shooter himself, and with the other shooters who may be present. They compare them to other cartridges on the market and to the old ones which they used in the 'good old days'. They wonder what technology has done to shooting while pitying their forefathers who claimed that a bird should not be shot at unless 'one could see its eye'. It was so in days of muzzle-loaders whose effective range was a mere thirty paces, but not today when birds are blasted out of the sky at three or four times that distance with ordinary cartridges.

Those who load their own cartridges need a lot of time since hand-loading cartridges is a laborious, time-consuming process. First of all, the shooter needs to buy raw material from the shop which sells shooters' goods, where the chat about birds and shooting is inevitable. Back at home, the shooter has to remove the used primer of every cartridge by means of a hand-operated gadget. He then gauges the cartridge to ensure that it fits into the barrel and fixes a new primer instead of the used one. The shooter then weighs the gunpowder and places a measure in each cartridge. A thin cardboard wad is then placed and pressed over the powder, over which, a thicker wad, usually of felt, is pressed in place. Another thin wad is placed before the cartridge is filled with a measure of lead shot, over which a final wad with the number indicating the shot size is placed. The cartridge is then closed, usually with a hand-operated machine.

A guest at a shooters' home is bound to be shown the collection of stuffed birds. The shooter will proudly explain what the birds are as well as when and where he shot them. He may go into a little more detail about particular birds, especially rarer, larger or more colourful ones. People are bewildered when they see so many birds. Most people do not believe that such a variety of birds pass over the Maltese Islands. In September, most birds and birds of prey are shot while people are sunning themselves on the beach. Otherwise, most shooting takes place when people are still asleep and by the time they go out in the countryside, there are very few birds, if any, left for one to see. Such situations favour the shooters, who will explain how able one has to be and how hard, expensive and time-consuming it is to 'catch' so many birds. At this point, shooters tend to exaggerate about the time they have to wake up in the morning, often claiming that they wake up at 3.30 am every day. This is done to impress their guests further and to show them how dedicated they are to their 'sport'.

Inevitably, the guest will be shown the gun cabinet, and may even be invited to handle a gun to see what it feels like. Some shooters like to keep the spent cartridges with which they killed the larger and rarer birds, and these may be shown to the guests as well. The evening is filled with stories and adventures about birds, big birds and shooting. And the shooter not only fills his time, but feels proud through being admired about his shooting feats.

In case the guests would not have noticed, the more obsessed shooter is bound to prove his affection and dedication to the pastime by telling them that even the name of his house is associated with shooting. House names bearing names such as *id-dura* (ie the shooter's hide), Hunter's House or bird names, are by no means uncommon. A weather vane with a shooter on it would not be amiss on a shooter's house while some shooters also paint bird names on their vans or trucks in a decorative manner.

Shooter's rituals

Certain activities of shooters are almost ritual-like: the preparation of things one needs to take out early the next morning; the setting of the alarm clock and watching the weather report; then the restless sleep and the dreams about the birds; waking up in the morning before the alarm clock rings; checking the weather through the bedroom window, while tea or coffee brews, then gulping it down in one breath, he grabs the gun and cartridges and off he goes. The drive or walk to a place for shooting is often interrupted by a stop at a reliable weather-vane for another check on wind direction. Arriving at the shooting place, the gun, dog and ammunition emerge from the car like a flash. The shooter then selects the first cartridges with which he loads his gun, wondering what he shall use them on as he walks to the shooting butt with the gun ready to leap to his shoulders or hugged across his chest. The tense expectant wait for the break of dawn and for birds is made longer with the nervous forefinger rhythmically tapping the trigger.

The first cracking of other guns fills the shooter with hope as he nervously stands in wait for birds within range – then the shoot itself, reloading the gun, retrieving the birds and waiting for more. Thoughts about the cartridges he used, their performance, his way of shooting and what cartridges he should use next converge on the shooter's mind.

Then comes the beating of the nearby trees, where the shooter walks slowly while throwing stones in the trees in an attempt to flush any birds that may be resting there. Later comes the chat with other shooters in the field, discussing the morning's shoot and comparing it with other shoots, other years and other weather conditions.

While walking back to the car – with the gun huddled under his arm or flung over his shoulder – the shooter is full of hope that an unsuspecting flock of birds might fly unhindered within his range. He constantly scans the skies around to ensure that his dream does not come partially true – with some birds passing without his seeing them. Such thoughts bring the shooter to his car, where, still scrutinizing the skies around, he hesitantly unlocks his car and reluctantly unloads the gun before sliding it into its cover and placing it on the back seat. Many shooters remove only the cartridge from the breech, leaving the magazine full, just in case they come across any birds on the way home when they will save themselves those precious seconds, as the gun can be reloaded by a single stroke of the hand.

The drive back home is often interrupted by a stop at a bar somewhere along the way where other shooters stop for a chat over a coffee. All of them talk about what they saw; some boast about what they shot, others bemoan their luck about the bird that got away or about the dog which flushed a bird in the wrong direction. Others complain about the weather or about not having seen any birds. Another stop may take place at the gun shop from where the shooter buys his goods. There he gets the latest news of who bagged what from where.

Finally back home, neighbours or passers-by might ask the shooter whether he 'caught' anything and he would display the ruffled feathers in his bag. Still thinking about the shoot, he then cleans his gun and refills the cartridge belt and game-bag. The morning ritual is repeated in the afternoon shoot. Then, in the evening, comes the chat at the village bar, this time with shooters who know each other more closely. Finally, back at home, the phone call to a friend, who lives and shoots in a different locality to enquire about how successful the shoot was on the other side of the island; then the preparation of things needed for the next day's shoot, and once again the setting of the alarm clock. . . .

Talk of the town

Maltese shooters are not conservationists, neither at heart nor in practice. They kill as much as they can. When spring is in the air and the birds arrive from the south, shooters start talking about the winds. They hope and pray for winds which bring the birds to our shores. Shooters become feverish with excitement. Loose cartridges and whole cartridge-belts start appearing on car dashboards and the only things that shooters talk about are birds and winds and cartridges and guns, even weeks before the first birds arrive. Yet shooters talk of shooting, think of shooting, even dream of shooting – endless flocks of turtle doves migrating through the sleeping minds of restless shooters, heaps of dead rare birds filling their bags and, later, their showcases. They thrill at the thought of talking about their kills, vividly describing each and every kill – as if it were an act of heroism – to envious ears whose owners remained asleep or who were at the wrong place at the right time the day the birds came . . .

In every town and village there is at least one bar or club where shooters meet to boast about their feats over a glass of wine or a bottle of beer. When a large bird is shot, the shooter usually takes it to the bar. There it becomes the main topic of conversation and other shooters will recount their experiences in shooting similar birds. The stories revolve on when and how the birds were shot, what the weather was like, the cartridges used and the altitude at which the bird was shot.

In the course of their explanation, shooters gesture, using their hands, arms and whole bodies to illustrate vividly what they are describing. They use their hands when talking about birds up to the size of a turtle dove and their arms when talking about bigger birds such as harriers.

From a crouched stance, the shooter sways as he uses the palms of his hands or his whole arms to describe the flapping wings of a flying bird. Then he rises from his seat or straightens himself, throwing his left hand in the air, and the right one in front of his face, as if he is actually shooting a gun. Then comes the '*pumm pumm pumm*', imitating the number of shots he fired while swinging slowly as if actually shooting at a bird in flight. And finally the clenched fist, quivering hand or rolling arms signifying the shot or dying bird falling to the ground.

Such dramatic scenes have to be seen to be believed. Yet they are commonplace and they can be witnessed not only in village bars and in shops selling shooters' goods, but almost anywhere shooters meet, be it in the field, or on the street or during social functions such as parties and wedding receptions where shooters meet other '*dilettanti*' and segregate themselves to talk about their favourite pastime.

Shooters' language

The word *dilettant*, which in the Maltese language stands for amateur, has a different meaning to the shooting community. To them, *dilettant* implies one who is fanatically interested in birds, that is, a shooter, a trapper, or a combination of both. The same can be said for the word *namra*, which means passion. To shooters and trappers, the word signifies one who has a passion for shooting or trapping birds.

Social historian Peter Burke wrote that different social groups use different varieties of language in different situations.[3] This is very true of shooters. They use strong words to describe their kills when discussing the subject amongst their kind – but talk with equivocation when conversing with others who do not form part of the shooting fraternity.

While talking to strangers, shooters talk of birds falling from the sky – *tajtu tir u waqa* – 'I shot it and *it* fell' they say, as if it is not their fault that the birds 'fall' dead or wounded. The verb 'to kill' is hardly ever used. Instead, shooters use the verb '*taqbad*' which means 'to catch', which does not imply killing. The birds which they shoot are 'caught' or 'captured'. The emphasis is on the skill, a sense of 'fair play' and the gentlemanly conduct of the shooter, and on his honest affection and admiration for the beauty of nature, which, they contend are the real reasons why shooters enjoy their 'sport'.

Yet, amongst their kind, the rituals of contemporary shooters betray uninhibited delight in the capture and killing of birds. The phraseology shooters use to describe their catches differs significantly from that which is used with the man in the street. Shooters speak about their catches using distinctly sadistic vocabulary. They speak in an emotionally violent way. According to their descriptions, the birds which they shoot are not simply killed, but blasted out of the sky. Apart from boasting about the altitude at which the bird was shot and its speed in flight, shooters use hyperbolic verbs which emphasise their performance in shooting.

I have heard shooters uttering phrases like: '*Sparajt għal kuċċarda, issussajtha bit-tir*', which means 'I shot at a honey buzzard, and lifted it with shot'; '*Qbadt seqer, thantu*', 'I shot a kestrel, and made mincemeat of it'; '*tajjart daqquqa, ġibta tabakk*', 'I flushed a hoopoe and made mincemeat of it'; '*sparajt għal buqrajq, ġibtu stoppa*', 'I shot a nightjar and turned it into oakum'; '*Li jidholli fit-tir, niskumnikah*', 'I destroy whatever comes within range'; '*Ħarġitli summiena, ġibta hara*' meaning 'I flushed a quail and turned it into shit!'; '*Sparajt għal gamiema, mank basset*' which means 'I shot a turtle dove and it didn't even have time to fart' (ie it was killed instantly); '*tajra safra ghamiltha raghad*' 'I shot a golden oriole and smashed it to smithereens'; '*Ġiet tajra kahla, ixxuttjajtha bit- tir*', 'I shot a cuckoo, and kicked it with the shot', '*dahalli seqer, qsamtu*' 'a kestrel came within range and I blasted it into two; '*Sparajt għal pespus, żelliġtu*', 'I shot at a meadow pipit and smeared it over the ground'. Talking about swallows, I have heard shooters say '*il-ħuttaf nifqgħu bit-tir*' meaning 'I shoot at swallows and burst them with the shot' and '*il-ħuttaf inġiddmu*', which means 'the swallows I shoot are plagued with shot'. I have heard a shooter say '*L-imlievez tihom ġo darhom*', which translated literally means 'hit the thrushes on the back' and '*Il-gamiem niehu gost inqattghu bit-tiri*' meaning 'I enjoy tearing turtle doves to pieces with shot'.

Words like '*qridtu*' (I destroyed it), '*dahhantu*' (I smoked it), '*fqajtu*' (I busted it), '*farraktu*' (I smashed it), '*kissirtu*' (I broke it to pieces), '*nixxiftu*' (I dried it), '*biċċirtu*' (I butchered it), '*tertaqtu*' (riddled it with shots), '*ġibtu rmied*' (I turned it to ashes), '*inhataf bit-tir*' (it shrunk with shot), '*intiftu fl-arja*' (I made its feathers fly off in the air, or its feathers were plucked in flight with shot), '*damdamtu*' (tore it open with shot), '*ġibtu gharbiel*' (peppered it with shots), '*kahhaltu*' (I plastered it), '*sammartu*' (I hammered it), '*inxartu*' (I shot it dead) and '*imbuttajtu*' (I pushed it) are frequently used to signify the way in which a bird was shot. The word '*ħraqt*', which means I burnt, has become very popular and has substituted the word '*sparajt*', which means I shot, in many shooters' vocabulary.

These strong phrases are nothing but a clear sign of a violent mentality. The verbs used, if taken literally, can be described as crude, but the intention is not so much an expression of crudeness as an expression of vulgar boasting and superiority.

On top of all this, in shooting circles, they have a 'hit-parade', whereby shooters rank in the list according to how many birds they shot in that particular season. Their desire is at least to break their own record of the previous year.

The shooting mania

Hunting, for most of the Maltese shooters, has only one rule: if it flies, shoot it. There is a craze for shooting and many shooters are simply trigger-happy. It is not only the winged creatures which are shot at. One can often see road signs, walls, doors and windows of buildings in the countryside as well as leaves of prickly pears and other cacti, peppered with shot. Some try to justify such shooting by attributing it to an inexperienced beginner who wanted to try out a cartridge to see what kind of shot pattern it has. But I have also seen shooters shooting at dragonflies, bats, butterflies, snakes, weasels and even each other's hats and shoes as these were thrown in the air in turn during tribal-like piques which arise following arguments of who is the better marksman or whose home-made cartridges are better. Some shooters often go to rubbish tips at night to shoot at rats.

Shooting of rats is becoming a common practice. At the rubbish tip of Xagħra in Gozo, groups of Maltese shooters who go there to shoot during the migration periods frequently organize rat shoots late in the evening and at night. Rat shooting also takes place at the rubbish tip at Magħtab, Malta, especially during summer and winter. The specialist paper for shooters and trappers, aptly called *Il-Passa* (ie 'the migration'), which at its launch in 1983 was said to have the full backing of the Shooters' and Trappers' Association,[4] recently carried a four-page article, starting on the front page and with a title, 'When we went rat shooting'. The article, which was lavishly illustrated with a number of pictures showing shooters posing with guns and holding dead rats, described vividly how a group of shooters went in a landrover and shot 'hundreds of rats'.[5]

It is common practice for some shooters to use air rifles (the use of which is illegal) to shoot at Spanish sparrows and starlings which perch on television aerials. The picture would be incomplete if no mention was made of when shooters were seen shooting at mullet fish at Salina Salt Pans and other places around the coast.[6] Reports of dead or dying dolphins as a result of shooting are quite frequent; while pets such as cats, which wander away from the safety of their home, often end up as victims of trigger-happy shooters.[7] Even racing pigeons are heavily persecuted and their shooting frequently results in quarrels between shooters and pigeon-fanciers. Parrots and aviary-bred birds such as budgerigars, or fowl bred on farms which escape from captivity, do not survive for long in the wild due to shooting.

Gulls and grebes which winter in harbours are frequently shot, or caught by fish hooks or nets. On more than one occasion I have seen people trying to catch black-necked grebes using large cup-shaped nets at the end of long poles or trying to hit them with oars or long sticks. On one occasion in winter 1988, I recall having seen a man shooting a pair of black-necked grebes with a harpoon at Vittoriosa. Spear-fishing is a very common pastime. Unfortunately the list of people who have a hunting and spear-fishing licence is not accessible to the public. It would be interesting to find out what percentage of those who practise spear-fishing are also bird shooters. My impression is that it would be high.

Surprisingly enough, bird shooting sometimes takes place even during clay-pigeon shoots. As a young boy I recall watching a clay-pigeon shooting competition at the Malta Shooting Club at Attard. On that occasion, a Maltese team was competing against a foreign team when two night herons flew over the range. One of the Maltese competitors shot them both while his team mates were shooting at clay-pigeons. On another occasion, while watching a trap shooting competition at the Mellieħa range in the 70s, a hoopoe flew through the range. Five or six shooters shot at it simultaneously. At the Dingli range, which is situated just below the panoramic road, I have on a number of occasions seen shooters shooting at swifts during clay-pigeon shoots – in full view of those present and of passers-by.

Other attitudes

The lack of respect for nature is reflected by the shooters' attitude, who consider the birds simply as targets. Mr J. R. Scicluna, the ex-President of the Shooters' and Trappers' Association, has recently referred to birds as 'a few feathers'.[8] With such attitudes, one cannot but conclude that hunting for pleasure in its various aspects is anti-educational. It confirms the old-fashioned image of man versus nature. Furthermore, its undemocratic position in this context prevents others genuinely seeking recreation through nature, from discovering and learning to appreciate it.

The social aspect of hunting as a means of recreation must not only be judged on the views of passionate nature lovers. One must also take into account the views of all those people who look for rest and relaxation in the limited area of our countryside. It must also be stressed here that the number of shooters is a small percentage of the total population. One must also take into account that the imposed subjection to the killing of birds, the noise of gunshots and the fear of being injured by shooters, can be an unnecessary worry for those seeking recreation on a physical as well as psychological level.

In his *Shooting Topics* series, A. Gauci also wrote about the relationship between shooters and the rest of the community. In his article entitled 'Merciless persecution', written when the number of shooters was half of what it is today, one reads:

> Today we have to witness armed men, young and old, parading the countryside as if Malta was at war with some other country and a sudden attack was expected from day to day. These armed patriots have no respect for the safety of other picnickers who have just as much right to enjoy the open countryside.[9]

Images of sexuality

There is something very manly about carrying a gun. The prevailing notion, that in olden days shooters shot only at 'game birds', is a far cry from the truth. The major difference is that they shot for the pot. Otherwise they differed little from those of today except that they were much fewer in number, they respected each other more and had more living targets available to them. They were also less macho, though they believed, as most still do, that shooting for sport was not only beyond reproach, but was almost a duty if one was to qualify as a real man.

Duffy sees hunting as satisfying sexual needs. She points out the sexual imagery in hunting and shows the hunt as a sexual pursuit. She argues that 'the point of hunting is to conquer by catching or killing. Whether fishing, fowling, coursing or the chase, it has, like a masturbation fantasy, two parts, the hunt and the kill even when that is symbolic as in the landing of a fish that is then thrown back'.[10]

Besides the macho element which exists in the Maltese Islands, one cannot but comment about the Maltese bird names. It is interesting to note that all species of birds which were and are still considered as edible species (with the exception of thrushes, which are also considered as songbirds, and snipe) have a feminine name: hence a turtle dove is called 'gamiema', a skylark 'alwetta', a golden plover 'pluviera', a lapwing 'venewwa', a woodcock 'gallina', a honey buzzard 'kuċċarda', a pigeon 'ħamiema', and a goose 'wiżża'. The generic name for duck is 'borka', also feminine. It is interesting to note that if a different word exists for the male, as in the case of the male turtle dove and quail, which can be called 'gamiemu' and 'summienu' respectively, the male name is hardly ever used. Somehow, shooters always seem to 'catch' a female.

On the other hand, all falcons, harriers, herons, finches and colourful birds, bear male names. With finches, it is evident that they bear male names because it is the males which are most sought for their song. Birds of prey were probably given male names due to their association with falconry and manliness.

Macho images

Today the manly attitude is much more evident in shooting. The younger generation of shooters is much more macho than shooters of a mere thirty years ago. This can be seen by both what the shooters wear and use, as well as their behaviour and vocabulary. While shooters used to wear plain khaki clothes and carry a twin-barrelled shotgun, today's younger generation wears camouflaged jackets, which can be bought from shops selling shooters' goods or which are made to measure. A double-cartridge belt and five-shot repeater shotgun, often with an attachment making the gun a seven shot repeater, are a common feature. The macho attitude of shooters was noted also by the late Albert Gauci, who wrote:

> How can you recognize this pest? Easy. He strolls like a mighty rebel through the countryside undaunted and unafraid of passerby, children and women who may be taking their share of God's fresh air on their days off. He shoots with a fearlessly straight aim at eagles, sparrows and swallows without the least fear of the possibility of being attacked in turn. Nothing which moves escapes his fire-spitting gun. His arms hug the shining automatic gun and a hundred and one peculiarities which he carries on and with him distinguishes

easily this pest from all other mortals, peaked cap, gaudy shirt and commando trousers, ammunition belt or belts, heavy boots, bag and all the rest.[11]

The macho mentality can be also seen through the exhibition of things related to shooting. Guns, cartridges and cartridge-belts are frequently left in places where they can be seen by passers-by in shooters' cars. Trophies, in the form of stuffed mounted birds, are often displayed in windows overlooking the street. Some shooters even hang stuffed heads of birds, especially birds of prey, from the rear view mirror of their car, while others hang cartridges. During the shooting season, one can often see men with cartridge-belts on near the village bars. They are shooters returning from a shoot, who keep their sign of manliness on even while stopping for a chat, a boast and a coffee.

The Rambo mentality

Thomas concluded that hunting stimulates warfare.[12] Local adverts for shooters' clothes often contain words like 'army clothes' and 'commando style'. The words printed on cartridges often have subtle and overt connections with military equipment. On more than one occasion, I have heard shooters say that the shooting of large birds like honey buzzards, would be more fun if the birds were armed with machine-guns under their wings.

Apart from what the shooters say and wear, some advertised shotguns resemble military weapons rather than conventional shotguns. Dr Michael Mallia, a magistrate who is a practising shooter, recently wrote, 'even the conventional five-shot repeater is aesthetically more connected to the military than to the traditional game-shooting gun.'[13]

A mere fifty years ago, shooters were also somewhat more modest towards fellow shooters and trappers. When shooters used to stay together or near each other they were careful not to shoot in the direction of footpaths, roads and other shooters. It was common practice for shooters to call or otherwise inform other shooters of an approaching bird. Today, not only do they not inform other shooters, but they even try to distract their attention so that they might have a better chance of shooting the bird themselves. If a bird settles close to another shooter without the latter realising it, instead of drawing the other shooter's attention to it, today's shooter tries to shoot it himself. Writing about the current situation, Magistrate Mallia wrote:

> Many times have I seen a poor bird being shot at by at least a dozen shooters and still being shot at while falling. The foul language and blaspheming that follows can best be imagined. This is not to say that this is the only source of argument; even the positioning of the shooter in the field is made with arrogance and selfishness.[14]

I have, on more than one occasion, seen shooters shoot at birds which others were trying to stalk or flush. There is no respect towards other shooters and arguments leading to serious quarrels and fights frequently arise when more than one shooter shoots and kills the same bird. There have been a number of cases where persons were charged in court

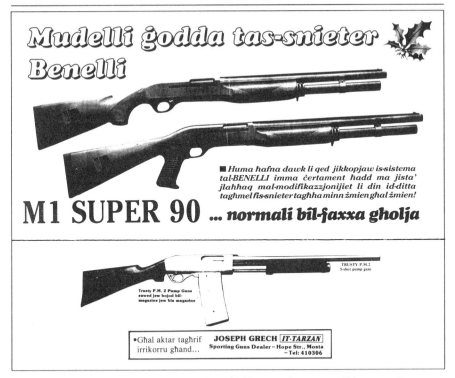

An advert showing new shotguns by Benelli. The captions says: 'Many are those who copy the Benelli system but certainly no one can keep up with the modifications it makes.' A pump action shotgun (below).

with attempting to seriously injure each other following quarrels on shot birds.[15]

Up to a few years ago, it was unheard of for shooters to shoot at birds which were flying towards a trapping site. Old-time shooters will readily tell you that, in pre-war years, shooters did not shoot at turtle doves early in the morning, but they looked for quails and left the early morning flocks of turtle doves for the trappers. Besides the fact that nowadays turtle dove trapping sites are surrounded by shooters, many trappers, being shooters themselves, carry guns. The shotgun has become a standard feature even at finch trapping sites. At places where finch trapping is most intensive, one frequently hears of quarrels arising when a trapper shoots at a bird which has just escaped his nets, thus not giving the adjacent trapper a chance of catching it himself.

In certain areas shooters do not allow shooters from other villages to shoot, even if the land is public property. Signs warning shooters, except those from Qrendi village, to keep out, can be seen daubed on the perimeter wall around the oldest free-standing prehistoric temples of Ħaġar Qim in Malta's south. Soon after the Government announced that it was considering turning the area around these temples into a national park, unknown persons daubed a gruesome message on the ground, *'namur jew ntajru'*, meaning 'it's either our hobby, or we'll blow up the temples'.[16]

Acts of vandalism by shooters, aimed at discouraging other shooters from going to shoot in 'their' areas are quite common. Vandalism, ranging from punctured tyres and scratches to the paint-work of cars to the throwing of hydraulic fluid, paint remover or acid on the cars of shooters who are new to areas where they are unwanted, are quite common practices. In extreme cases, windscreens are known to have been smashed and cars shot at. In some places, nails are strewn on certain parts of the road so that the unwanted shooters end up getting flat tyres. At Miżieb, the land which is 'managed' by the Shooters' Association, pieces of wood with nails pointing out were buried in the parking area while more nails were strewn around the place. People who went to the picnic areas in Miżieb ended up with multiple punctures.[17]

Poisoned bait aimed to kill other shooters' dogs is frequently strewn in some places. Such acts of vandalism do not effect only shooters, but also other people using such areas. The demolition of shooting hides used by shooters and the burning of trees and other vegetation are amongst other forms of vandalism which occur before, during and after each migration period.

Shooters and the law

Most shooters are also unafraid of the law, of which they make a mockery. Deep down they know that there is no law enforcement. Some shooters even boast of their immunity due to their links with Members of Parliament, whose alliance with shooters is not as innocent as it seems. For some politicians, the sponsorship of certain shooting activities and the association with shooters is often an indirect show of force. Shooters boasting of the immunity claim that they always know beforehand if the police are going to make any 'surprise' visits to protected areas. Such statements have a good measure of truth since, whenever the police made raids at Buskett Gardens, a bird sanctuary, some shooters who are usually present, were absent on days when the raids took place. It seems that one can almost know if the police are going to make a raid or not depending on whether one sees certain shooters (or their cars) or not. To make matters worse, it is common knowledge that when the police do take action and some guns are confiscated, the guns are frequently returned to the law-breaking shooters even before they are charged in court – and in some cases, prosecution does not even take place.

Shooters in and around Buskett Gardens can be seen, even in the main road leading to the gardens. Shooters shoot from the street in full view of passers-by, killing birds and peppering picnickers with lead shot in the process.

The attitude of law-breaking shooters can be best illustrated by the photograph showing the shooters in the dinghy. These people were shooting at herring gulls and cory's shearwaters, which are protected birds, near the Islet of Filfla, a bird sanctuary, during the closed-season. When

Top left: Armed to the teeth, a shooter and his dog show off a golden oriole. *Right:* A robin trap. *Centre:* Dishevelled and looking miserable, this robin is just a decoy with which many others are trapped. *Above:* To mobilise public opinion, over 70,000 spent cartridges were strewn at the main entrance of the capital city Valletta on 10th September 1988 by members of the environment group *Zgħazagħ għall-ambjent*. Such actions are no longer being held. Environment groups are being courted and manipulated – yet the killing goes on.

Top left: The *raghaj*, a decoy which is tethered to the ground but which is not required to flutter. It is more commonly used for luring wintering finches which gather in flocks to feed. *Top right:* The result of spite and envy amongst shooters frequently results in burnt trees. *Above:* Sheer waste of life, a dead bee-eater rots in the warm spring air. The hopes of spring are shattered by the urge to pull the trigger.

Opposite above: A hoopoe shows the real meaning of a near miss. The real fun of shooting is not the kill, shooters argue. *Below:* Part of a typical collection of stuffed birds. Most shooters have such a collection.

Top: Christmas decorations in a shopwindow of a shop selling shooters' goods. Baby Jesus is surrounded by stuffed birds of prey (which are protected birds), cartridges and guns. *Above:* In spite of the fact that gunpowder and guns were invented many years after the birth of Christ, in Malta shooters are represented even in the Christmas crib! The above are different figurines of shooters which can be seen in cribs.

The Church has a finger, if not a whole hand, in the pie. Apart from the fact that the shooters' mass is said at a number of villages, shooters fire salutes from the roof of the parish priest on the feast of Our Lady of Victory, and from the roof of the church on the Feast of St Julian.

Above: A pied flycatcher and a spanish sparrow died a long, slow, cruel death after being caught in a vertical net, in which they were left to die.
Opposite: During the week, birds are sold from shops in villages while on Sundays they are sold on the open air market at Valletta in Malta and at Rabat in Gozo.

Bird-song devices with small cassettes with songs of most types of birds are available at relatively cheap prices. Their effectiveness in luring birds more than justifies their cost.

Opposite left: If it moves, shoot it. If it doesn't, shoot it just the same. *Opposite right:* Bar sign. Macho shooters are more likely to sport a T-shirt with an advert for cartridges. They are more likely to shoot at anything as well. *Above:* With no more birds around to shoot, shooters gather to chat and boast of their feats before going home. The drive back home is usually interrupted by another stop at a bar along the road, where shooting is again the topic of conversation.

Above: Typical shop signs advertise the brand name of the cartridges which are produced by that shop. Other shops who just sell a variety of accessories for hunting usually bear a name which is associated with hunting. Like the word *Dilettant*, *In-Namra* (which means passion), is used to signify someone who is interested in hunting. *Opposite:* The nonchalant attitude of Maltese shooters – unafraid of the law – can be seen from such pictures. The shooters were shooting during the closed season at herring gulls and cory's shearwaters, protected birds, near the Islet of Filfla, a bird sanctuary. When they realised that their illegal activities were being photographed, they drew closer and one of them pulled down his pants. They were acquitted because of "lack of supporting evidence"!

Top left: Female finches are tethered as fluttering decoys. When the trapper pulls the string, the perch to which they are tethered rises and when it is released, the perch falls and the bird flutters giving the impression of a bird alighting on the ground.

Above: A clockwork skylark decoy made by Manufrance and a home-made version by a Maltese shooter.

Top: Turtle doves which are used as fluttering decoys are kept hooded throughout the hunting and are fed mouth to mouth by the shooter or trapper who uses them.

Above: The ordeal is not yet over for this kestrel. Birds of prey which are wounded are often kept alive. Crammed in a small cage or chained by one of their legs, they spend the rest of their lives in a most miserable way.

A shooter and his dog wait for migrating birds.

Just as bars, cars and cartridges are named after aspects of shooting, so too are shooters' houses.

A dead kestrel – like most birds of prey that fly over the Maltese Islands, it never lived to tell the tale. Birds of prey are protected only on paper.

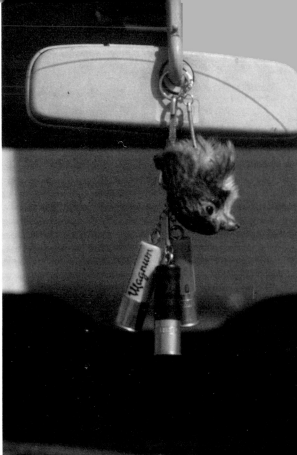

Top: Metaphors of masculinity. A stuffed head of a kestrel and heavy gauge cartridges hang from the rear view mirror of a shooter's car. Stuffed heads of birds of prey and occasionally woodcocks, can be seen as the alternative to a soft toy or furry dice.

Above: Names of birds are often painted on vans and trucks belonging to shooters. Bird names and other items associated with shooting are also common as house names.

Right: Heavy-gauge cartridges – every effort is made to kill birds at high altitudes.

Top left: In some places, hunting butts are erected amidst trees planted for bird-shooting purposes.

Top right: Spent cartridges at Buskett, a bird sanctuary turned into a shooting reserve for those who shoot there with impunity. The arm of the law is too short to reach them.

Above: A hooded turtle dove ready to become a fluttering decoy while an assistant holds a freshly trapped turtle dove and the trappers relay their nets.

Right: Trapped turtle doves in the trapper's sack.

Top left: Spring-operated nets have an effective catching volume almost 3 times that of conventional clap-nets. They are becoming fashionable. *Right:* Plastic decoys of golden plover and lapwing are used by trappers and by some shooters. *Centre left:* Duck decoys. *Right:* Round whistles of different sizes are used for luring skylarks, meadow pipits, yellow wagtails and song thrush, although cassettes are fast replacing them. *Above left:* Golden plovers are lured by a reed pipe whistle. *Right:* Imitating the call of the lapwing.

they noticed that their illegal activities were being photographed, they drew closer and one of them stood up, back to the camera, and pulled down his pants.

Marked changes: wordage on cartridges

The manufacturing industry which provides paraphernalia for the shooting community, has long sensed this trend of machismo. If one were to take a look at cartridges produced some 60 years ago, one would find that most of them were plain, without any motifs or else having just the brand name and the name of the powder with which they are loaded. Some time later, animals and birds which were considered as game, such as deer, rabbits, ducks or partridges, started appearing on cartridge cases. Birds of prey also featured, as they still do, on some of the cartridges. Gradual changes started taking place and cartridges were then being loaded by 'The best smokeless powder and chilled shot' and 'Super Ballistite'. Words like 'Heavy Load', 'Long Range' and 'Express' were soon to find their way on to cartridge cases.

Thus, if one were to compare cartridge cases, not to speak of their performance, one notes significant changes. Manufacturers use words which attribute special characteristics to the cartridge. The emphasis today is on the high velocity, the special load, the long range and the impact. Cartridges with the words super calibre, super match, *super chasse, grande chasse,* flash, concorde, victory, saga, turbo, anvil, semi-magnum, baby-magnum or magnum cartuccia speciale, are very easy to come by. Names with obvious military connections are mirage, super jet, speed fire and challenger. It is becoming increasingly fashionable for manufacturers to make cartridges with black bases. Formerly, cartridge bases used to be made of brass or a copper-plated alloy. Although there may be reasons such as cutting down costs behind the black bases, the choice of black is not accidental. It gives cartridges a sinister appearance. Recently introduced Italian cartridges, being dark, dull olive green with a black base, resemble ammunition used by special squads rather than hunting ammunition.

Indeed, the macho shooter might be more eager to try out a cartridge which gives the impression of a heavier load, with which birds are not simply killed but blown out of the sky. The examples mentioned show the extent of the macho attitude. A French firm produces cartridges on which one reads the words *la nucléaire* amidst a star symbolising an explosion!

Locally-made cartridges are no exception and words like 'Super', 'Special' and 'High velocity' also feature prominently on them. One particular shop produces cartridges called Pattern. Names associated with birds, such as Flamingo, Pelican and Wings are also popular. Brand names such as Punch, Tarzan, and MX, are amongst the most popular of locally-loaded cartridges.

It is interesting to note that the cartridges called MX appeared on the local market during the mid 1980s, shortly after the controversy which ensued when the Reagan administration gave the go-ahead for the production of the intercontinental ballistic Missile X, known as MX for short. History repeated itself quite recently during the Gulf crisis, when allied troops waged war to liberate Kuwait. Stories about Iraqi Scud missiles being shot down by Patriot missiles filled the news. It came as no surprise that cartridges with the name Patriot splashed onto them appeared in local shooters' shops. A Patriot is capable of destroying a missile, let alone a bird. . . . Such is the philosophy of the shooting fraternity.

Other changes

Among other changes that have taken place over the past few years, one can mention the construction of the *dura*, the shooting butt. Few shooters today bother to build their *dura* of rubble stone, traditionally used for rustic construction. Most shooting butts are today built of *franka*, the stone used for house building and in spite of the fact that they are frequently white washed with grey cement they do not blend at all with the surroundings in which they are built without permits. Occasionally one can come across shooting butts which have graffiti of birds, guns and retriever dogs painted on them.

The use of neatly cut stone has also enabled shooters to build high shooting butts and one can often see these butts or towers in places where trees are high or in valleys such as Lunzjata in Gozo and Wied Żembaq in Malta. In some places, high shooting hides are built on pylons. At Wied l-Isqof, close to Buskett Gardens, and at Il-Kunċizzjoni, limits of Rabat, I have seen such hides which were over seven meters high.

In the past, shooting at night used to take place only infrequently on cloudless moonlit nights, when some rabbits or ducks used to be shot. Today, powerful battery-operated lights are used for shooting rabbits at night. Such lights are also used by shooters to shoot at birds roosting in trees or to shoot birds which are flushed before the break of dawn. Water reservoirs, ponds and seasonal pools are frequently scanned with such lights and waterfowl, waders and other birds are shot at night. The use of artificial lights as well as shooting at night, is illegal.

Shot-proof glasses are now also available. These not only protect the shooter's eyes from stray pellets, but also improve sight due to having a yellow tint which improves contrast, and hence vision.

Publicity material for shooting goods today is more widespread. It ranges from adverts in the press to stickers and T-shirts with names of shops, which are also found on the cartridges produced by them.

Time off for hunting

Absenteeism from work during the shooting seasons is another factor which seems to have increased greatly over the past few years. It is a known fact that a number of shooters go out on sick-leave during the month of April. This was also mentioned in Parliament by Dr Philip Muscat, a practising shooter who was then Minister of Education.[18] People taking sick-leave have to report sick by 8 am and shooters who take sick-leave to go to shoot, return home by 9 o'clock, knowing that the company doctor would not visit before that time.

The weekly statistics of sick-leave reveal that there are peaks in the numbers of persons reporting as sick during the 1st week of March, the 2nd, 3rd and 4th weeks of April and the first three weeks of May. In autumn, there are peaks during the 2nd, 3rd and 4th weeks of October and the 2nd week of November.

The first week of March coincides with the peak of the finch trapping season, while April and May are the times when bird shooting is at its peak. October and November are the times when finch trapping is again in full swing, while shooting of thrushes and woodcock is also at its peak.

Gauci, stated that sometimes, building contractors found it difficult to keep up with their work due to the fact that shooters took long spells of time off or leave from work so that they can spend a longer time shooting birds.[19] This was confirmed by the then Prime Minister of Malta, Mr Dom Mintoff. In his foreword to a book about the birds of Malta which was published by the Museums Department, he wrote: 'During the two migration periods, absenteeism in the building industry, in government employment and in the new industries reaches frustrating peaks'.[20]

I have heard a car mechanic in Gozo, who is also a shooter, saying that he will no longer employ people who are shooters or trappers. He argued that they take excessively long leave and very often they turn up late or even fail to go to work without prior notice during the migration periods.

Apart from all this, one cannot fail to mention the special arrangements which are often carried out by certain employers to accommodate shooters during the shooting season. Cases in point in 1991 were the Malta Shipbuilding, where a new shift was introduced in April and a number of sections within government departments who made similar arrangements, enabling shooters to report late for work, and then make up for it in the evening.[21]

The graph on p. 100 shows that the amount of sick-leave claims increase by 9% during the shooting season and may give an indication to the loss of labour due to shooting and trapping. When one considers that over 50% of the sick-claims are for 1–2 days, and that during the shooting season shooters take a number of single days sick-leave, the increase in the number of claims takes on added significance. With about 15,000 sick-leave claims made due to shooting, the government is losing more than it gains in import duty on material related to shooting!

Killing sprees

Another novelty is tourism for hunting, both domestic and international. Many Maltese shooters now travel to Gozo to shoot and today one can really speak of local tourism during the months of April and May and to a lesser extent, in late October and November. Due to the fact that Gozo is somewhat less urbanised and therefore has more countryside, hundreds of Maltese shooters go to Gozo in mid-April and, to a lesser degree, in November. There they rent a flat which they might share with other shooters, and stay for a week or two (some even spend three or four weeks), during the peak migration periods, to shoot birds. Some shooters even go

TABLE 8

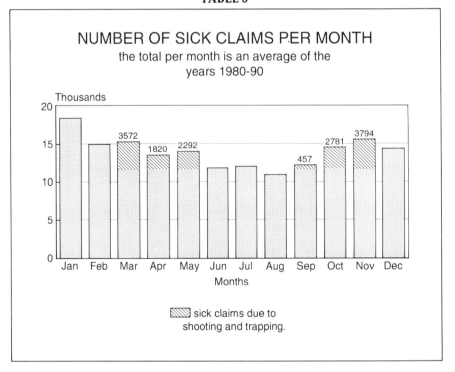

NUMBER OF SICK CLAIMS PER MONTH
the total per month is an average of the
years 1980-90

sick claims due to
shooting and trapping.

* A sick-leave claim is made each time a person reports as sick.

The total and average of the summer months were calculated from the months of June, July, August and September, during which months all government employees and most employees in the private sector work half days. The number of people taking sick-leave on half days is significantly lower than other months of the year, and hence reflects more accurately the number of real sick-leave claims than other months.

The months of December, January and February were not taken into consideration as during these months, people are more prone to infectious diseases such as colds and thus more claims are made.

Note the increase in the amount of sick-leave claims during the peak trapping and shooting seasons in March, April and May and in October and November. In September, during which shooting takes place, shooters do not take much sick-leave as most shooting takes place in the afternoons, when they are still working on half days.

The total number of sick-leave claims above the summer average taken between March and May and between September and November amount to 14716 claims, an increase of 8.8% during the shooting seasons.

to Gozo for weekends and it is not unusual to come across shooters who sleep in the open air or in their own car for two consecutive nights before returning home on Sunday night.

During the early part of the migration season there are always those days in which there is rather a strong passage of harriers, especially with mild to strong southerly winds. On such days, some shooters go to Gozo for the day and return with a ferry late at night having bagged a harrier or two –

or more – depending on how strong migration has been.

The number of Maltese shooters going to Gozo has been increasing steadily over the past few years. Some Gozitans saw them as a source of income, as undoubtedly many shooters were spending money while living in Gozo. But some Gozitan shooters argue that Maltese shooters were costing more than they were actually spending, both in terms of trampling and stealing of crops, as well as their conduct in the field. Letters expressing such concerns frequently appeared in the shooters' paper *Il-Passa* [22]

In April 1991, leaflets against the presence of Maltese shooters in Gozo were strewn along many streets in Gozo,[23] while words like 'Maltese shooters out' could be seen daubed on a number of prominent walls. In places such as San Lawrenz, poisoned meat was laid out to kill the dogs of shooters who went there.

Exporting shooters

Others, who are better-off financially, go to shoot abroad, and shooting trips to Bulgaria, Italy, Great Britain, Scotland, Yugoslavia, Russia and Egypt take place – such tours being advertised from time to time. Articles boasting of the large number of kills made by Maltese shooters are easy to come across in the shooters' paper. According to such articles, over 10,000 turtle doves were shot by a group of five Maltese shooters in a week in Egypt, while other articles boast of large bags of grouse, pheasants, crows and duck in Scotland.

The tours to Egypt seem to have stalled following action taken both in Malta, but more so in Egypt. In April, Egyptian authorities raided a hotel which was being used as a base by Maltese shooters. They confiscated more than 150 carcasses of protected species which included black-shouldered kites, little owls, kestrels, cattle egrets and little green bee-eaters.[24] Following this action, the Egyptian Government stopped hunting in the El Fayoum region, where Maltese shooters went on their bird killing sprees.[25]

I shall not, however, dwell too much on this aspect of shooting since shooting outside the Maltese Islands, even when committed by Maltese shooters, is not within the scope of this work.

Chapter 7

Trapping

Finch migration

The movements of finches in the Mediterranean from late autumn to early spring, have not yet been well studied. In Malta there are years in which there are large influxes of certain finches, while in other years, some finches are conspicuous by their absence. In some winters, for example, greenfinches pass in very large numbers, and keep passing through all winter, while siskins are hardly seen at all. Sometimes, serins are seen in large numbers in January and none, or very few, are seen in spring. Some finches try to winter in considerable numbers.

A day in the life of a bird trapper

The previous chapter outlined the routine which shooters follow and how it evolved making shooting their way of life. Although there is a difference in attitude between shooters and trappers, both can be extremely obsessed with their pastime. In an appreciation, written by a friend of a renowned trapper who had died a few weeks before at the age of seventy-two, one reads that the only wish that the trapper had was to die on his trapping site, happily holding a freshly-trapped greenfinch.[1]

Trappers follow certain patterns in their daily life. Bird trapping is more time-consuming than shooting, for while a shooter can easily go out shooting for an hour or two before going to work, a trapper needs a longer time, first to set the nets and the live bird decoys and then he has to wait, since most finches arrive late in the morning and in the afternoon. Trappers spend whole days at the trapping site. They have to take time off from work to be able to do so; unless they have a job as watchmen or unless they work shift duties, which many of them seek in order to have more free time to trap and shoot birds.

One cannot but mention that the rising standard of living, which brought more free time, was one of the main factors for the increase in bird trapping and one can draw many parallels between the way of life of trappers and shooters. In summer, trappers try to cross-breed finches with canaries in order to get hybrids, which are usually better songsters. Then they wait impatiently for summer to end so that finch migration will start. During this time, many trappers indulge in the laborious process of making the tiny cages for the finches they anticipate trapping, or to sell them to others.

A few weeks before migration begins, they start gathering in bars and chatting with shooters, who would have started taking their toll of birds a good month before it is the trappers' turn to do so. They start preparing their nets, the poles, ropes and decoys. Then they clean the trapping site, from which they remove all the wild plants and they use weed killers to ensure that no grasses grow in the area where the nets are laid. Very often, the trapping site is enlarged or some of the gadgets which operate the nets are changed or modified. If the trapping site is enlarged, the trapper has to make a new set of nets, which he meticulously checks and dyes so that they match the colour of the earth on which they are later laid. He also refurbishes the hide, making it more comfortable, better and in many cases bigger, before each and every season.

Then the birds arrive and trappers, who would have been eagerly waiting for them in their minds for a few months, and who would have been sitting impatiently in their hides for long days on end, start having their field days. The trapping activity itself is a time-consuming process. Early in the morning, there is the setting of nets and placing the decoys in strategic positions; the testing of the nets and fluttering decoys to see that all functions well; then the wait in the hide, making tea or coffee while listening and enjoying the song of the caged birds. The nervous crouched wait, with the rope that triggers the nets in their hands, ready for the slightest sign of an approaching bird; the soft whisper or murmur to a companion in the hide not to move, telling him what the approaching birds are; the pulling of the string to make the right decoy flutter and finally, the vigorous pull of the rope, the closing of the nets which trap the birds, and the exuberant run towards the nets to recover the trapped birds from under the nets; the rush to take them out from under the nets before any may escape, the first hurried look at the birds to see whether they are males or females before placing them in a large shallow cage called the *gabjun*, which is made purposely for keeping the freshly-trapped birds, the re-setting of the nets, and checking the decoys; then back to the hide, waiting for more birds; thinking about the ones he just trapped, how they came, what he did, which decoys he used, which songster performed best and how many he trapped of the flock which came, while waiting and hoping for more birds, and grumbling that the coffee he poured some time ago has become cold. . . .

Then he drives back home, already looking forward to the next morning, hoping that the weather, and his catch, is even better. At home, he takes a closer look at the birds he trapped that day, and chooses the ones to keep and the ones to sell. The feeding and cleaning of birds' cages, the buying of bird seed, the chat at the bird seed shop and at the village bar and the maintenance of the nets – all form a part of the routine of the trapper's life. The visit to the Valletta Sunday market, or as it is popularly termed *il-monti*, is inevitable. There the trapper has a chance to see, buy and sell birds, while exchanging small talk and passing time.

Some trappers show a lot of affection for the birds they trap. They claim that birds are better off in their care than left to the mercy of nature. They argue that birds face many hazards in the wild – 'birds of prey, snakes, large sea-crossings on migration and the weather take a huge toll out of birds;

they have to look for food and water while in cages they have food, water and shelter provided for them' they argue. Of course, trappers conveniently forget that freedom is of crucial importance to any living being. Many trappers and bird keepers claim that they spend a lot of money on the birds. Undoubtedly, the birds themselves will fare much better if the money is not spent on them in that way. But still, one has to admit that most trappers do love their birds. They just happen to express their love in a negative way.

Although one can sometimes see a small model of the *gabbjetta*, the cage in which finches are kept, hanging from the rear-view mirror of a trapper's car, generally speaking, they are more modest and less macho than shooters. They do not boast of their catch, since they fear that other trappers might be tempted to set a trapping site next to theirs or that their trapping site is vandalised by jealous trappers. Trappers envy each other but they do not boast in terms of the numbers they catch; they boast of the quality of their songsters or the size or colour of the birds they catch. I have heard them boasting of having trapped a greenfinch which was 'as large as a thrush' or which is 'as yellow as gold', or a linnet which is 'as red as a robin'!

Most trappers prefer finches which are '*tal-passa*', that is, migratory ones, rather than imported birds.

A historical perspective

It is not known by whom and from where bird trapping was introduced to our islands. The Arabs, who ruled Malta for almost 200 years after the year 870 AD, gave a number of words to the Maltese language and through etymology, one can often trace origins of things. The Maltese words for net – *xibka* – and trapping site – *mansab* – have been derived from Arabic. Thus, a form or forms of bird catching may have been taking place, at least since the Arabs came to Malta in 870 AD.

During the time of the Order of St John, the *regna* (a form of vertical net) and other nets were used, and various edicts made it illegal to use nets for catching birds during the closed-season which was in force at that time. Edicts regulating hunting, which specifically mention the use of nets, may be traced back to February 1655.[2] Nets were used for catching falcons, migratory birds, as well as rabbits. People were permitted to trap birds at certain times of the year outside areas reserved for the Grandmaster. An edict dated 29th March 1773, for instance, permitted people to catch 'migratory birds and turtle doves' with nets.[3]

However we have no evidence of the use of any clap-nets, similar to those which were in use in Italy and France, which were described by Olina,[4] Raimondi,[5] Arkstee,[6] Diderot[7] and others.

In his dictionary of 1750, De Soldanis gives the meaning of the word *mansab* as a place where nets are laid to trap migratory birds.[8] He also mentions trapping sites for turtle doves, falcons, short-toed larks and pigeons. This may be the first implication of the use of clap-nets, since it is difficult to imagine how short-toed larks could be trapped with nets other than a form of clap-nets.

Ciantar[9] mentions the catching of birds by nets, but he fails to specify what types of nets were used and what kinds of birds were taken. However, the birds must have been caught for the pot since he wrote that the birds were 'delicious prey'. The net which Ciantar talks about was most probably the *regna*, since it was a type of vertical net which could be set and left unattended. At that time, people were too busy working hard to earn a living and few, if any, could afford to spend their days trapping birds. Ciantar also wrote that peasants climbed down sea cliffs and used cup-shaped nets attached to poles to catch pigeons as these flew out of their nesting sites.[10]

De Boisgelin[11] wrote that birds were taken with nets, but he too failed to specify what kind of birds were taken and what types of nets were used. Schembri,[12] the father of Maltese ornithology, does not mention any forms of trapping. In 1864, Wright[13] was the first to describe clap-nets, which he referred to as 'platform nets' when he wrote about the trapping of turtle doves and yellow wagtails. In another instance, where he refers to 'a man netting of larks', he implies that clap-nets were used since, as said De Soldanis, it is difficult to envisage larks being trapped with other nets.

Wright[14] was also the first to describe the 'nets spread on the standing corn' which were used for catching quail. He also wrote about the garden warbler and other warblers, popularly termed *beccafichi*, which were netted in large numbers. He remarked that as many as 'a hundred dozen' frequently ended at the market stalls.[15] Adams[16] wrote that in a single spring, just from two opposite stalls at the Valletta market, 'about 100 dozen whitethroats and garden warblers had been disposed of, not to mention scores of nightingales and other soft-billed birds which are eagerly sought after'. He also states that 'the bird catcher is hard at work filling his cages with hundreds [of yellow wagtails], all of which will be dead and eaten before another day'.[17] Cooke[18] wrote that 'enormous numbers of birds, too, are annually trapped or netted, and sold in the markets, or hawked about the streets for ridiculously small sums of money per dozen'. Gulia[19] wrote that the meat of *beccafichi* had an excellent flavour and was thus eagerly sought.

Finch trapping

From the information available, it is evident that birds were caught for the pot and that the use of clap-nets as well as finch trapping are other developments of the 19th century.

Some nobles probably kept caged birds in the middle of the 17th century since bird seed was imported at that time. Quarantine records show that 8 consignments of bird seed were imported from Magherbi ports between 1654 and 1665.[20] It may well be that more bird seed was also imported from European ports, since the mentioned records were kept for countries to which quarantine control applied during the plague.

But the fact that there are no descriptions of clap-nets before those of De Soldanis,[21] who did not mention finch trapping, coupled with the fact that there are no paintings or lithographs of trappers, implies that finch trapping was introduced sometime in the middle of the 19th century. The keeping of songbirds in cages started becoming popular during that time and it is hard to tell whether finch trapping was the cause or the effect of this new fad.

Finch trapping has become a popular pastime during the past forty years. The licence for the use of the clap-nets as we know it today was introduced in 1932.[22] Hawfinch, greenfinch, goldfinch, chaffinch, linnet, serin, siskin and ortolan bunting are the most sought. Bramblings are sometimes trapped and some trappers also trap short-toed larks and dunnocks. Crossbills, are also trapped and their flocks are decimated in a few days following their arrival.[23]

During the Debates of the Council of Government in November 1916, G. Zammit spoke in Parliament against the protection of the short-toed lark, stating that the wool-carders of the village of Zurrieq would die of want, being deprived of their means of subsistence during the months in which they are unemployed.[24]

Trapping by the use of clap-nets and bat-nets was a common practice and Despott[25] stated that 'hundreds of dozens' of linnets were caught and sold as *beccafichi* at the Valletta Market or were 'more quickly consigned to the pot of the netters themselves'. Finches were severely persecuted and were taken both by nets and by gun. Despott[26] wrote that it was said that many people earned a living by capturing finches.

The number of trapping sites has increased greatly over the past few years. In Gozo, for example, there were over one thousand six hundred finch trapping sites in 1989 while in 1944, their number was less than a hundred.[27] This increase may be attributed to a number of factors. Firstly, finch trapping has become more popular through the increase of leisure time. Finch trapping is a time-consuming activity and a mere twenty years ago people worked for longer hours, leisure time was very limited and they could not take time off from work very easily. Nylon nets, which were introduced in the mid-fifties for fishing, created a revolution. Such nets were more convenient to use since they were much less fragile than those made of hemp which were in use at that time. Nets became more readily available, and at a much cheaper price too.

Formerly, the number of trapping sites was also limited. Finch trapping sites were situated only on *garigue* areas or on land which could not be cultivated. Each and every piece of arable land was tilled and every patch of soil was utilised. It was unheard of for trapping sites to be situated on arable land, occupying about 100 square meters of land which could be used for growing produce. Today, agriculture has lost much of its former importance and has changed greatly. For instance the number of neglected fields has increased and consequently one finds a number of trapping sites both on uncultivated and farmed land.

The use of clap-nets

Undoubtedly, the commonest way to trap birds is by using clap-nets. In 1936, that is four years after the licence to use a clap-net was introduced, 700 people held such a licence.[28] The number of licence holders in 1990 stood at

1,528.[29] However this figure does not reflect the actual number of trappers since there are many more who trap birds without paying a licence fee. It suffices to note that the number of trapping sites which I counted from the photographs taken in connection with an aerial survey of the Maltese Islands in 1989 stood at 5,309, while just over 1000 people had a trapping licence. The official statistics at the end of the 80s show that there was a decrease in the number of trappers while the number of trapping sites is increasing – which means that many more people are trapping birds without a licence. This is most probably due to the lack of enforcement of the regulations.

Clap-nets usually have two nets about 15 metres long and 2 metres wide. However, nets much larger then these are often used nowadays and they have become somewhat more fashionable. The nets are laid out flat on the ground and the space left between the nets is wide enough so that when the nets are operated they overlap on each other by a few centimetres.

The birds are caught either when they fly across the trapping site, or as they settle in the catching area amongst the decoys. The migrating finches are lured towards the trapping site by the caged decoys which are placed around the nets. When the finches approach the nets, the trapper makes use of the fluttering decoys. This gadget is made of a stick or twig about 50 centimetres long. It is hinged to the ground in a way that when the string in the trapper's hide is pulled, the twig rises.

A harnessed bird, usually a female, is tethered at the end of the stick. The decoys are trained to flutter and when the trapper pulls the string, the stick rises from its horizontal position and the decoy finch sits on the perch. When

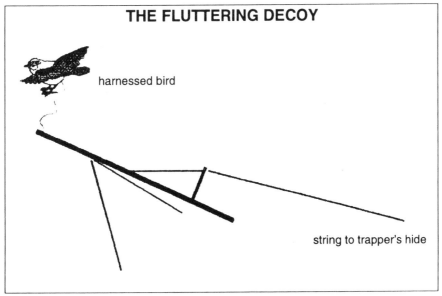

THE FLUTTERING DECOY

harnessed bird

string to trapper's hide

The stick rises every time the trapper pulls the string. When the trapper releases the string, the bird flutters giving the impression of a bird about to settle on the ground.

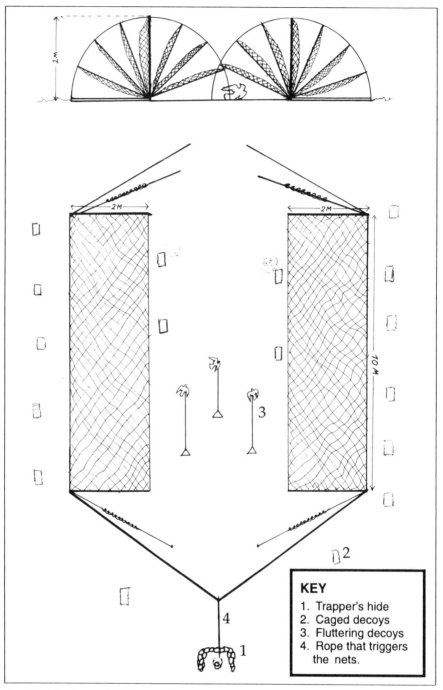

An old style clap-net with nets of 10 × 2 m, the effective trapping volume is 125 m³.

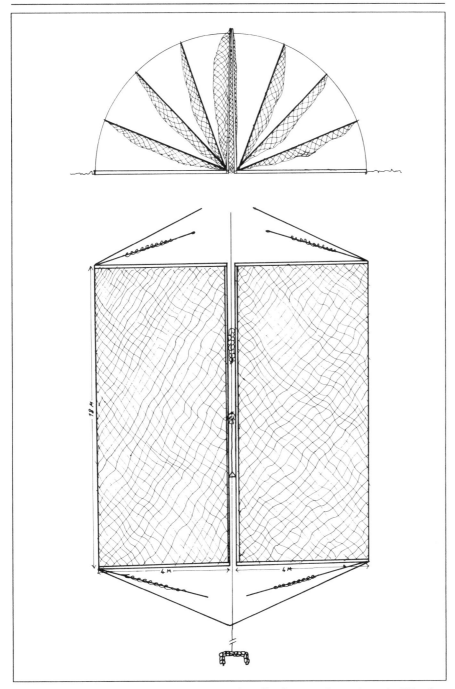

The new breed of nets with nets 18 × 4 m, the effective trapping volume is 452 m³ – over 3½ times the older ones!

the trapper releases the string, the stick falls to the ground and the finch hovers gently giving the impression of an alighting bird.

Wild birds are attracted by fluttering decoys and as they try to alight near them, the trapper pulls the rope which triggers the nets. The nets spring from their rest position, sweep through the air in a semi-circular movement and overlap each other on the ground by a small margin. Thus the finches can be trapped even in flight, as long as they are within the catching area of the nets.

Trapping sites are usually situated in the open, however some have trapping sites in wooded areas for hawfinches and siskins, which tend to prefer such habitats. Many trapping sites have added attractions to birds.

Most trappers plant food plants which are known to be attractive to some species of finches. Thistles are planted for goldfinches while White Wall-rocket (*Diplotaxis erucoides*) and Sweet Alison (*Lobularia marittima*) are frequently planted for linnets and serins, which like to feed on them. A water-hole in the middle of the netting area is a common feature.

Trapping sites often do a lot of damage to the ecosystems in which they are situated. Firstly, many trappers use weedkillers and kerosene to clear the trapping site of the vegetation which grows in it when it is not being used. Such chemicals not only destroy the vegetation, but in some areas may find their way into the water tables, contaminating them in the process.

In garigue areas, trapping sites are very frequently levelled by means of stones, rubble and soil. The trapping sites are literally built over large patches of garigue habitat and large numbers of wild plants, such as orchids, and other species of flora in this habitat are destroyed. A case in point happened with a very rare species of iris, which is found in only three sites in Malta. One population of this iris was nearly completely eradicated by a bird trapper[30].

Further damage is done because trappers drive with their cars as close as possible to the trapping site, since they have a lot of paraphernalia to carry. In *The Malta Structure Plan Report* one reads: 'In addition to the destruction of birds, animals and flora, vehicles create unofficial tracks to the hides, which further damage the vegetation and intrude on the landscape'[33].

In places where there are dolmens and other archaeological remains, the trappers' hiding place is frequently made out of stones taken from the temples. At Wied Moqbol, in the south-west, at Ġebel Ciantar, limits of Dingli and at Ta' Marżiena in Gozo, there are a number of trappers' hides which are built around and amongst dolmens. At Clapham Junction, limits of Buskett, a trapping site is built over pre-historic cart ruts.

Many trappers simply lay claim to vacant public land and construct their trapping hut to the exclusion of everyone else. Pembroke is a prime example where a concentration of trapping sites has sprouted on the disused rifle range and on the garigue itself.

Number of finches trapped

Trapping of finches takes place between early October and late March, though some trappers keep trapping until the first weeks of April. The largest numbers of finches are trapped in October, November and March.

In some years, finches keep passing through all winter, and the number of finches trapped is significantly higher. In winter 1990 for instance, the number of finches trapped was so large that shops ran out of their stock of *gabbjetti* – the small cages in which finches are kept – and their price practically doubled from 65 cents to Lm1.

The number of birds which one can see for sale at pet shops, on the Valletta Market on Sunday mornings, and at the Cirkewwa quay on Fridays, where some Gozitans come to trade some of the birds trapped in Gozo, may give an indication of the number of birds which are trapped.

It is more difficult to estimate exactly the number of finches that are trapped each year than it is to estimate birds shot. Trappers, unlike shooters, tend not to disclose the numbers of birds they catch. Some localities, such as Dingli Cliffs, Għar Lapsi and Delimara, are renowned as places where large quantities of finches are trapped. One can easily note which sites these are by looking at the density of trapping sites.

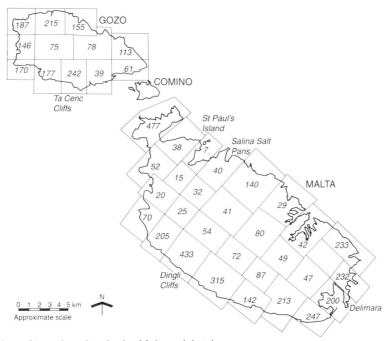

Number of trapping sites in the Maltese Islands.

Sultana and Gauci[32] stated that 'the finches trapped in Malta must run into hundreds of thousands, the largest number caught being linnets followed by serins, greenfinches and chaffinches in that order'. Magnin[33], working on the estimate by Sultana and Gauci[34] that there are 15,000 bird trappers, stated that: 'It is very difficult to estimate the number of finches trapped annually, but a total of 3 million birds (i.e. an average of 200 birds per trapper in one year) is a conservative number. In a year in which finches appear in larger numbers, the yearly catch exceeds the 4 million mark.' The figure of trapped finches, given by Magnin as 200 birds per trapper per year, is an underestimation. The figure of trapped finches is more likely to be in the region of 200 to 400 birds per year – that is, 100 to 200 birds per season.

The estimate that there are some 15,000 trappers may be a bit too much. On the other hand, the number of licensed trappers does not reflect their actual number since many people trap without a licence. The fact that there are over 5300 bird trapping sites, implies that there must be at least as many bird trappers. Most trappers use their trapping sites for a short time each season, and they may then be used by other trappers, usually close friends or relatives. Therefore the actual number of bird trappers may be about twice the number of trapping sites.

Since the number of trappers is unknown, it might be safer to work on the number of trapping sites for estimating the number of finches which are trapped. Finch trapping takes place from October to mid-May. However, it is most intensive during October and early November and from mid-February until mid-April. If one were to assume that each trapping site is used for only two months in a year (i.e. March and October only), and that during these times an average of two to five birds is trapped each day at each site, with a peak of 10 birds trapped on two days (ie a day in March and a day in October), then the total number of trapped finches ranges between 1 to 2.8 million finches each year.

One must bear in mind that this figure is an underestimation since many trapping sites are used for over two months in a year. To the number of trapping sites seen on the map at page 111, one must add a large number of temporary sites which are built to trap finches known as 'tal-post', (ie wintering birds). One must also take into account the considerable number of birds which are caught by traps and mist-nets, details of which are given later.

Intensive trapping

Finch trapping is more intensive along the coast but finch trapping sites are frequently found inland as well. The nets vary in colour depending on the season and on where the trapping site is situated. Nets are usually similar in colour to the land on which they are laid out; this renders them as invisible as possible. Thus a trapping site situated in a field or on ground with a covering of soil is likely to have brown-coloured nets while a trapping site situated on rocky terrain is likely to have light-coloured nets. Nets are dyed in a variety of ways, the most primitive ones involve the use of boiled pomegranate or tea. More recently it has become fashionable for trappers to dye their nets black with used engine oil mixed with kerosene.

A trapping site is rather conspicuous, especially when seen from the air and most trappers believe that the birds can actually see the nets. Trappers say that birds that would have already seen clap-nets in action are very cautious and are not easily lured into the netting area, unless the nets are well camouflaged.

Live decoys

A number of decoy birds are placed in small cages around the trapping site and around the nets. The number of birds which a trapper employs at the trapping site varies according to the size of the nets, the distance which he has to carry the trapping equipment, the number and proximity of other trapping sites and the number of finches which he has in stock. A normal size clap-net is usually surrounded by at least thirty decoys while trappers who have a lot of birds may have up to fifty decoys.

The trapper carries his decoy finches in a special square-shaped sack, at the bottom of which he carries the *gabjun*, a large shallow rectangular shaped cage with two or three compartments, which is used to keep the trapped finches of the day. The decoy cages are stacked above the *gabjun*.

The decoys are kept in small cages, measuring some 19 cms by 13 cms by 11 cms. The caged decoys are usually males since they are better songsters. The trapper places his best songsters strategically around the trapping site so that migrant finches are attracted into the trapping area and are not held just out of reach of the nets by the better songsters. Decoys of goldfinches are usually placed by a patch of thistles inside the space which is covered by the nets when these are closed. Serins, siskins and ortolan buntings are usually placed either inside the netting area or immediately next to the nets. In any case, it is usual to find finches in cages inside the netting area, especially if a fluttering decoy of that species is not used.

Since it is known that caged finches stop singing while they are moulting, some finches are placed in small cages and left in a dark place for a period of time, since this encourages them to moult. Some trappers pluck the flight feathers and all the tail feathers to induce moult. This cruel practice is also common in Italy.[35] The local term for closing finches in the dark is *jinkaxxawhom* which literally means boxing them, since finches are placed in small cages and four such cages are usually kept covered by a cardboard box. Since the cages to which they are confined are small, and the birds would have been in them for quite a while, they could easily find their way to food and water, albeit in total darkness.

Linnets and greenfinches are usually boxed in late June and are kept in a dark place until mid-September, just before the autumn migration. Those finches which are not boxed in this way are usually released in the *guva* (a large aviary), during the hot summer months. Most trappers usually have at least one large aviary which is usually a room on the roof enclosed with wire netting.

In an article in *Il-Passa*, the monthly paper for shooters and trappers, it was stated that research based on a five year study revealed that 80% of the goldfinches, 75% of the linnets, 70% of the serins, 45% of the greenfinches, 30% of the siskins and 10% of the chaffinches died in captivity after their capture.[36] These gruesome figures of death speak for themselves and go a long way to explain why there is an insatiable demand for finches caught from the wild. They also highlight the sheer waste of bird life which takes place in the name of a 'traditional sport', which is not traditional, and even less sporting.

Use of hybrids

Crosses between male siskin, goldfinch, linnet and greenfinch and female canary are frequently used as decoys. Hybrids are considered to be better songsters and are frequently trained to imitate the call of a particular finch. A hybrid of a goldfinch and a canary can be trained to call like a greenfinch. The secret lies in placing the hybrid in the company of greenfinches as soon as it fledges, so that it will learn their call. The trappers place newly fledged hybrids with finches whose call they want them to imitate. They are careful not to let hybrids hear the call of the canary, as otherwise the hybrid will learn that call and be worthless as a decoy for finch trapping.

Hybrids are expensive because they are often exceptional songsters. Prices range from Lm25 to Lm100, depending on which call the hybrid imitates best and its performance as a songster. Hybrids of linnets are amongst the most expensive since they are more difficult to obtain.

It appears that this habit of crossing finches has been carried out for a very long time. In 1864 Wright[37] mentioned that siskins were 'often crossed with the canary by the native bird-fanciers' and Despott[38] wrote about a cross between greenfinch and canary in 1912. Some trappers try to breed finches in captivity and a number of greenfinches are bred successfully in this manner each year.

Fluttering decoys

Earlier this century, finches were tied by the leg instead of being harnessed[39]. When pipits were used as fluttering decoys, an incredible amount of cruelty was involved. Two primary feathers were plucked from their wings, knotted together and the quills were passed through the bird's nose. They were then attached to the stick which rose each time the trapper pulled it[40]. The bird had to flutter while tied from its nose.

Today, harnessed birds are used as fluttering decoys in the middle of the trapping site. Female finches (commonly linnet, chaffinch and greenfinch), being cheaper to buy and therefore more dispensable, are commonly used. The greenfinch decoy is used instead of any finch for which fluttering decoys are not available. Being tame, greenfinches are usually the best decoys. The linnet is the next most common decoy. During strong migrations in certain years, trappers would be prepared to use a male as a decoy, but only if they thought that they would have better prospects of catching more birds if they use a male. Male greenfinches, being more conspicuous due to the bright yellow markings on the wings and rump, are used as fluttering decoys, in these instances. I know of a trapper from Attard who dyes female greenfinches with a yellow antiseptic liquid for this purpose. In Gozo, the habit of using a male greenfinch as a fluttering decoy seems to be more widespread.

Although there are no hard and fast rules, a trapping site in October would have at least three fluttering decoys, a greenfinch, a chaffinch and a linnet. A goldfinch may be added in November. In December, the decoy chaffinch is replaced by a serin. In March, only fluttering decoys of linnet, greenfinch, chaffinch and possibly serin are used. The species used as fluttering decoys depends on when trapping is taking place. Since chaffinches stop passing through in December and serins arrive, a serin replaces the chaffinch fluttering decoy.

Importation and sale of birds

Finches were often imported from Sicily. Wright[41] mentions that immature goldfinches were imported from Sicily in August and kept as song birds.

Some trappers are against the importation of finches so that locally-trapped finches may fetch higher prices. Until recently, the Trade Department of Malta used to issue import licences for 'song-birds'. The list of 'song-birds' included birds such as the jackdaw, which is not a song-bird. It also included two species which are protected locally. Import licences used to permit the importation of up to twelve birds per person per year for personal use, however some people obtained licences under different names and imported significant quantities of birds. It is positive to note that import licences for birds which are protected at the country of origin are no longer being granted, but considerable quantities are still being smuggled. Large numbers of exotic birds are also imported.

Finches are often kept as pets and it is quite common to see caged finches in houses. Sometimes men can be seen with a caged finch under their arm,

MALTA NEWS — Monday September 25, 1978

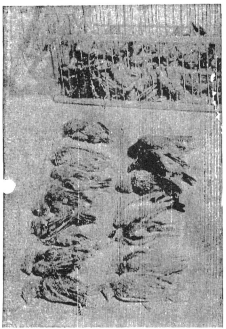

A NUMBER of birds suffered a cruel death after being put into a small cage in great quantities and hidden underneath heavy ropes on the deck of a ship.

The aim of the person or persons hidding the cages there was obvious: they wanted to escape detection by Customs officials.

The birds were found yesterday evening when a ship entered the Grand Harbour with merchandise from Tunis. Customs officials detected the birds, as also a quantity of cigars and cigarettes and a portable television set.

SMUGGLED BIRDS SUFFOCATE

The birds, about 100 of them, were all greenfinches and goldfinches. Informed sources said that these birds are bought cheaply in Tunisia but fetch high prices in Maltese markets.

About forty of the birds were dead or dying, (see picture) the remainder were set free this morning.

Attempts to smuggle finches are quite common. The above shows customs officers discovering an unsuccessful attempt to smuggle birds from Tunisia.

as if it were a portable radio. The greenfinch is the most common finch to be seen carried in this manner, but goldfinches and more seldom chaffinches, can be seen as well.

Those carrying greenfinches usually keep a few hemp-seeds in their pockets and from time to time they can be seen amusing themselves demonstrating the tameness of their birds by giving them individual seeds through the wires of the cage.

There is brisk trade in finches. Besides the large number of shops which sell birds and bird-seed, the open air market in the outskirts of Valletta has a stall for bird sellers every Sunday morning. At these stalls, pet shop owners who import birds and who buy birds from trappers, as well as trappers themselves, come to trade birds. On Sundays, the bird sellers in the market start selling as early as 6.30 am, and before mid-day they would have sold practically their whole stock.

Competition for stalls on the market is so stiff that during the peak times of the trapping season, some bird sellers go as early as 3.30 am to secure one of the most advantageous places on the stalls. Prices of finches are practically the same at all stalls and those who have large quantities try to seek the best stalls. Dealers from Gozo often arrive in the evening and sleep in their vans to secure the best places. Just to give an indication of how brisk bird business is, on one Sunday morning in November 1990, a Maltese bird dealer sold over 200 greenfinches in an hour while a Gozitan dealer next to him sold over a thousand birds in three hours. The Valletta Sunday market is not the only place where finches are sold. During both migrations a small bird market is set up at the quay where the Gozo ferry berths at Cirkewwa on Friday mornings. The birds which are not sold on Friday are brought over to the Valletta market.

It is interesting to note that in March 1991 the place where bird dealers sell their birds on the market was changed. They are no longer on the main road leading to the capital city, but are now buried away at the far end of the market. There has been no official explanation for this but it is very probable that bird dealers were removed from the public eye and transferred to a place where it is unlikely that tourists see them to avoid complaints. Nevertheless, the atrocities continue.

Male finches are usually more sought after for their song and thus fetch higher prices. An ortolan bunting fetched 4s 6d in 1938.[42] A male greenfinch was comparatively more expensive in 1949, when it fetched 2s 6d.[43] Today it fetches Lm3 to Lm20 depending on its abundance during the particular season. A female greenfinch costs between fifty cents and Lm2, and may fetch over Lm4 in years when they are very scarce. Goldfinches sell between Lm8 and Lm10, but up to Lm20 can be paid for a good songster. When a male linnet fetches Lm1.25, a female fetches 10 cents, and one can often buy a bag containing 10 to 20 females for the price of a male.

Serins may sell anywhere between less than Lm1 to Lm5 while chaffinches sell between Lm2.50 and Lm5. As with all other finches, the price depends on the numbers trapped and much higher prices are paid for good songsters.

The hawfinch is the most expensive of the migratory finches. Gibb[44] states that a hawfinch cost over £5 in 1949. A male can now cost between Lm16 and Lm35 while a female costs between Lm14 and Lm30. Siskins may be as expensive as hawfinches but their price usually falls when larger numbers are caught while the price of hawfinches usually holds. A case in point happened during winter of 1990. Before migration started, hawfinches and siskins were selling for Lm40 each. When large numbers of both were trapped, the price of the hawfinch went down to Lm16 while siskins sold for Lm3.

New methods

Recent innovations in trapping methods include the use of springs, similar to the ones used in some garage doors, or strong elastic bands. These help in operating the nets faster. In the past, some turtle dove nets were made to operate faster by the use of weights. Stones were hung in a sort of well dug out for that purpose. One end of the rope was tied to a stone or a sack containing stones, and the other end was tied to the poles which held the net at the far end of the trapping site. When the trapper pulled the rope which triggered the net, the weight of the stones helped the nets to close much faster than those without them. Such trapping sites are locally called 'tal-mażżri'.

Today, the use of powerful springs enables trappers to use nets which are much wider and longer than the conventional ones which were never more than 10×2 metres. In a study about bird catching in Italy, Bondietti[45] describes the *paretaio*, which is a similar netting system with minor variations.

Clap-nets which close against each other in mid-air are also being used and they are gaining in popularity. These are usually spring-operated and are capable of trapping many more birds since they have a catching volume which is three-and-a-half times bigger than the conventional trapping nets (see figures on pages 108 and 109). Some birds trapped by spring- or elastic-operated nets are killed because of the strong blow they receive from the nets on impact.

The 'Bird song' electronic devices, which have already been mentioned when discussing the use of whistles, are now used by many trappers and have proved their efficiency in trapping finches like serins which fly right up to the speaker emitting their call.

One must also point out that while finch trapping in general has increased in popularity over the past ten years or so, finch trapping in spring has become a common practice even more recently. In the early sixties, finch trapping in Gozo during spring was practised by no more than a dozen individuals,[46] the reasons probably being that people had practically no free time and that hardly anyone knew that finches migrated in large numbers in spring. Men worked from 8 am until 4.30 pm on week-days and half-days on Saturdays. Thus, while they may have had some time to shoot before going to work, they certainly had no time to set their nets, lay their decoys and sit in wait for migrating finches.

Wintering finches are trapped by clap-nets. At Imriehel, instead of fluttering decoys, a decoy known as *raghaj*, that is a shepherd, is often used in winter. The 'shepherd' is a decoy bird which is tied to the ground and is not required to flutter. Wintering finches are attracted to feeding areas from where they are trapped, both by scattering bird-seed, as well as by the presence of decoys. Such trapping is done after the trapper identifies an area where wintering birds gather to feed. The majority of birds which are trapped in this way are mainly serins which, if given the chance, would winter in considerable numbers and possibly breed in the following spring.

In years when finches are trapped in unusually large numbers, some trappers release some of the female linnets and chaffinches which they trap. They release them to avoid having to feed them. Before the birds are released, they pluck their tail feathers. This is done so that the birds will not migrate and will serve to attract other migratory finches to flock with them, thus improving the chances of trapping some of the finches which might have otherwise kept migrating.

In spite of being illegal, Japanese mist-nets are frequently used for finch trapping. Most of these nets have found their way into Malta from Australia through emigrants who have relatives on these islands, and they may sometimes be seen for sale at the Valletta Sunday market. Some try to trap roosting finches by means of cup-shaped nets and artificial lights. This practice, although widespread, is not very common. It is also illegal.

Pipits, wagtails, sparrows and other birds

Some trappers also trap tree pipits and yellow wagtails in spring and autumn. Being very gregarious by nature, yellow wagtails are lured to the trapping site simply by calling them and using any bird as a fluttering decoy. Flowers of Crown Daisy (*chrysanthemum coronarium*) or Cape Sorrel (*Oxalis pes-caprae*), are frequently tied to the stick of the fluttering decoy and are as effective as a decoy bird in luring other wagtails to the trapping site. Some white wagtails and meadow pipits are also caught in winter. Some might trap them just for fun and then release them again, often with many feathers, especially the tail ones missing. Others trap them to give away or to try and keep them alive, an exercise which always fails. In former times, such birds ended in the pot. Occasionally, some still do as some trappers still kill such birds to cook them. Red-throated pipits and tawny pipits are also trapped by some trappers. Pipits and wagtails have been protected since 1936.

Because of their habit of eating flies, yellow wagtails, vernacularly called *pappamosk* (i.e. fly-eater), used to have their longer primaries clipped and were kept in shops and houses to catch flies.[47] This remained a common practice in some villages until the mid-70s and it may occasionally still be encountered both in Malta and in Gozo.

In the summer months, trapping of sparrows takes place using a small single clap-net over man-made water holes. The net is usually hidden in a small clearing immediately next to the water-hole. Dry leaves are often placed over the net to hide it and the sparrows are trapped when they come to drink. This practice was more common before the 80s, when sparrows were trapped for trap shooting purposes or to end up in pies. Despott mentions that people netting for sparrows, often trapped other birds[48], as they still do nowadays.

A number of dunnocks are also trapped, and these may be seen for sale at the market along with other protected and unprotected birds. The short-toed lark, which is a very common migrant and a breeding summer resident, is relentlessly trapped by many trappers, especially during the spring migration. Short-toed larks can be commonly seen for sale for ridiculous prices in pet shops as well at the Valletta Sunday Market. Sultana and Gauci[49] state that the trapping of short-toed larks has greatly decreased in recent years, but they do not give any supporting evidence. From personal observations in the field as well as at the Valletta Market and visits to pet shops, it is evident that trapping of short-toed larks is still a very common practice.

The use of vertical nets

De Soldanis[50] mentions the *ragnaja*, but fails to describe it. It may well have been a sort of vertical net as described by Wright,[51] who noted: 'Great numbers [of nightingales] are taken in nets, which are thrown over a low-spreading carob-tree selected for the purpose, and the birds driven from other trees into it – a mode of capture very successfully adopted for most of the warblers and other small birds.'

Despott[52] mentions that the use of the net called *regna* was a common practice, especially in the south of Malta. Nightingales and other small birds were caught to be eaten. Despott[53] also mentions the taking of linnets in November by the bat-net. Despott does not describe what this net was and how it was used but, most probably, it was the English name which he gave to the *regna* since a regulation in 1916 made illegal the use of 'bat-net (*ragna*)'.[54]

However, the bat-net could also have been a net which was held between two poles and which was used at night. The poles were used to hit the tree in which birds were roosting and the roosting birds flew out into the net.

The use of vertical nets today

Although the use of vertical nets is illegal, large vertical nets (similar to mist nets used for bird ringing) and nets which are rigged up in trees, are often used.

Long and high nets held between two or more poles are usually set in valleys or between trees. These nets, which are often over 30 metres long and up to 10 metres high, are usually set and left there day and night throughout the migration periods. They are primarily set for catching turtle doves in spring and thrushes in autumn, but many other birds like cuckoos, golden orioles, scops owls as well as many small birds get caught.

The *regna*, the net which is rigged up around or hung from trees, though illegal is again being commonly used in certain areas, especially in the south. These nets are often very conspicuous, but most birds get caught in them at night. One can very often come across such nets in valleys and in small clusters of trees which are planted for shooting and trapping purposes. Old nets which would have been worn out having been used as clap-nets are then often used as a *regna*. These large nets are rigged in such a way that they have slack, loose pockets of net, in which the birds get entangled.

The people who set the nets check them during the migration period to retrieve the birds which are caught. During and after the migration periods, many small birds are caught and never retrieved. As in the case of mist-nets and vertical nets, apart from turtle doves and thrushes, for which the nets are primarily set, many small birds such as warblers, flycatchers, and sparrows are caught. The birds which get caught late in the evening or at night, usually die by the following morning. Many of those which survive the nets, die at the hands of the trappers, who very frequently kill the small birds by pulling off their heads to make their removal from the nets easier.

Both because they are usually old nets as well as because of the way they get entangled in the trees, these nets are very difficult to remove without being torn apart, and thus they are frequently left in place even after the migration period is over. When migration stops, the nets are not checked anymore and birds which get caught remain entangled in the nets where they die a slow, cruel death. Once the birds get caught, they have little or no chance of escaping and the more they struggle, the more helplessly entangled they get in the nets, where they are left to die.

Another type of net which is sometimes used is a sort of funnel shaped net, which is secured to the ground at one end, while its other ends are supported on two high poles. A decoy bird is often placed under the net. When migratory birds fly under the net, the attendant releases the net which falls rapidly to the ground because of to the weights attached to it. This type of net is mainly used for turtle doves.

Flap-traps and cage-traps

Flap-traps and cage-traps are used for trapping finches such as hawfinch, siskin and sometimes greenfinches. These traps usually consist of a cage compartment where the decoy bird is kept. The other compartments are the catching compartments and have an open side with a spring-loaded catching flap. Flap-traps come in all sorts of odd shapes and sizes, the most common being squarish or rectangular and having one or two catching compartments. Traps with four catching compartments are by no means uncommon, while I have even seen a large one having ten. Some cage-traps are even more effective since they often have a small flap net on the top of the cage.

Whatever the shape or size, a perch is set in a way which when sat on, releases the latch which slams shut the catch flap by means of a spring.

Many people make these traps themselves. In the 1950s, in Gozo, a trapper informed me that he had made a clockwork-operated cage-trap. The trap consisted of a cage for the decoy, a compartment for the trapped birds and the catching compartment with a revolving door. It was designed so that when a bird was caught, it was automatically placed in a closed compartment while the trap remained set.

These traps were very commonly used when there was less free time, since they could be set and left unattended; only to be checked in the evening when the trapper returned home from work. They are still used and can often be seen set on specially-made wooden platforms in gardens, orchards and even on roof tops. Flap-traps are often baited with bread and used to trap Spanish sparrows. Some use them to trap robins.

Robin trapping

Sultana and Gauci[55] wrote that robin trapping has 'always been popular'. However, this practice seems to be another innovation of this century. Schembri,[56] does not mention anything about robin trapping. Wright, who frequently mentions various forms of shooting and trapping, does not mention any robin trapping and in one instance he even wrote about robins 'singing merrily'.[57] It was Despott[58] who in 1917 noted that 'many traps were set for their capture'. He later wrote: 'Those few robins which winter in Malta without falling victim to some boy are indeed lucky'.[59] In 1948, Gibb wrote that 'robins are caught by children for amusement in traps 'baited' with a live decoy'.[60] In 1966, the SPCA Inspector estimated that 5000 robins were trapped during the month of November.[61]

It is not known who introduced robin trapping to our shores. Arrigoni degli Oddi[62] mentions, amongst other implements, *trabocchetti* when he wrote about hunting methods which were used in Italy in 1902 and it is most probable that robin traps came to Malta via Italy or Sicily. If not the traps themselves, their name has most certainly come that way. In a study related to Spain, published in 1860, one finds descriptions of cage-traps, variations of which are used locally.[63]

One can often see children, and quite often adults, walking with a sack or bag containing a squarish object. If this is seen during the months of October, November and December, the squarish object is probably a *trabokk*, the local word for a robin trap. Robin traps are also known as *trabokk tal-kampnar*, or *trabokk tal-pitirrossi* or *g̱harix*. *Kampnar* means steeple while *g̱harix* means tent, and the traps are so called because of their shape.

In spite of the fact that it is illegal to use, keep or sell robin traps, one can frequently see them for sale at the Valletta Sunday market, at shops which sell shooters' and trappers' goods, pet shops and some ironmongers' stores.

There are various types of robin traps, but the most commonly used are flap-traps which are triangular in shape. Essentially, they all have a flap-net on either side, and this net may either trap from the top of the trap to the bottom or vice-versa. There are variations of the triggering mechanisms. Most commonly, the triggering mechanism is a perch, on which the robin sits. The weight of the bird causes the perch to fall; this unhinges the flap holding the net, which springs and traps the bird. Sometimes, the triggering mechanism is a wire mesh along the whole side of the trap. The flap-net slams shut on being triggered by the displacement of the latch which holds the flap-net in its set position.

Being territorial, robins will readily fight off other robins which intrude on their territory. In the Maltese Islands, this behaviour costs many a robin its freedom, and often its life. A live robin is placed inside the trap. The trap is then set and placed in a prominent place close to a tree where a robin is heard calling or singing. The free robin will, in no time, try to engage the intruding robin in a territorial fight. At some point during the course of the fight for his territory, the free robin will sit on or hit the perch that triggers the mechanism which traps it.

Sometimes, if a person does not have any robins from the previous year, a dead or stuffed robin is used to catch the first robin, with which many more are then trapped. A piece of mirror is also sometimes used when the trapper lacks a starter robin. The free robin is attracted to the cage-trap containing the mirror either by whistling or by imitating its ticking call. Up to 1972, when Malta's currency was still one based on shillings and pence, the ticking call was often imitated by two penny pieces. They were held between the forefinger and thumb of one hand in such a way that they overlapped with each other partially. The fingers of the other hand were flicked rhythmically against the bottom penny, which was held further out than the upper one.

A home-made finger-operated call made out of the crown of a soft drink bottle is also used. Such a call is made by wrapping a piece of string around a crown, whose cork or plastic seal has been removed. A nail is then fixed in the string in such a way that the ticking call of the robin is imitated when the fingers are flicked across the nail which hits the crown repeatedly.

The free robin usually comes to investigate the call and on seeing the stuffed robin, or itself in the mirror, tries to engage in a fight and gets caught. A split prickly pear fruit or pomegranate is also sometimes used to lure robins into the cage-traps.

The use of *turmentina*, a type of glue similar to bird lime, is sometimes also used. A decoy robin is placed in a small cage while a stick coated with glue is placed on the cage containing the decoy. Robins are caught when they try to perch on the glue-covered perch. Fortunately, this practice is neither very widespread nor too common.

Although such practices are carried out mostly by children, it is not uncommon to see adults, accompanied by their children, trapping robins. In Gozo, the typical robin trap was introduced in the early 1970s, when communications between the two islands started improving.[64] Robin trapping grew in popularity as artificial animal food became available. Previously, robins were trapped and fed on pomegranates or prickly pears and died when such food was no longer available. My father recalls that sometimes robins were kept alive by crushing roasted chick peas and *galletti* (i.e. hard-baked biscuits) and working it in the shape of a dome by mixing it with some water.

Being insectivorous and not recognizing as food the artificial food given to them in captivity, many robins starve to death a few days after being trapped. One can often see them dead in the gutter, frequently just outside the house in which they died.

Other trapping methods

Apart from the triangular-shaped traps with flap-nets on both sides and cage-traps which are also used for finch trapping, another sort of net-trap which is sometimes used for robins is a flat board with a small compartment for the decoy bird. A spring-operated flap-net surrounds the tiny decoy compartment and when the latch is released, the net covers the entire floor area. This type of trap is locally known as *ċattra* (raft) or *tilar* (pan) due to its flat shape. In Gozo, this trap is called *trabokk tax-xibka*, meaning a trap with a net.

Children also use nets in the form of a small bag attached to a long pole to catch sparrows while nesting in ventilators of houses. The net is placed outside the ventilator, blocking the only way out of the nest and the children hold the net there and wait until the bird flies out of the nest and ends up in the net. Although this practice is decreasing, it may still be met with in some villages in rural areas, especially in Gozo.

'Game' bird trapping – quail trapping

The trapping of quail, which used to be a common practice up to twenty years ago, has decreased because quails are shot long before they can be located by the trappers.

Quail trapping takes place both in spring and in autumn. In spring only male quails are trapped, for they are lured by the call of the female. To trap quails, the trapper goes into the countryside and listens for quail calls. If he hears none, he imitates the call of the female, using the quail call. Upon hearing a quail, or when a quail replies to his calls, he identifies the field in which the quail is heard calling. He then spreads the net in that field or in an adjacent one. The net is spread loosely over the crop, be it cauliflowers, silla, corn, barley or whatever it might be. An area covering at least a hundred square metres is covered by such nets.

Quails are mostly trapped early in the morning. The trapper sits in the field with the end of the net on his lap. He then uses the *kirjolin* to imitate the call of the female quail. The trapper usually has at least two quail calls, one louder than the other. The one emitting the loud call is used when the quail is still far off, the softer one is used when the quail is nearer to the trapper. In Malta, a call carved out of soft stone or made of lead, was also used to imitate the call of the male quail.

In spring, the male quail rushes to find the female whose call he hears. Quail trappers say that as soon as the male quails hear the call of the female, they fly towards the call 'as if someone threw a stone'. As the quail lands on the net, its legs get caught in the large mesh and is unable to spring up and take flight. It is then simply plucked from the net.

Sometimes, the quail skulks in the vegetation and walks towards the trapper, who hits incessantly at the quail call. Those who can use the *kirjolin* well are able to draw the quail to their laps. They say that when a quail walks towards the trapper in this manner, on seeing him it springs up in an attempt to fly away and ends up in the net. That is the reason why trappers secure the end of their net on their laps, otherwise, the quail will fly upwards past his face without getting caught.

During the past thirty years or so, trappers started using female quail decoys for attracting males in spring.

September is the best time for catching quail and both males and females are trapped. As in autumn there are no crops on which the nets can be laid, they are spread out on pieces of reed and raised pillars of stone. These props are usually some half a metre high and they just keep the net off the ground. Trapping sites are quite large and a large number of caged decoys, often exceeding thirty in number, are placed around the site. Caged female quails are placed in the area covered by the net.

Before the trapper sets out, he places the male quail decoys near the females 'to stimulate them'. Then he covers each of the cages containing male quail with a dark cloth. Some trappers think that male quail keep calling even after the break of dawn because they would have been stimulated, yet it is more probable that quails keep calling because the dark cloth tricks them into thinking it is still night time, thus they continue to call even after daybreak. Hard boiled eggs are also given to quails because trappers believe it helps quails call better.[65]

In autumn the trapper is usually on the trapping site at about 4 am. At the break of dawn, bent double, the trapper and an assistant walk slowly towards the net and make faint rustling noises with a milk tin containing some soil and small stones. In this way, quails skulking near the netting site are driven under the net. When the trappers reach the open end of the net, they secure it to the ground and the driven quails are thus trapped below the net.

On many occasions, to make trapping easier, the vegetation at inaccessible places where quails are likely to seek shelter is burnt thus the birds will have to seek shelter in places where they are more exposed and can be easily shot or trapped. Many of the quails trapped are kept alive as decoys. Quails are easily bred in captivity and a number of people breed them in significant numbers.

Turtle dove trapping

In former times, turtle dove migrations were larger and trapping used to take place on a much larger scale. Trapping was indeed more economical and efficient than the use of the gun. Schembri[66] wrote that many turtle doves were taken. Wright[67] noted that with nets which were laid out over 'an area of (say) 24 feet by 8 or 9, twenty or thirty doves, and upwards, are frequently caught at one haul'. Payn,[68] wrote that 700 turtle doves were netted by one man alone in spring 1935. Gauci[69] wrote that he knew of people 'who can boast of netting 500 turtle doves in one morning'.

Turtle doves are trapped only in spring – between mid-April and late May. Trappers complain that they are usually surrounded by shooters who shoot at turtle doves, without giving them a chance with their nets.

Nowadays, trapping of turtle doves is carried out using two or three fluttering decoys, although Wright[70] mentions that five decoys were frequently used. The decoy birds are kept hooded for most of the trapping season and the hood is taken off for a brief period each day when they are mouth-fed. The trapper holds an amount of corn in his mouth and after opening the bird's beak, he inserts the grains of corn into the bird's mouth using his tongue.

On the trapping site, one of the fluttering decoys is placed in a depression built in the 'ċakija', a shallow heap of stones built in the middle of the trapping site. It runs parallel to the nets, which are spread out on either side. Another decoy is placed close to the decoy in the depression. This stationary decoy gives the impression of a sitting dove and is the only decoy which remains visible to migrating turtle doves when the fluttering decoy is lowered into the depression and disappears from sight. The other fluttering decoys are placed at the edge of, and further away from, the nets. All fluttering decoys are kept in low rubble constructions so that they cannot be seen unless they are made to flutter. If these decoys are conspicuous the wild turtle doves usually settle next to them, instead of alighting in the trapping area.

The decoys are used successively when turtle doves are sighted, the distal one being made to flutter first, then the proximal one at the end of the nets. When the turtle doves are about to alight close to the edge of the nets, the one in the middle of the nets is made to flutter and the turtle doves usually swerve to alight near it. When they do so, the trapper pulls the rope that operates the clap-nets and the birds are trapped. More often than not, a shooter stays close by to shoot at the birds which escape the nets.

Some breed turtle doves in captivity. Very often they are crossed with Barbary doves and the offspring are sometimes used as decoys. Since they are tame and need less attention than turtle doves, their hood can be removed each day so they can feed by themselves, thus saving the shooter or trapper plenty of time.

Plovers and lapwings

Golden plover and lapwings are also trapped but the number of trappers who specialise in 'game' bird trapping is very small since the gun offers an easier and less time-consuming option. There are a number of renowned places for plover trapping. Clap-nets for plovers are about 40 metres long and about 25 caged decoys are used on such sites. Plastic decoys and stuffed ones are used together with caged live birds and the cassettes described earlier. A Barbary dove whose tail is cut short to give it a more wader-like appearance is often used as a fluttering decoy for plovers. Although daily catches are not significantly large, there are days when over a dozen plover are trapped on a trapping site. Plover trapping starts in late October and lasts until mid-January. Some trap over a hundred birds in a season. A golden plover sells for Lm18–25. Nowadays it is easy to keep such birds in captivity due to the introduction of artificial foods. Up to a few years ago, when such food was not available, birds like thrushes and plovers were kept alive on snails and grain. Thus it was neither easy nor popular, to keep them in captivity.

Other birds in captivity

Birds which fly across the trapping area are also trapped. Snipe, thrushes, larks and hoopoes are frequently netted. Some individuals trap starlings with small clap-nets, especially in olive groves and other plantations where starlings gather to feed. Birds of prey, such as kestrels are also frequently trapped after being lured by the fluttering decoys. At trapping sites which are situated near the coast, waders such as sandpipers, little ringed plovers and little stints, are frequently trapped. Such birds often die a slow, lingering death from starvation when they are placed in an aviary or when they are released in a back-yard after having their wings clipped.

Birds which are shot and wounded are sometimes kept in captivity. The great majority of these birds suffer painfully due to untreated or improperly treated gunshot wounds such as broken legs or wings or other internal injuries.

Furthermore, it is not unusual for birds up to the size of a kestrel to be placed in cages, where they beat themselves against the wire of the cage. Passerines invariably damage the sides of their beaks and many rub their foreheads raw. Birds of prey damage their cere as well as their wings when they flap helplessly. It is quite common to see song thrushes with badly bruised, bleeding faces or kestrels with overgrown beaks and a large clot of dried blood where the cere used to be.

Larger birds of prey such as harriers, falcons and honey buzzards which are caught injured, are often kept tied by one of their legs. This practice almost always results in badly bruised and sprained leg muscles since the birds flap helplessly in an effort to set themselves free.

The birds' natural diet is substituted by an artificial one and many birds, especially insectivorous species (such as hoopoes), starve to death. People who keep live birds of prey often shoot small birds to feed them. But later, when the plumage of raptors starts getting ruffled and when its keeper starts losing interest, they are fed on scraps of meat bought from the butchers – usually bits of lung and other scraps unfit for human consumption. The nutritional value of such food is so low that the birds start suffering from dietary deficiencies resulting in loss of colour of the legs and the cere. Such birds have little resistance to infectious diseases, to which they eventually succumb.

Amongst the commonest diseases suffered by birds in captivity one can mention scaly legs, locally called *pullagri*. It is a common disease in the case of thrushes, plover and finches. Bumble foot, is common with raptors. Bird trappers and keepers try to invent medicines to cure birds from scaly legs. The legs of infected birds are dipped in solutions of iodine, alcohol, 'Dettol' and other antiseptics. Village chemists will readily tell you that trappers frequently come to ask for medicine or vitamins for their birds.

Old-timers tried to cure such diseases by dipping birds' legs in kerosene. Birds which had eye infections had their eyes treated with pure honey.[71]

Nests and nestlings stolen

It is common for nestlings to be taken whenever nests are found. De Boisgelin[72] wrote that people climbed down cliffs using ropes to take nests of pigeons and other birds. In his description of Malta and Gozo, the French historian Lacroix[73] quotes a letter dated 8th January 1749, written by Commander Godeheu de Reville to M. de Reaumur, which describes how Maltese people used to climb down to caverns in the cliff faces to take the young pigeons from their nests.

Nowadays, some people climb down sea cliffs to steal the young of the blue rock thrush, which are then sold to be hand reared, thus becoming tame. Again, this is not a practice of our times since Wright[74] recorded blue rock thrushes breeding 'in ruined buildings, in which case its progeny are sure to be taken by the country lads, who find a ready sale for them in town as cage birds'. He added that 'fabulous prices are sometimes given for a good songster' and states that 'he knew of a noble lady who considered herself fortunate in securing one for £7 10s'.

Nestlings of corn buntings and short-toed larks are also sought to be hand reared. Albeit to a lesser extent, nestlings of Spanish sparrows are also taken as are warblers'. However, these are not usually searched for since it is known that they die within a short time, and those which are taken are usually mistaken for the young of corn buntings or short-toed larks.

The few finches which attempt to breed usually end up having their young taken from the nest. If the nest is not found or is inaccessible, the adults may succeed in rearing their young but these fall victim to nets at water-holes as soon as they fledge in summer. Despott[75] noted that linnets were 'very often robbed of their nestlings'.

Nests of other species, like the barn owl, are also taken, whenever found. The birds are usually sold to collectors as happened to a nest containing four young, which was found on a sea cliff in Gozo in 1987. The young, together with their mother and an egg, were sold for Lm20 to a Maltese collector.

While mentioning nests and nestlings, one cannot fail to mention egg collecting. Although I have seen a small number of egg collections, such collections are, most fortunately, very rare. It is seldom that one sees birds' eggs in collections except maybe the odd egg next to a stuffed bird. However Despott mentions egg collectors twice: once in relation to corn buntings, when he attributes its decrease 'perhaps due to the great demand for its eggs among dealers on the continent',[76] and another time with reference to the serin, when he wrote about a nest which was obtained by an egg-collector.[77]

Eggs of cory's and manx shearwaters and herring gulls used to be taken for food, especially by fishermen, but this practice seems to have now ceased. However, some fishermen still take the young of herring gulls and cory's shearwaters to hand rear them.

Chapter 8

History of Hunting and Bird Protection Legislation

The earliest hunting laws

During the years 1239–1240, Emperor Frederick II linked Malta to Sicily and appointed a person known as *Paulino de Malta* as his proctor.[1] On 5th May 1240, the Emperor sent falconer Guljermo Ruffino and a team of eighteen falconers to report on the number of falcons he had on the island, how many were caught and how they were kept.[2] This implies that some sort of legislation related to the catching and keeping of falcons existed at that time. Since Malta was under Sicilian rule, the laws which applied to Sicily applied locally, and thus one can say that the first legislation related to hunting was that of Sicily.

In mediaeval times, the noble classes used trained falcons to hunt other birds. Falcons were considered to be the property of the King and one needed special permission to catch and keep a falcon.

Bresc wrote that the mediaeval administration of the 1400s was responsible for paying the *falconiere*, a civilian who played an important role in the island life. He also noted that the only significant expense of the administration was on the capture, feeding and shipment of falcons to Sicily for the King.[3]

Sultana[4] and Sultana and Gauci[5] wrote that the first hunting laws in Malta date 'as far back as 1499'. In fact, the first local legislation dates back to May 1492, when the Viceroy of Sicily recognized the privilege of keeping *paragni* – places reserved for hunting by means of nets and trained falcons. Seven years later, King Ferdinand reaffirmed the privilege of hunting and of keeping falcons.[6]

Hunting laws under the order of St John

It is interesting to point out that during the 13th century, that is before the Knights came to Malta, the practice of hunting was forbidden to the Knights on all the territories controlled by the Order.[7] This seems to have been revised at some point in time since, when they came to Malta in 1530, they attached considerable importance to hunting. From time to time the matter was discussed in the Council of the Order and regulations were issued. A secret ballot taken in March 1650 introduced the concept of the closed-seasons. It was forbidden to hunt between 1st March and the end of June. The penalty of 2 months imprisonment was contemplated.[8] A number of edicts published later declared hunting as prohibited between the middle of December and July of the following year.[9] Game wardens were obliged to report any transgressions of the law, failing which they were dismissed and exiled.[10]

The edict of 22nd June 1530 was the first law regulating hunting enacted by the Knights. It reserved the hunting of partridges for the Grandmaster and the penalty for breaking the law was a fine of 10 *oncie*.[11] The Knights took possession of Malta in October and this edict was enacted almost four months before they took actual possession of the islands!

Grandmaster Pietro del Monte (1543–35) issued an edict prohibiting the hunting of partridges and hares in Malta, Gozo and Comino. The penalty was 3 lashes and a year on the galley bench for first time offenders and a life sentence for second time offenders. Village Captains had to report anyone infringing the law. Moreover they had to sever the ligament from one of the legs of any dog found on a hunting spree.[12]

In February 1588, Grandmaster La Vallette ordered that nobody could hunt or get firewood from Comino and nobody could land there except in case of emergency. The penalty was a fine of 25 *scudi* and the confiscation of the boat. Those unable to pay had to spend two years on the galley bench. The person reporting the contravention was given half of the fine and pardoned if an accomplice.[13]

The edicts regulating hunting published under the various Grandmasters were not very different in substance from each other – they established closed-seasons between December and July, declared that no one could hunt partridges, rabbits and hares or disturb their nests and that no one could sell or buy protected species. Buskett Gardens and Comino are among the areas which are frequently mentioned as areas reserved for the Grandmaster. The picking of snails and the cutting of grass from reserved areas were also forbidden. Fines or the galley bench were contemplated for anyone who hunted without a licence or who hunted in sown fields or in reserved areas. The confiscation of the firearm and ammunition was contemplated for anyone passing through forbidden areas with a loaded gun.

The shooting of pigeons was also prohibited by a number of edicts while other edicts stated that no one could trap falcons. A number of edicts declared that a bounty was to be paid to anyone who consigned heads, legs or eggs of jackdaws, which were considered as pests because of the damage they did in orchards, fruit gardens and fields.[14]

Towards the end of the 1700s, the Knights were ousted by the French, who, in turn, were driven out by the Maltese and the British in 1800.

Hunting and bird protection laws under British rule

The first legal provision related to hunting under British rule can be found in an edict dated 30 January 1801. This edict listed five privileges which could be enjoyed by those who joined the infantry or the artillery. The last of the five privileges was that those who subscribe in the militia can carry a firearm for hunting purposes without needing to apply for a permit.[15]

The first Government Notice concerning bird protection was a regulation regarding 'sporting and fishing' published in The Malta Government Gazette of 22nd May 1872, which prohibited the use of the *regna*.[16]

Bird protection regulations underwent many fluctuations. Amongst promoters of bird protection one finds the noted Maltese Naturalist Giuseppe Despott, John H. Cooke, editor of *The Central Mediterranean Naturalist* as well as other officers of the British Forces stationed in Malta. Amongst the foreign organizations involved, one cannot fail to mention the RSPB, which in the early 1900s was trying to set up a section of their society in Malta, the RSPCA as well as the Smithsonian Institution.

Those opposing bird protection were, as usual, shooters, mainly from the upper classes. They often used their positions in organizations such as the Agrarian Society, to torpedo any moves towards bird protection.

Closed-seasons reappear

In spite of opposition, regulations published in 1916,[17] re-introduced the concept of the closed-season which was first introduced by the Knights. These regulations had schedules listing the protected species.

Political pressure against these regulations was rather strong especially in the Council of Government. The arguments used by shooters then are still in use today; namely that there is hardly anything to shoot at and that shooters have a right to shoot and stuff birds.

Following the publication of new regulations in November 1936[18,19], some shooters, notably those from high society, rallied together to protest against the laws regulating hunting. An advert urging 'sportsmen and land owners' to attend appeared in the *Times of Malta*.[20] Rosario Frendo Randon, the honorary life president of the *Societa Economico Agraria*, was one of the promoters. The meeting for shooters and trappers was held at Palazzo de la Salle in Valletta and Rosario Frendo Randon, Professor Vassallo, the Hon L. Galea and Major Alfred Sant Manduca were chosen to sign a memorandum on behalf of the shooters and trappers present.

This memorandum, which was submitted to the Governor, objected to, amongst other things, the inclusion of several areas as bird sanctuaries. The regulations were amended – the golden oriole was included in the list of protected species while seventeen localities consisting of railway stations, public gardens, sports grounds and cemeteries, were again declared as protected areas but lost their no-shooting boundary zone. The regulations of 1937 remained in force (with minor alterations) until 1980, when they were replaced by a new law.

The trail to the laws of 1980

During 1962, The Malta Ornithological Society (MOS) was formed on the initiative of Mr Domnic Cutajar, who sought RSPB's help to set up a bird protection movement. Together with Mr Joe Attard and a handful of other conservationists, some of whom had often voiced their concern about the killing of birds, as well as help from overseas, the MOS was set up.[21]

The efforts of this organisation, as well as those of the Natural History Society of Malta (now SSCN) and the Malta Society for the Prevention of Cruelty to Animals (now SPCA), created pressure which brought about a number of changes to the regulations related to bird protection.

In spite of a number of minor amendments to the law, Malta badly needed a complete revision of the hunting laws. Pressure against the killing of birds was growing both from within the Maltese Islands, as well as from overseas. The Maltese dailies of the 70s were literally inundated with letters and polemics about shooting. The number of letters against bird shooting, however, by far outnumbered those written by shooters. Editorials frequently appeared urging the Government to make a move and enact adequate legislation for the protection of birds.

In 1972, the local shooters, fearing that something radical was about to happen to their 'sport', formed an association which they called *Ghaqda Nazzjonali Kaccaturi w Nassaba* (National Association of Shooters and Trappers). According to Mr Albert Gauci,[22] the first secretary of this association,

> it was hailed by some optimists as the future teacher of good manners and correct behaviour among the rather copious local community of shooters, snarers and what have you. In time, this aim may or may not be reached, but as far as the present times are any indication of the future, we can safely say that we should not let ourselves be kidded by false hopes.

The Malta Ornithological Society was, at that time, very vociferous and effective. The awareness of the general public grew, so much so that the weekly article *Shooting Topics* in *The Times of Malta*, was replaced by one pro-conservation. The number of tourists coming to Malta also increased. Tourists started coming face to face with birds in cages and shooters firing at birds which were protected in their home country. Protests from tourists were plentiful.

As a result of economic growth in the country, Maltese people started earning more money and the introduction of the 40 hour week gave Maltese workers more free time. Thus shooting and trapping grew in popularity while people who were neither shooters nor trappers started visiting the countryside more frequently. Consequently, shooting became much more evident.

These pressures might have been the cause that made Mr Dom Mintoff, then Prime Minister, to ask the police to study the question of bird shooting. In January 1977, the police set up an internal committee which consisted of Assistant Commissioners John Cachia, Laurence Pullicino and Anthony Mifsud Tommasi as well as Police Inspectors Alfred Calleja (a shooter, who now is the Commissioner of Police) and Joe Attard (one of the founders of the Malta Ornithological Society).

The first draft

Draft regulations drawn up by these officers included the introduction of two closed-seasons for shooting and trapping. They also suggested that the trapping of finches in spring was to be prohibited but turtle dove trapping allowed. The draft legal notice also contained schedules listing the birds that could be shot or trapped and the places which were to be declared bird sanctuaries.

In spite of some shortcomings, the draft was a great leap from the regulations of 1937 which were then in force. The draft was forwarded to the Shooters' and Trappers' Association, the Malta Ornithological Society and the Malta Section of ICBP, which was then composed of the Society for the Study and Conservation of Nature, Men of the trees, RSPCA, and the MOS. However, pressure by shooters as well as by government ministers who were themselves shooters, led to a gradual dilution of the law.

The Government brought over Dr Fulco Pratesi, the vice-chairman of the Italian section of ICBP, who together with Dr A. Chelini produced a report about the draft legislation.[23] They advised against a long open season in spring and remarked that the shooting season should end on 30th April at the latest. They also suggested that the open season in spring should be reduced by ten days each year so that eventually, spring shooting of migratory birds will be abolished. They suggested that rabbit hunting should only take place using net and ferret.

In July 1977, the internal police committee amended the original draft and included some points regarding the methods of catching wild rabbits, but while the draft was awaiting the approval of the Prime Minister, the Shooters' Association sent further proposals. They again asked for the inclusion of herons, cranes, bustards, honey buzzards, scops owl, cuckoos and terns in the list of birds that may be shot.

Back-tracking

In the meantime, the conservation movement was not consulted over any of the new changes, while the Shooters' Association had another meeting with the Commissioner of Police on 12th June 1978. This was a very fruitful meeting for shooters as most of the amendments which they proposed were accepted and through these, a number of loopholes were created. Their suggestion that the prohibition of shooting in the territorial waters should be reduced to the prohibition of shooting within 3 km offshore was accepted by the police. A type of net hitherto unknown, which they termed as *xibka wieqfa ghall-imlievez* (ie a vertical net for thrushes), was introduced as a legal means to take birds. The introduction of this type of net meant that all types of vertical nets could be used under the pretext of being for thrushes.

The Shooters' Association kept insisting that herons, scops owls, cuckoos and swifts should be included in the list of birds that may be shot while the short-toed lark should be included in the list of birds which may be trapped.

The association also requested to be informed prior to the publication of the regulations so that they could inform their members.

Following this meeting, herons and egrets appeared on the drafts of the police for the first time and the concept of a closed-season in spring was dropped. Some of the shooters' proposals seem to have received the support of the curator of the Natural History Museum, who was a shooter and a keen collector of stuffed birds. At that time, the MOS was in conflict with the curator of the Natural History Museum over the issue of bird-ringing.

In May 1979, the police sent a copy of the draft final version of the regulations to the Shooters' Association, something the shooters themselves had requested during the meeting of the previous June. The shooters submitted fresh proposals with further amendments, amongst which they again requested that swifts, scops owls, cranes, bitterns and bustards be included in the list of birds which may be shot. They also wanted the prohibition of shooting within three kilometres offshore to be replaced by the prohibition of shooting in any harbour or bay. For once the proposals of the Shooters' Association went unheeded.

The best words that describe the actions of the Shooters' Association are those of the Commissioner of Police of that time, who wrote: 'Most of the requests of the Shooters' Association were implemented; if *all of them* were accepted the regulations would not have been issued at all. I regret to say that they were not always consistent in their opinions and their only aim was to delay, as much as possible, and even nip in the bud, any controls aimed at preservation.'

Last minute changes were effected when the Director of Civil Aviation requested that places where transmitting stations were situated should be declared as bird sanctuaries 'to avoid damages by game hunters to the installations or even injuries to the personnel working therein.'

Following a series of debates which took the best part of a month's parliamentary sittings, Act XVII of 1980[24] was enacted by Parliament. Although being described as 'a very mild law' by Dr Philip Muscat,[25] then Minister of Education and a practising shooter, this act and the subsequent regulations were a badly needed step forward and a milestone in the history of bird protection legislation. It had been over forty years since proper bird protection legislation existed.

The act and regulations of 1980

The new act came into force on the 30th May 1980. It introduced the badly needed, albeit too short, closed-seasons. The closed-season for birds was between 22nd May and 31st August while a closed-season for wild rabbit was established between 1st January and 31st May. Thus due to the overlapping of both closed-seasons shooting is totally prohibited between 22nd and 31st May.

The 1980 amendments, which are still in force today, also prohibit the discharge of firearms within three kilometres off shore; the discharge of firearms within 200 metres from any inhabited area and within 50 metres of any street. These amendments also introduced the licence for taxidermists and for birdringers.

The Commissioner of Police is empowered to issue regulations to control the shooting and trapping of birds. In fact, Legal Notice 68 of 1980, which came into force on 8th August, replaced the bird protection regulations of 1937 *in toto*.

These regulations, entitled *Protection of Birds and Wild Rabbits Regulations of 1980* apart from including the closed-season defined in the Code of Police Laws, protected nests of all species of birds. They made it illegal to shoot at, take or disturb any nest or its young and forbade the keeping, selling or exposing for sale of robin traps, birdlime, mist-nets and blind live decoy birds. The release of birds for shooting purposes and the use of lead shot larger than 3.2 mm in diameter, were also made illegal.

Two schedules, one listing the birds which can be shot at and the other listing the birds which can be trapped, appear in these regulations. The birds which can be shot at are: collard doves, curlews, dottorel, egrets, golden plover, herons, lapwings, nightjars, quails, rails, crakes and coots, skylarks, snipes, Spanish sparrows, starlings, stock doves, stone curlews, thrushes (except blue rock thrushes), woodcock, wood pigeon and wild duck.

The birds which can be trapped are: chaffinches, golden plover, goldfinches, greenfinches, hawfinches, linnets, ortolan buntings, quails, serins, siskins, skylarks, Spanish sparrows, starlings, thrushes (except blue rock thrushes) and turtle doves.

Parts of the law are very difficult to enforce. If a police officer stops a shooter who is in possession of a freshly-killed protected bird, he cannot charge him with having contravened the regulations unless he actually sees him shooting it. The same can be said to the three kilometre zone where one cannot shoot from any foreshore. The law states that no one can shoot but does not prohibit the carrying of firearms. Thus the police cannot apprehend anyone carrying a gun unless a person is actually seen shooting.

For better and for worse

The first amendment to these regulations appeared in Legal Notice 25 of 1983.[26] This amendment deleted the vertical net – '*xibka wieqfa ghall-imlievez*' – from the implements that can be used for trapping purposes. This amendment came about after pressure from the Department of Environment, which was supported by the Curator of the Natural History Museum and the MOS.

Another amendment to the 1980 regulations was effected by Legal Notice 18 of 1987.[27] This Legal Notice was published in February 1987, and it shortened the closed-season for birds to between 1st June and 14th August. Due to the fact that the closed-season had been established by an Act of Parliament (Act XVII of 1980), it could only be changed by another Act of Parliament and the amendment by the Minister of Justice was claimed to be *ultra vires*. This was explained in detail by the conservation movement in a joint press conference, in which they appealed to the Government to repeal the Legal Notice. But the authorities ignored all appeals.

The Legal Notice was finally challenged in court by Louis F. Cassar and Christian Holland in their own name and as representatives of the environmental pressure group Żgħażagħ għall-Ambjent (now *Moviment għall-Ambjent*). The First Hall of the Civil Court decreed that such a change could not have been made since the Minister was not empowered to make it. It further declared that the regulation was null as far as the shooting of birds was concerned. However, it was not irregular with regard to bird trapping since the closed-season for bird trapping was not stipulated in the Code of Police Laws but was part of the regulations.[28] Nevertheless, this case has been in the court of appeal following an appeal filed by the Shooters' and Trappers' Association.

The current situation

Currently, the laws and regulations of 1980 are still in force but they are never respected and hardly ever enforced. It seems that on those rare occasions when they are enforced, the judgments which are delivered are so poor that they verge on the ridiculous. Very often, the accused is only reprimanded and acquitted or fined a small amount of money. Shotguns are hardly ever confiscated.

For infringements of hunting laws, poor judgments have prevailed. To give a few examples: in 1969 a man was prosecuted by the police at the request of the RSPCA. He was charged in court for trapping birds without a licence. The case was dismissed because the man claimed that although he had no trapping licence, he was trapping birds on behalf of a person who had a licence.[29]

In August 1970, a man from Mellieħa was prosecuted by the police, again at the request of the RSPCA for keeping five fledglings of blue rock thrush. He was found guilty and fined £1.[30] At that time, a blue rock thrush sold illegally for £10. More recently, a man was charged in court for having shot an eagle. The court found him guilty and fined him Lm10.[31] An eagle can easily sell for at least Lm50. Another man who was charged for having shot and killed a male widgeon at Għadira Bird Sanctuary, was found guilty and fined Lm10. A male widgeon can fetch up to Lm30 for collection purposes. In October 1991 a griffon vulture was shot. The shooter, whose name was even published in a section of the local press, was offered Lm1900 for the bird.[32] He was never charged in court – but if he were, he would have been liable to a maximum penalty of Lm50!

The fines that shooters have to pay, if they are caught, charged in court and found guilty, are ridiculous. They do not provide enough compensation for the administrative costs involved, let alone for the harm done to the eco-system.

To make matters worse, the Shooters' and Trappers' Association – which has recently added the word Conservationists to its title – is constantly voicing its 'concern' while criticising the Government for declaring too many reserves. Instead of condemning the illegal activities of shooters

and asking for strict penalties to discourage illegal activities by shooters
and trappers, the Association constantly criticizes the Government for
not consulting it on matters related to shooting. In spite of the fact it
is a corresponding member of FACE (the Association of Shooters of EC
Countries), the local Association constantly opposes the signing of the Berne
Convention.

In 1984 the Association submitted proposals to the Government for
changes in the hunting law. These are the same ones they harp on today. A
summary of these proposals was published in the shooters' paper *Il-Passa*.[33]
The following is a synopsis of the article entitled 'The Proposals of the
Shooters' and Trappers' Association':

> To the schedule of species which can be hunted, the Association wants to
> add: rock pigeons, honey buzzards, gannets, cormorants, ruffs, oystercatchers,
> glossy ibis, swifts, owls, cuckoos, harriers, shanks, cranes and geese.
> The closed-season should be between 1st June and 14th August [a time
> when there is no bird migration!]. The Association wants that in the case
> of Spanish sparrow, the closed-season does not apply. [Shooters want this
> modification so that they will be able to shoot legally all year round.]
> The Association also wants shooters to be allowed to shoot next to any
> road and to carry a loaded gun on any road and also wants to decrease the
> distances that shooters have to keep away from bird sanctuaries. They also
> want to have exclusive use of public land during the shooting season.
> In addition to the 50 cents they receive from every licence shooters have
> asked to receive a further Lm1.50 so that they can assume the role of an
> aviculture society. The Shooters' Association want any infringements to the
> hunting regulations to be considered as contraventions and not as crimes –
> thus the penalties should be lowered.
> The Association is of the opinion that shooting competitions using live
> birds should be permitted and want that Buskett Gardens and Ta' Qali be
> open for shooting until noon on weekdays and until 9.00 am on Saturdays
> and Sundays. The Shooters' and Trappers' Association feels that the present
> number of bird sanctuaries is more than enough to cater for the needs of Malta
> and Gozo, and hence, no more bird sanctuaries or nature reserves should be
> declared.

Following the publication of these proposals, A. Gauci, who was the first
secretary of the Shooters' Association, wrote: 'We have an association of
shooters and trappers which unlike similar associations to be found elsewhere, seems to have no wish to impose restrictions on its members. The
principal aim of the local association seems to be that of engaging in
polemics with people on the other side of the fence.'[34]

The conservation movement

On the other side of the coin there are a number of environment pressure
groups with a combined membership of over 5000. Public awareness on
environmental problems is growing. So is opposition to hunting. However
the majority of the population suffers in silence. It does not constantly
threaten politicians like the Shooters' and Trappers' Association, which
claims that shooters and trappers are worth '20,000+++ votes'.

It is interesting to point out that while the Association always claims to have over 20,000 members, the number of licensed shooters and trappers combined does not exceed 14,000. In spite of boasting about its membership, the Shooters' and Trappers' Association is constantly appealing to shooters and trappers to become members. In an unpublished report to FACE, the local shooters' association has declared itself as having 1069 members in 1985,[35] while in 1991, only 13% of the shooters were members.[36]

Some of the environmental groups are doing their best to make the general public aware of the consequences of hunting. Protests, talks, fora and seminars related to environmental issues are sometimes organised by some of the environmental groups. The Shooters' Association is constantly opposing efforts made to instil in school children the love and respect of nature and constantly label environmental education as 'brainwashing'. Yet, one is pleased to note that more children are learning to appreciate wildlife in its natural environment. This is due both to the work of those organisations who strive for the protection of the environment as well as the increased amount of wildlife documentaries being shown on local and foreign television stations which are received in Malta.

In April 1990, the MOS and the Shooters' Association reached an agreement which was hailed as 'historical' by Dr Yves Lecocq, Secretary General of FACE.[37] Some saw this agreement as a severe blow to the conservation movement as it came at a time when the Government had shown its clear intentions of joining the EC. In fact Government applied for membership on 16th July of that same year.

While these meetings were in progress, the customary slaughter of protected birds went on unabated but a dead silence against such killings was conspicuous. In December 1990, following a published interview with the Parliamentary Secretary for the Environment, a letter from the MOS president appeared in a local paper to clarify a point on such talks.[38] The Shooters' and Trappers' Association was quick on the draw and in a reply letter to the press announced that the meetings with the MOS had been suspended, claiming that the MOS had violated the gentlemen's agreement.[39]

According to Mr C. L. Farrugia (the treasurer of the Shooters' Association) '. . . from the very first meeting it was decided by both sides not to criticise each other's association until the end of meetings as a sign of goodwill'.[40] This statement was repeated at the annual general meeting of the Shooters' Association.[41]

The reply of the MOS Director by-passed the question of whether there was an agreement as alleged by the shooters.[42] The Shooters' Association, through its secretary again replied, confirming the alleged breech of the gentlemen's agreement.[43]

In view of Malta's application to join the EC, the conservation movement has precious little to gain by discussing with shooters. On the other hand, shooters gained a measure of credibility and as a direct result of these talks, Dr H. Kalchreuter a hunter and game biologist, was brought to Malta twice to conduct 'studies' on hunting and migration. His first report was the subject of a lengthy editorial in a local daily[44] and was commented favourably upon by another section of the press.[45]

It was also quoted by the Prime Minister during the election campaign of 1992. The Prime Minister countered statements against Malta's entry into the EC by quoting from 'the foreign expert's report' which 'confirms that migration is minimal' and that 'a number of birds that migrate through Malta are not important to sustain a healthy migratory population'.[46] In another instance the Prime Minister again quoted this report and stated that 'in Malta there are no problems with regards to bird trapping and shooting'[47] and that 'bird hunting and trapping could be tolerated'[48].

Apart from the statements quoted by the Prime Minister, the report repeated many of the well-known lines of local shooters, such as that more money and land should be given to the Shooters' Association. Dr Kalchreuter also wrote that the 'trapping of several species of finches could be tolerated from the population dynamics point of view'.[49] In a country where the opinion of foreigners is given weight, such reports cannot but have a negative impact on conservation – both because they are inaccurate and also because of the underlying motives.

In spite of the negative repercussions of such talks, it is indeed surprising that the MOS keeps saying that it is more ready to meet shooters when it is evident their conservation policies are only skin deep.

Malta and the EC

Malta has applied to join the European Community. A report by the EC Directorate to the Prime Minister of Malta stated that 'it is appreciated that certain measures could have an initial negative reaction from particular sectors, as, for example, the measure for the protection of wild birds which could considerably change the habits of Maltese hunters and trappers', adding that 'all measures which are for the protection of the environment should be considered as a positive effect on Malta as a result of her membership'.[50]

If Malta joins the EC, then Malta will have to adopt a number of Directives – amongst which there is Council Directive 79/409/EEC, dealing with the conservation of wild birds. This directive binds the member states to create protected areas, re-establish destroyed biotopes and create new ones. It also compels the member states to establish a general system of protection for all species of birds, prohibiting in particular the keeping of species the hunting and capture of which is prohibited.

The local legislation will have to be amended by the inclusion of a closed-season to cover migratory birds while they are returning to their breeding grounds in spring. The shooting season will have to be in line with that of other European countries and thus the shooting of certain species will only be allowed between September and March 10th at the latest.

There are a number of Annexes in this Directive. The species of birds listed in Appendix I are the subject of special conservation measures. In this Annex, one finds a number of species, such as herons, crakes, stone curlew and dottorel which are not protected in the Maltese Islands. Birds of prey are also in this annex, and although these are protected under Maltese legislation, they are shot at by one and all. As shown throughout this study, the law is never respected and hardly ever enforced.

The species listed in Annex II may be hunted under national legislation. The species listed in this annex can be hunted but member states are to ensure that the hunting of these species does not jeopardise conservation efforts which are taken in the distribution area of the birds concerned.

In Annex II/2, one finds a number of species which are protected but which may be hunted in some of the members states. As an example, shooters in Italy, France and Greece, can shoot a number of migratory species which are protected elsewhere within the EC. In these countries, turtle doves, some thrushes and quail may be shot between mid-September and 10th March.

Member states have different shooting seasons, which often differ according to species. The longest hunting seasons within the EC member states are those prevailing in France, Greece and Italy, which like Malta, are Mediterranean countries. However, the hunting season in these countries closes on 10th March and from then until mid-September, bird shooting is not allowed. The emphasis lies on the protection of the breeding populations.

Apart from the closed-seasons during which no hunting can take place, some of the EC member states have local legislation which prohibits hunting on specific days during the open season. In Italy, for example, hunting is prohibited on all Tuesdays and Fridays. Hunters cannot hunt for more than three days in a week and not more than 65 days per season. In Great Britain hunting is prohibited on Sundays and Christmas day. In Greece hunting is forbidden on all Tuesdays and hunters can only hunt for three days in a week.[51]

There is no EC country in which finch trapping is allowed, thus, finch trapping will have to be phased out – or at least restricted. The use of tape-recorders, artificial lights, nets, traps, automatic weapons and fast boats, all of which are widely and wildly used in the Maltese Islands, are forbidden by the EC Directive.

In addition, member states have to send to the Community all relevant information on practical application of their hunting regulations. But this will not be a difficult thing to do for the Maltese Government – if there is the will to change.

Malta and the Maltese

Whether Malta joins the EC or not is a political decision and irrespective of this decision, the Maltese Government will have to live up to expectations. Malta has been the driving force behind international initiatives for the protection of the common heritage of mankind. It is more than evident that migratory species form part of this international heritage too. It is not only the ozone layer and the extra territorial space which need protection, but also migratory birds, which know no boundaries.

People coming from countries where birds are dearly protected and who spend substantial amounts of money to save them and their habitats, frequently voice their concern about the killing of birds which goes on unabated in the Maltese Islands. Letters of complaint from tourists who see *their* garden birds being caged or shot at, appear regularly in the local press.

Picnickers and those who frequently go to the countryside to seek relaxation, especially on weekends and public holidays complain about the risk of injury from shooting and the arrogance of shooters and trappers.

On 10th September 1990 a new unit known as Administrative Law Enforcement Branch was formed within the Police Corp. This branch has a section which deals with environmental legislation. When this section was established, it was spearheaded by Inspector Jimmy Abela and three policemen.

Commenting about this section of the police and their actions, an editorial entitled *Protecting Wildlife* read: 'The police caught 25 offenders and 24 others were caught infringing regulations on bird trapping devices. Given the number of hunters and trappers known to exist, this must be only the tip of the iceberg. Too many shoot close to inhabited areas in the early morning and Buskett and similar areas continue to be happy hunting grounds. . . . The earnest hope of all is that, like many others before it, the police drive will not be a once-only effort that will simply fizzle out after a short period.'[52]

Anyone who knows anything about local politics knew that Inspector Abela's days in that section were numbered. He was transferred to a district police station a few months later and another inspector now sits in the hot seat. This section is still understaffed, overloaded and clearly ineffective.

In Malta steps forward in environmental matters are taken only on paper. A case in point is the publication of the Environment Protection Act 1991[53] published in February. This Act enables the Minister responsible for the environment to issue regulations related to various aspects of the environment. Months have passed and regulations affording protection to birds and nature are nowhere in sight. It is such a pity that politicians fail to realise the sense of urgency. Please help to wake them up as there is no time to loose. Enough time and bird life have already been lost.

As I write, I can hear shots ringing out from a nearby valley and I wonder whether the bird being shot at is a thrush, a woodcock, a kestrel or a crane. Shots are still ringing out, but they will pass unnoticed, taken for granted as part of the daily noise of Malta.

The 4% of the population which has a licence to kill, seems to dictate. It is a case in Malta where the gun is still mightier than the pen showing the people's will.

This is Malta in the 1990s. The best is yet to come.

Selected Bibliography

MANUSCRIPTS

All manuscripts referred to are preserved at the National Library of Malta. To avoid repetition, I have summarised some of the references as follows:

AOM means Archives of the Order of Malta
Libr. means Library Manuscript
Ms means manuscript
Univ. means Università Manuscript
DMC means *Daily Malta Chronicle*

a. Manuscripts found in the Archives of the Order

AOM 262 Liber Conciliorum Status
AOM 269
AOM 428 Liber Bullarum
AOM 625 Indice delle bolle dal 1346 al 1662
AOM 1184 Suppliche (1630–1649)
AOM 1190 Suppliche (1758–1765)
AOM 1192 Suppliche (1771–1777)

b. National Library Manuscripts Collection.

Libr. Ms 49 *Traduzione di un ms. in lingua Latina che comprende varj Capitoli generali dell'Ordine Gerosolimitano celebrati in Gerusalemme ed altrove, fino al VII celebrato in Rodi nel 1344.*

Libr. Ms 149 *Collezione di Bandi dal 1641 al 1724.*

Ms 291 Usages et Éthiquettes observeés à Malte, à la Cour du Gr. Maitre, au Conseil, a l'Eglise ainsy que un détail de ce qui concerne les Devoirs, les Préminences, et prérogatives de Diverses Personnes de l'Ordre de Malte 1762.

Libr. Ms 355 *Indirizzi che facevano i giurati della Notabile al Gr. Maestro, al suo possesso, prima che presentasse il giuramento e ricevasse le chiavi di quella città.*

Libr. Ms 429 *Bandi e prammatiche della Gran Corte della Castellania.* 9 vols. (1) 1722–36, (2) 1736–1744, (3) 1744–56, (4) 1756–65, (5) 1765–72, (6) 1772–79, (7) 1780–84, (8) 1784–94, (9) 1794–98.

Libr. Ms 430 *Bandi e prammatiche della Corte Capitanale e primi appellazioni notabili* Vol 1 1790–1805.

Libr. Ms 431 *Bandi Gran Corte della Valletta.* Vol 1 1800–1803.

c. Università Manuscripts

Univ. 7

PRINTED WORKS

Abela, G.F. 1647 *Della Descrittione di Malta Isola nel mare Siciliano, con le sue antichita, ed altre notizie* Libri Quattro, Malta pp.573.

Adams, A.L. 1870 *Notes of a Naturalist in the Nile Valley and Malta.* Edmonston Douglas, Edinburgh pp.295.

Azzopardi, A.E. 1985 *The Maltese Shooters' Handbook*, Midsea Books Ltd. Malta pp.254.

Bannerman, D.A. & J.A.
Vella Gaffiero. 1976 *Birds of the Maltese Archipelago* Museums Dept. Valletta. pp. 550.

Ciantar, G.A. 1772 *Malta Illustrata* Stamperia del Palazzo di S.A. Serenissima, Malta.

Despott, G. 1913(a) La Berta maggiore del Mediterraneo. Puffinus kuhli – Ciefa: una specie che si estingue. *Archivum Melitensis* 2 (13–16):91–92.

Despott, G. 1913(b) Lista delle nuove specie di uccelli da me osservate. *Archivum Melitensis* 2 (13–16): 97–100

Despott, G. 1916(a) Ornithological report for the Maltese Islands July–December 1915. *Zoologist*, London 20:378–388.

Despott, G. 1916(b) Ornithological report for the Maltese Islands January–June 1916. *Zoologist*, London 20:441–452.

Despott, G. 1916(c) Ornithological notes for the Maltese Islands July to December 1916) *Archivum Melitensis* 2 (21–24):251–256.

Despott, G.1916 (d) The breeding birds of Malta. *Zoologist*, London 20:161–181.

Despott, G. 1917(a) Notes on the ornithology of Malta *Ibis*, ser.10 5:281–349, 466–526.

Despott, G. 1917(b) Ornithological notes for the Maltese Islands (January–June 1917). *Archivum Melitensis* 3 (2):83–90.

Despott, G. & Conti Meli T. 1931 Continuazione dell'irruzione dei Crocieri (Loxia curvirostra curvirostra, Linn.) a Malta durante l'estate e l'autunno del 1930. *Rivista Italiana di Ornitologia* Anno I, Ser II:184–185.

Despott, G. 1932 2 Ornitologia delle Isole Maltesi. *Rivista Italiana di Ornitologia* Anno II, Ser II:5–16, 65–77, 119–136, 218–24.

Despott, G. 1933 Ornitologia delle Isole Maltesi. *Rivista Italiana di Ornitologia* Anno III, Ser.II:1–15

Despott, G. 1934 Ornitologia delle Isole Maltesi. *Rivista Italiana di Ornitologia* Anno IV, Ser.II:77–80

Gibb, J. 1951 The birds of the Maltese Islands *Ibis* 93:109–127

Magnin, G. 1986 *An assessment of illegal shooting and catching of birds in Malta.* ICBP Cambridge pp 38.

Ortner, S.B.& Whitehead, H. 1981 *Sexual meanings – the cultural construction of gender and sexuality.* Cambridge University Press 1981.

Payn, W.H. 1938: Some notes on the spring migration in Malta and Gozo *Ibis* (14) 2:102–110

Pope John Paul II (1990) *Message of His Holiness Pope John Paul XXIII for the celebration of the World Day of Peace.* January 1.

Roberts, E.L. 1954 *The Birds of Malta* Progress Press. Malta pp.xvi+168.

Roberts, E.L. 1987 A Mediterranean venture. *Bokmakerie* 39(2) pp.34–36.

Sant, C. 1986 *Natural Environment: the biblical perspective* oration delivered at the graduation ceremony of the faculty of Theology on 20th December (pp. 13).

Schembri A (1843) *Catalogo Ornitologico del Gruppo di Malta* Anglo-Maltese pp. 136 + III.

Scicluna, J.R. (1986 ?) *Comments on the ICBP study report on the shooting and catching in Malta.* (undated report sent to FACE in 1986.)

Sultana , J. 1981 Outlines of the new bird protection legislation in in Malta. *Gozo Year Book* pp. 27–31.

Sultana J., Gauci C., & Beamen M., 1975 *A Guide to the birds of Malta* Valletta: Malta Ornithological Society xvi+191 pp.

Sultana J., and Gauci C., 1982 *A new guide to the birds of Malta* Valletta: The Ornithological Society pp. 207.

Thomas, K. 1983 *Man and the natural world* Middlesex: Penguin pp.426.

Vella, A.P. 1979 *Storja ta' Malta* Vol I *Klabb Kotba Maltin.* pp. 390.

Woldhek, S.1980 *Bird killing in the Mediterranean.* [2nd edition] European Committee for the Prevention of Mass Destruction of Migratory Birds: Ziest/Netherlands. pp.iv+62.

Wright, C.A. 1863 A visit to the Islet of Filfla, on the south of Malta. *Ibis* 20 (15):432–440.

Wright, C.A. 1864(a). List of the birds observed in the Islands of Malta and Gozo. *Ibis* 1 (6): 42–73, 137–157.

Wright, C.A. 1864(b). Appendix to a list of the birds observed in the Islands of Malta and Gozo. *Ibis* 1 (6): 291–292.

Wright, C.A. 1865. Second appendix to a list of the birds observed in the Islands of Malta and Gozo. *Ibis* 2 (1): 459–466.

Wright, C.A. 1869. Third appendix to a list of the birds observed in the Islands of Malta and Gozo. *Ibis* 2 (5): 245–256.

Wright, C.A. 1870. Fourth appendix to a list of the birds observed in the Islands of Malta and Gozo. *Ibis* 2(6):488–493.

Wright, C.A. 1874. Fifth appendix to a list of the birds observed in the Islands of Malta and Gozo. *Ibis* 3(4):223–241.

REFERENCES

Chapter 1.

1. Cooke, J.H. An important question *Public Opinion*, September 17 1892.
2. Goodwin, D. Bird-life on Malta, Agric. Mag. 54 1948 p.57; Carmel Borg pers. comm.
3. Cachia, W. P. & Taliana, M. Fate of Lead in Maltese Soils, unpublished B.Sc dissertation, University of Malta 1991 pp.51–2, 63.
4. Vella, A.J. *L-effetti ta' l-ambjent fuq is-sahha tal- bniedem* paper presented at MZPN national conference entitled 'L-Ambjent dmir mhux moda' 3–5 May 1990 p.4.

5. Lautier, M. Il-Berne Convention *In-Nazzjon Taghna* November 19 1990.
6. Fenech, N. Aktar dwar il-Berne Convention *In-Nazzjon Taghna*, December 3 1990.
7. Central Bank of Malta *Quarterly Review* March 1991 Vol 24:1 p.80.
8. Central Bank of Malta *Twenty-Third Annual Report and Statement of Accounts* 1990 p.16.
9. Malta Structure Plan Report of Surveys 1990 Vol 1 p.G3.
10. Central Bank of Malta 1991 p.12.
11. Sisman, D. Green Tourism in Malta – issues and opportunities, Green Flag International Ltd, 1991 p.16.
12. Taylor, K. The bird black hole, *BBC Wildlife Magazine* 9(5) May 1991 pp.324–9.
13. *Bird's Eye View* 1983 Marching at Buskett p.4.
14. Gauci, V.M. A sad incident, *Times of Malta* September 6, 1979.
15. Nastasi, E., and Fsadni, M. *Il-Madonna tal-Għar, santwarju mirakoluż* Lux Press 1957 pp.39–41.
16. Fsadni, M. *Our Lady of the Grotto, priory, church and sanctuary* Dominican Publication, Rabat 1980 p.41.
17. Fsadni, M. 1980 p.56.
18. Attard, L.E. Rabat Dominicans and the 'Grotto' tradition *The Sunday Times*, December 7 1986.
19. Azzopardi, A.E. Is-salut tal-kaċċaturi in: *San Ġiljan Programm tal-Festa*, Kumitat Festi Ċentinarji, (ed Borg. A.) San Ġiljan 1990 p.21.
20. Fenech, N. In honour of Saints, *The Sunday Times*, September 1 1991 p.28.
21. Pope John Paul II *Message of His Holiness Pope John Paul II for the celebration of the World Day of Peace.* January 1 1990 pp.3, 7, 9.
22. Aquilina, J. *A comparative dictionary of Maltese proverbs* The University of Malta, 1972 pp.liii+694.
23. Azzopardi, A.E. *The Maltese shooters handbook* Midsea Books Ltd. Malta 1985 pp.222–3.
24. Bondietti, P. *Lasciateli Vivere, raccolta d'informazioni sulla cattura degli uccelli in Italia e il loro destino.* Lugano 1974 p.35.
25. Anthony Briffa pers. comm.
26. Attard, J. Problems of bird protection in Malta *Bird Notes* Vol 3 No 4 1962 p.126.
27. Testaferrata Abela, G.E. The brutal scramble *Times of Malta*, August 13 1974.
28. Attard, J. 1962 p.126.
29. Scicluna, J.R. Hunters and intruders *The Times*, February 11 1989.
30. *The Sunday Times* The Sunday Times Interview: Dr Stanley Zammit, December 9 1990.
31. *The Times* Bank sponsors hunters' association, February 4 1987.
32. *The Times* MLP mass meeting at Mellieħa, April 27 1987.
33. *The Times* MLP leader accuses US, UK, France of interfering in Gulf crisis, December 3 1990.
34. *The Times* Party not responsible for mistakes by officials – MLP Leader, March 18 1991. *The Times* MLP leader queries utility of church radio station, March 15 1991.
35. Bannerman, D.A. & Vella Gaffiero J.A. *Birds of the Maltese Archipelago* Museums Dept, Valletta 1976 p.iv.
36. Dom Mintoff pers. comm.
37. *The Times* Talks to formalise handing over of public land to hunters, May 2 1991.
38. *The Times* PM holds first public dialogue in series 'Building our country together', February 10 1990.
39. *Il-Mument* Gvern iehor tal-PN ikompli jikkonsolida dak li nbeda dwar l-ambjent. Darryl Grima jintervista lil Eddie Fenech Adami. January 19 1992.

40. Wright, C.A. Fourth appendix to a list of the birds observed in the Islands of Malta and Gozo. *Ibis* 2(6) 1870 p.493.
41. Govt. Dept. Reports 1907.
42. Despott, G. La Berta maggiore del Mediterrerraneo. Puffinus kuhli – Ciefa: una specie che si estingue. *Archivum Melitensis* 2 (13–16) 1913 p.92.
43. Despott, G. Notes on the ornithology of Malta *Ibis*, ser.10 5 1917(a) p.282-3.
44. *DMC* The indiscriminate shooting of birds, May 19/20 1931 p.4.
45. Payn, W.H. Some notes on the spring migration in Malta and Gozo *Ibis* (14) 2 1938 p.103.
46. Gibb, J. The birds of the Maltese Islands *Ibis* 93 1951 p.110.
47. Roberts, E.L. *The Birds of Malta* Progress Press. Malta 1954 p.xv.
48. Brockman, E. *Last bastion, Sketches of the Maltese Islands* Darton, Longman and Todd Ltd. London 1961 p.73.
49. Hogg, G. *Malta Blue-water Island* George Allen & Unwin Ltd. London 1967 pp.44, 83.
50. Gauci, A. Pause and hope *Times of Malta*, April 8 1974.
51. Turner, S. Bird conservation in Malta *Diplomatic Service Ornithological Society* 3 1979 p.11.
52. Gauci, A. Prelude to the new season *Times of Malta*, August 19 1974.
53. Gauci, A. Crux of the argument, *The Times*, July 25 1983.
54. Legal Notice 68 of 1980 published in in the supplement of the Malta Government Gazette No. 13756 of the 8th August 1980. at pp.B251-260.
55. Information Division: Police Report (signed L. Pullicino, Commissioner) in *Report on the working of Government Departments for the year 1983*. DOI 1983 p.16-17.
56. Mallia, M. Shooting as a sport *The Sunday Times* March 26 1989.
57. Sultana J., and Gauci C., *A new guide to the birds of Malta* Valletta: The Ornithological Society 1982 p.26.
58. Farrugia, C.L. Statistika realistika *Id-Dura*, 4 November 1988 p.6-7.
59. *Il-Passa* Wasal zmien il-gamiem, April 1990 p.8-9.
60. Bannerman, D.A. & Vella Gaffiero J.A. 1976 p.xiii.
61. Wright, C.A. 1870 p.493.
62. Memorandum dated 23rd March 1988 signed by JR Scicluna, president of the Shooters' Association.
63. Azzopardi, A. Kills to cartridges *Times of Malta*, April 22 1974.
64. Despott, G. The Breeding Birds of Malta, *Zoologist*, London 20 1916 p.167-8.
65. Gauci, A. Flying pellets . . . *Times of Malta*, September 16 1974.
66. Gauci, A. Tales of mystery *Times of Malta*, November 19 1973.
67. Borg, S. The Woodcock, *Times of Malta*, February 9 1976.
68. *Il-Passa* Qed jinxtraw 19 il-senter kull gimgha, December 1990 p.1-2.

Chapter 2

1. Evans, J.D. *Prehistoric antiquities of the Maltese Islands: a survey*. Athlone Press London 1971 p.239. Bonanno, A. A socio-economic approach to Maltese prehistory. The Temple Builders. In *Malta studies of its heritage and history*, Mid-Med Bank Ltd., 1986 Malta p.31.
2. Godfrey Wettinger pers. comm.
3. Azzopardi, A. Hawking *Times of Malta*, June 3 1974.
4. Huillard-Bréholles, F.A.& De Albertes de Luynes, H. *Historia Diplomatica Frederici Secundi* (ed. Bottega d'Erasmo) Torino, 1963 Vol. V(ii) pp.969-71.

5. Wettinger, G. The Militia watch roster duties of 1417, *Armed Forces of Malta Journal* No 32, October 1979 p.27.
6. Abela, G.F. *Della Descrittione di Malta Isola nel mare Siciliano, con le sue antichita, ed altre notizie* Libri Quattro, Malta 1647 p.134.
7. Ciantar, G.A. *Malta Illustrata*. Stamperia del Palazzo di S.A. Serenissima, Malta 1772 p.392.
8. Bresc, H. The 'Secrezia' and the royal patrimony in Malta: 1240–1450 in *Mediaeval Malta: studies on Malta before the knights*, (ed. A. Luttrell) The British school at Rome, London 1975 p.138.
9. Godfrey Wettinger pers. comm.
10. Mifsud, A. *Sulla caccia in Malta nel passato* in *Archivum Melitense* III 1917 p.118.
11. Abela, G.F. 1647 p.810.
12. Porter, W. *History of the Knights of Malta* Longman & Brown 1858 p. 470.
13. Liber. Ms 291 p.35; AOM 262 f.3; AOM 269 f.44r, f.80.
14. AOM 625 f.8v.
15. Bosio, I. *Dell'Istoria della Sagra Religione et Illustrissima Militia di San Giovanni Gieroolimitano* Napoli 1683 Part 3 p.241.
16. Galea, J. *Art Twelidi* PEG 1984 p44.
17. Libr. Ms 291 p.34–38.
18. AOM 1184 f98; AOM 1190 f449; AOM 1192 f122.
19. Bosio, I. 1683 p.819.
20. Bosio, I. 1683 p.816
21. AOM 428 f.36.
22. Univ 188 f.153v.
23. Abela, G.F. 1647 p.134.
24. Ciantar, G.A. 1772 p.392.
25. Agius G.P.F. *Il Gozo Antico-Moderno e Sacro-Profano, Isola Mediterranea Adiacente A Malta Africana* 1746 MS 145 p.48.
26. De Soldanis G.F.Agius, *Damma tal-kliem Kartaginis mscerred fel fomm tal Maltin u Ghaucin.* 1750 Ms 143 p.(M)1.
27. De Caro, L. *Storia dei Gran Mastri e Cavalieri di Malta* Vol 2 1853 pp.625–632.
28. Haskins, C.H. *Studies in Mediaeval culture* Frederick Ungar Publishing Co. New York 1929 pp.107–123.
29. Kraus, E. *The Adventures of Count George Albert of Erbach, a true story.* (translated from the German of Emil Kraus by Beatrice, Princess Henry of Battenberg). John Murray, London 1891 pp.167–8.
30. Agius G.P.F. 1746 p.47–8; Farrugia, G. Ghawdex bil-grajja tieghu. Stamperija tal-Gvern, Malta 1936 p.49.
31. Ciantar, G.A. 1772 pp.391–6.
32. Libr. Ms 149 p.176.
33. Proclamation No.1 10th March 1854 Laws and Regulation of Police pp.17–18.
34. Ciantar, G.A. 1772 p.393.
35. Wright, C.A. 1864(a) p.43.
36. Wright, C.A. 1870 p.493.
37. Adams, A.L. *Notes of a Naturalist in the Nile Valley and Malta*. Edmonston Douglas, Edinburgh 1870 p.103.
38. Cooke, J.H. Birds and Insects *Supplement to the Malta Stand ard*, September 14 1892. Cooke, J.H. An important question *Public Opinion*, September 17 1892.
39. Despott, G. 1917(a) p.295.
40. Despott, G. 1917(a) p.285.
41. De Boisgelin, L. *Ancient and modern Malta*, Richard Philips, London 1805 p.106.
42. Wright, C.A. 1864(a) p.47.
43. Wright, C.A. 1870 p.493.

44. Adams, A.L. 1870 p.90.
45. Despott, G. 1917(b) Ornithological notes for the Maltese Islands (January–June 1917). *Archivum Melitensis* iii (2) p.89.
46. Wright, C.A. 1864(b). Appendix to a list of the birds observed in the Islands of Malta and Gozo. *Ibis* 1 (6) p.291–292.
47. Adams, A.L. 1870 p.90.
48. Seddall, H. *Malta past and present* Chapman and Hall London 1870 p.353.
49. Ganni Borg pers. comm.
50. Payn, W.H. Some notes on the spring migration in Malta and Gozo *Ibis* (14) 2 1938 p.109.
51. Charles Galea Bonavia pers. comm.
52. Gauci, A. Drawing a balance *Times of Malta*, May 28 1973. Gauci, A. Game as a present *Times of Malta*, June 4 1973.
53. Wright, C.A. 1864(a) p.58.
54. Ganni Borg pers. comm
55. Joe Sultana pers. comm.
56. *Il-Passa* Stejjer tal-kaċċa mill-Baħrija, January 1991.
57. Despott, G. 1917(a) p.469.
58. Wright, C.A. 1864(a) p.50.
59. Despott, G. 1917(a) p.467.
60. Despott, G. 1917(a) p.472.
61. Despott, G. 1916(b) Ornithological report for the Maltese Islands January–June 1916. *Zoologist 20*, London p.444.
62. Despott, G. 1916(a) Ornithological report for the Maltese Islands July–December 1915. *Zoologist 20*, London p.386.
63. Despott, G. 1916(b) p.445.
64. Despott, G. 1916(a) p.387.
65. Despott, G. 1932 Ornitologia delle Isole Maltesi. *Rivista Italiana di Ornitologia* Anno II, Ser II p.134.
66. Despott, G. 1916(b) p.443.
67. Despott, G. 1917(b) Ornithological notes for the Maltese Islands (January–June 1917). *Archivum Melitensis* iii (2) p.89.
68. Payn, W.H. 1938 p.103.
69. Despott, G. 1916(a) p.381.
70. Wright, C.A. 1864(a) p.73.
71. Azzopardi, A. Kills to cartridges *Times of Malta*, April 22 1974.
72. Ganni Attard pers. comm.
73. Salvu Borg pers. comm.
74. Bondietti, P. *Lasciateli Vivere, raccolta d'informazioni sulla cattura degli uccelli in Italia e il loro destino.* Lugano 1974 pp.22, 81.
75. Wright, C.A. 1864(a) p.46; Payn, W.H. 1938 p.109.
76. Schembri, A. *Catalogo Ornitologico del Gruppo di Malta* Anglo–Maltese 1843 p.16.
77. Gulia, G. Il calendario del cacciatore Maltese *Guida Generale di Malta*. G. Muscat Malta 1910 p.11.
78. Sultana, J. and Gauci, C. L-Agħsafar, Malta Ornithological Society 1979 p.80.
79. Despott, G. 1916(b) p.447.
80. Despott, G. 1917(a) p.283.
81. Mifsud Bonnici, C. Disraeli in Malta *DMC* January 28 1936.
82. Schembri, A. 1843 p.103.
83. Schembri, A. 1843 p.84.
84. *DMC* More B.P.' s memoirs, November 22 1932.
85. Despott, G. 1913(a) p.91–92.
86. *DMC* Malta Gun Club, December 27 1887.

87. *DMC* Malta Garrison Gun Club, March 9 1888.
88. *DMC* Malta Garrison Gun Club, May 5 1888; *DMC* Malta Garrison Gun Club, December 7 1888.
89. *DMC* Malta Gun Club, December 16 1887.
90. *DMC* Malta Garrison Gun Club, November 27 1888.
91. *DMC* Muscat's Shooting School, November 26 1907.
92. *The Malta Herald* Muscat's Shooting School, December 2 1907 p.1.
93. *DMC* The Malta Shooting Club, August 27 1908.
94. *DMC* Malta Shooting Club, March 31 1909.
95. *DMC* Malta Shooting Club, May 19 1915.
96. *DMC* Malta Shooting Club, February 4 1915.
97. *DMC* Malta Shooting Club, June 9 1910.
98. *DMC* Malta Shooting Club, June 8 1923.
99. *DMC* Formation of a new shooting club, June 19 1937.
100. Azzopardi, A.E. *The Maltese shooters handbook* Midsea Books Ltd. Malta 1985 p.15–16.
101. Government Notice No. 427 published in *The Malta Government Gazette* No. 8096 of the 28th October, 1935 at p.935.
102. Government Notice No. 505 of 1955 published in *The Malta Government Gazette* No. 10676 of the 16th September 1955 at p.1380.
103. Act No. XVII of 1980 published in the Supplement to *The Malta Government Gazette* 13736 of the 30th May 1980 at pp.A173–177.
104. *It-Torca* Juzaw ghasafar flok plattini, August 12 1973.
105. Rosario Fenech and George Zammit Maempel pers. comm.
106. Gauci, A. Flying pellets *Times of Malta*, September 16 1974.

Chapter 3

1. Ciantar, G.A. 1772 p.393.
2. Libr. Ms 149 p.176.
3. *Il-Berqa*: Il-Ġvern u l-kaċċaturi (4/10/43) p.4; Kif isir il-black market (5/11/43) p.2; Licenzja tal-kaċċa u skrataċ(16/3/44) p.2; l-iskrataċ (14/4/44) p. 2; bejh l-iskrataċ (26/6/44) p.4.
4. Azzopardi, A. Hand-loading *Times of Malta*, 25 March 1974. Ganni Borg, George Zammit Maempel pers. comm.
5. Rosario Fenech pers. comm.
6. Rosario Fenech pers. comm.
7. Ganni Borg pers. comm.
8. Rosario Fenech pers. comm.
9. *Il-Passa* Franwin advert, March & April 1989; *Il-Passa* Gun and Rod advert, April & May 1991.
10. *Il-Passa* PUNCH . . . ix-xogħol wara dak l-iskartoċċ March 1986.
11. Azzopardi, A. Hand-loading *Times of Malta*, 25 March 1974.
12. Gauci, A. Topsy turvy world *Times of Malta*, September 30 1974.
13. Same as reference 11.
14. Same as reference 12.
15. De Boisgelin, L. *Ancient and modern Malta* Richard Philips, London 1805 p.106.
16. Scicluna, J.R. 1986 *Hunting, trapping and conservation of wildlife in Malta*. (address given at a seminar organised by the International Environment Institute-Valletta, the text of which was privately distributed).
17. Carmelo Borg pers. comm.

18. Rosario Fenech and Carmelo Borg pers. comm.
19. George Zammit Maempel pers. comm.
20. Franceschi, G. *Manuale del cacciatore* Hoepli Milan, 1905 p.78.
21. Carmelo Borg pers. comm.
22. Rosario Fenech & George Zammit Maempel pers. comm.
23. George Zammit Maempel pers. comm.
24. George Zammit Maempel pers. comm.
25. Franceschi, G. 1905 p.77–8.
26. George Zammit Maempel pers. comm.
27. *Il-Passa* Rivulozzjoni tal-cassettes, December 1989.
28. Gulia, G. Il calendario del cacciatore Maltese *Guida Generale di Malta*. G. Muscat Malta 1910 p.8.
29. Franceschi, G. 1905 p.78.
30. Gauci, A. Alwetta *Times of Malta*, December 17 1973.
31. Sultana and Gauci 1982 p.113.
32. Libr. Ms 429 (6) f.120, f.296; (8) f.39.
33. Roberts, E.L. 1954 p.xv.
34. Zammit, T. In-nassaba *Lehen il-Malti* No 5, July 1931 p.5–6.

Chapter 4

1. Ciantar, G.A. 1772 p.394.
2. Wright, C.A. 1864(a) pp.436–8.
3. Wright, C.A. 1863 p.438.
4. Schembri, A. 1843 pp.116–7.
5. Gulia, G. 1910 p.11.
6. Despott, G. 1913(a) pp.91–92.
7. Charles Galea Bonavia pers. comm.
8. Gauci, A. Hard facts *Times of Malta*, December 16 1974.
9. Antoine Agius pers. comm.
10. *Il-Passa* Jissogra hajtu biex jaqbad papra (jew 55)! January 1984.
11. *Il-Passa* Il-kaċċa tal-borok, March 1984.
12. *Il-Passa* Il-kaċċa fuq il-baħar . . . l-avventura, il-periklu, il-pjaċir, October 1984.
13. Antoine Agius pers. comm.
14. Sultana J., and Gauci C., 1984–85: An unsuccessful breeding attempt by the short-eared owl. *Il-Merill* No.23 p.14.
15. Same as reference 10.

Chapter 5

1. Bannerman, D.A. & Vella Gaffiero, J.A. 1976 p.317.
2. *DMC* Revision of sanitary laws, 19 December 1933.
3. *L-Orizzont* 1967: Għandu record ta' ibbalzmar, October 23 p.7.
4. Coles C.L. (1982?) *A visit to the hunters and ornithologists of Malta* unpublished report by C.L. Coles (Game Conservancy and Conseil International de la Chasse) [The report by Mr Coles is undated, however the report was compiled in 1982, the year when Mr Coles visited Malta] p.4.
5. Magnin, G. *An assessment of illegal shooting and catching of birds in Malta*. ICBP Cambridge 1986 p 15.
6. Scicluna, J.R. (1986 ?) *Comments on the ICBP study report on the shooting and catching in Malta*. (undated report sent to FACE in 1986.) pp.5–6.
7. Despott, G. 1917(a) pp.283–5.

8. Bannerman, D.A. & Vella Gaffiero, J.A. 1976 p.471.
9. Vincent Sammut pers. comm.
10. *Alternattiva* Ta' Ċancu u l-Griffon October 19 1991 p.12
11. Attard, J.M. 1966 Nicola Ardoino (1817–1903) an Ornithologist of the 19th century. *The Natural History Society of Malta incorporating the Malta Ornithological Society Report of the working of the committee for 1966.*
12. *DMC* Malta University Museum of Natural History, January 23 1913.
13. Despott, G. 1917(a) pp.283–5.
14. Despott, G. 1917(a) p.288.
15. Wright, C.A. 1864(a) p.291.
16. Wright, C.A. 1864(a) p.149.
17. Wright, C.A. 1869. Third appendix to a list of the birds observed in the islands of Malta and Gozo. *Ibis* 2 (5), pp.52–3.
18. Wright, C.A. 1869 p.254.
19. Despott, G. 1917 p.293.
20. Despott, G. 1917(a) p.304.
21. Despott, G. 1917(a) p.326.
22. Despott, G. 1917(a) p.468.
23. Despott, G. 1917(a) p.504.
24. Sammy Borg pers. comm.
25. Sultana J., and Gauci C., 1982 p.185.
26. Raymond Busuttil pers. comm.
27. Sultana J., and Gauci C., 1982 p.185.
28. Scicluna, J.R. (1986 ?) pp.1–8.

Chapter 6

1. Gauci, A. The Fever *Times of Malta*, April 10 1973.
2. Gauci, A. The Beginning *Times of Malta*, December 10 1973.
3. Burke, P. and Porter, R. (eds) The social history of language. Cambridge University Press 1987, pp.3–4.
4. *The Times* 1983: Bird shooters now have their own publication, December 30.
5. *Il-Passa* Meta morna għall-kaċċa tal-ġrieden, March 1990.
6. Fenech, N. Slaughter in a protected place, *The Times* August 30 1979.
7. Sciberras, M. Wrong prey, *The Times*, January 4 1989. *The Times* Wrong Target, April 29 1991. Desira, M. Trigger Happy, *The Sunday Times* August 11 1991.
8. Scicluna, J.R. Hunting referendum, *The Times*, December 14 1990.
9. Gauci, A. Merciless persecution *Times of Malta*, March 18 1974.
10. Duffy, M. Beasts for pleasure In S. Godlovitch and R. Godlovitch and J. Harris (eds) *Animals, men and morals* London Gollancz 1971 p.115.
11. Gauci, A. Our sins are many *Times of Malta*, April 15 1974.
12. Thomas, K. *Man and the natural world* Penguin 1983 p.426.
13. Mallia, M. Shooting as a sport *The Sunday Times* March 26 1989.
14. Same as reference 13.
15. *Malta News* Everybody's Prey, October 20 1973; *L-Orizzont* Kaċċaturi jiġġieldu fuq Kuċċarda, October 20 1973; Tilwima dwar Kuċċarda twassal kaċċatur fil-Qorti October 20 1973. *L-Orizzont* Żewg kaċċaturi jisparaw għal-xulxin dwar tajra April 14 1982; *L-Orizzont* Sparati tiri f'incident bejn kaċċaturi, May 3 1991; *The Times* Hunters clash, May 6 1991.
16. *The Times* Proposal to turn site into nature and archaeological park, October 9 1991 p.6.
17. *Alternattiva* Il-Miżieb Vjetnam June 1 1991.

18. *Debates tal-Kamra tad-Deputati* Seduta Nru. 371 18 ta' Marzu 1980 Kamra tad-Deputati Malta, p.812.
19. Gauci, A. The Fever *Times of Malta*, April 10 1973.
20. Bannerman, D.A. & Vella Gaffiero J.A. 1976 p.iv.
21. Fenech, N. Bird shooting in Malta and abroad. Are there parallels to be drawn? *The Times*, April 26 1991.
22. *Il-Passa* Il-kaċċaturi li jigu Għawdex, January 1991. Il-verita toffendi, M'għandna xejn kontra dawk li għandhom dura, Ix-xogħol m'għandux x'jaqsam mal-kaċċa, Il-verita dwar il-kaċċaturi f'Għawdex, Inrabbu l-għaqal – March 1991.
23. *The Times* Gozo hunters 'declare war' on Maltese shooters April 24 1991. *Il-Gens* Inkomplu fuq l-agħsafar May 17 1991.
24. Taylor, K. Maltese caught holding the bag. *BBC Wildlife Magazine* Vol 8. No.7 July 1990 p.486.
25. Taylor, K. Mean men of Malta, *BBC Wildlife Magazine* Vol 8, K. No. April 1990 p.264. *The Times* MLP leader accuses US, UK, France of interfering in Gulf crisis, December 3 1990.

Chapter 7

1. *Il-Passa* Apprezzament, in-nassab Ċikku Bezzgħani, September 1990.
2. Libr. Ms 149 p.67.
3. Libr 429 (6) f.32.
4. Olina, G.P. *Uccelliera, ovvero discorso della natura, e proprietà di diversi uccelli e in particolare de que' che cantano, con il modo di prendergli, conoscergli, allevargli e mantenergli.* Andrea Fei, Roma 1622 pp.XXII + 81.
5. Raimondi, E. *Delle Caccie Libri Quattro aggiuntovi in questa nuova impressione altre caccie che sperse in altri libri andavano.* Venice 1630 pp.284–381.
6. Arkstee, M. *Amusements de la chasse et de la pêche* Amsterdam & Leipzig 1753 Vol 1 pp.xiv+391+55 plates.
7. Diderot, M. *Encyclopédie ou dictionnaire raisonné des sciences, des arts et des métiers,* 1753 Vol 2 (2) pp.1–31, Vol 3 pp.224–230.
8. De Soldanis G.F. Agius, 1750 Ms 143 p.(M)1.
9. Ciantar, G.A. 1772 p.393.
10. Ciantar, G.A. 1772 p.394.
11. De Boisgelin, L. 1805 p.106.
12. Schembri, A. 1843 pp.136+III.
13. Wright, C.A. 1864(a) p.48, 138.
14. Wright, C.A. 1864(a) p.140.
15. Wright, C.A. 1864(a) p.67.
16. Adams, A.L. 1870 p.101.
17. Adams, A.L. 1870 p.108.
18. Cooke, J.H. An important question *Public Opinion*, September 17 1892.
19. Gulia, G. 1910 p.11.
20. Cutajar, D. The Malta Quarantine Shipping and Trade 1654–1694, Mid-Med Bank Report of Accounts, 1987 p.50–51.
21. De Soldanis G.F. Agius, 1750 Ms 143 p.(M)1.
22. Government Notice No. 111 published in The Malta Government Gazette No. 7539 of the 6th April, 1932 at pp.301–303.
23. Caruana Gatto, A. Sulla straordinaria comparsa in Malta della Loxia curvirostra L. *Archivum Melitensis* 1910 Vol 1 pp.15–17. Despott, G. & Conti Meli T. Continuazione dell' irruzione dei Crocieri (Loxia curvirostra curvirostra, Linn.) a Malta durante l'estate e l'autunno del 1930. *Rivista Italiana di*

Ornitologia 1931 Anno I, Ser II pp.184–185. Fenech, N. Crossbills – protected but not saved *The Times*, August 13 1990.

24. Debates of the Council of Government, Sitting 101, November 4 1916, p.371.
25. Despott, G. 1917(a) p.299.
26. Despott, G. 1917(a) p.300.
27. Joe Attard pers. comm.
28. Govt. Dept. Reports 1937.
29. Parliamentary Question 28509 Sitting 544.
30. Lanfranco, E. The Flora. In: Schembri, P.J. & Sultana, J. (eds) *Red Data Book for the Maltese Islands*; Valletta, Malta Department of Information, 1989 p.41.
31. Malta Structure Plan Report of Surveys 1990 Vol 2, p.N25.
32. Sultana J., and Gauci C., 1982 pp.207
33. Magnin, G. *An assessment of illegal shooting and catching of birds in Malta.* ICBP Cambridge 1986 pp.38.
34. Sultana J., and Gauci C., 1982 p.171.
35. Bondietti, P. 1974. p.34; Consiglio, C. *No alla caccia.* Savelli Editori 1980 p.19; Belletti, P. and Francone, M. *La caccia – un sadico e egoistico esercizio di rapina della fauna.*, Satyaraha Editrice, Torino, 1990 pp.15–16.
36. Gauci, G. Kemm jgħixu l-agħsafar ta' l-għana fil-magħluq? *Il-Passa* March 1991.
37. Wright, C.A. 1864(a) p.54.
38. Despott, G. 1917(a) p.297.
39. Roberts, E. L. 1954 p.xv.
40. Zammit, T. *In-nassaba. Leħen il-Malti* No 5, July 1931 p.6–9.
41. Wright, C.A. 1864(a). p.54.
42. Payn, W.H. 1938 Some notes on the spring migration in Malta and Gozo *Ibis* (14) 2, p.105.
43. Gibb, J. The birds of the Maltese Islands *Ibis* 93, 1951 p.110.
44. Gibb, J. 1951 p.110.
45. Bondietti, P. 1974 p.24.
46. Joe Sultana pers. comm.
47. Wright, C.A. 1864(a) p.63. Gibb, J. 1951 p.110.
48. Despott 1917a, p.301.
49. Sultana J., and Gauci C., 1982 p.111.
50. De Soldanis G.F. Agius, 1750 Ms 143 p.(M)1.
52. Despott, G. 1932 Ornitologia delle Isole Maltesi. *Rivista Italiana di Ornitologia* Anno II, Ser II, p.134.
53. Despott, G. 1916(a) Ornithological report for the Maltese Islands July–December 1915. *Zoologist*, London 20, p.386.
54. Government Notice No. 262 published in The Malta Government Gazette No. 5852 of the 13th October, 1916 at pp.666–668.
55. Sultana J., and Gauci C., 1982 p.128.
56. Schembri, A. 1843 pp.136+III.
57. Wright, C.A. 1864(a) p.67.
58. Despott, G. 1917(a) p.346.
59. Despott, G. 1932 p.135.
60. Gibb 1951, p.110.
61. D'Hugo, H. 1966 Bird life in Malta, *Times of Malta* 1966.
62. Arrigoni degli Oddi, E. 1902 *Atlante Ornitologico, Uccelli Europei con notizie d'indole generale e particolare.* Hoepli, Milan. Part I pp.165 Part II, p.61
63. Salvador Archiduque L. 1870 *De la caza, pesca y navegacion* Mossen Alcover, Palma de Mallorca, p.23.
64. Joe Sultana pers. comm.
65. Mario Camilleri pers. comm.

66. Schembri, A. 1843 p.78.
67. Wright, C.A. 1864(a) p.138.
68. Payn, W.H. 1938 p.110.
69. Gauci, A. Turtle Doves *Times of Malta*, December 11 1972.
70. Wright, C.A. 1864(a) p.138.
71. Joe Sultana pers. comm.
72. De Boisgelin, L. 1805
73. Lacroix, F. *Malte et le Goze* Firmin Didot Paris, 1835 p.13.
74. Wright, C.A. 1864(a) p.64–5.
75. Despott, G. 1916 The breeding birds of Malta. *Zoologist*, London 20, p.11.
76. Despott, G. 1916 p.12.
77. Despott, G. 1916 p.10.

Chapter 8

1. Luttrell, A.T. 1975 Approaches to Mediaeval Malta in *Mediaeval Malta: studies on Malta before the knights (ed. Luttrell) pp.1–70. Vella, A.P. 1979 Storja ta' Malta* Vol I p.93 *Klabb Kotba Maltin*, Malta.
2. Huillard Breholles, F.A.& De Albertes de Luynes, H. *Historia Diplomatica Frederici Secundi* (ed. Bottega d'Erasmo) Torino 1963.
3. Bresc, H. The 'Secrezia' and the royal patrimony in Malta: 1240–1450 *Mediaeval Malta: studies on Malta before the knights.* (ed Luttrell), The British school at Rome, London 1975 pp.126–162.
4. Sultana , J. Outlines of the new bird protection legislation in in Malta. *Gozo Year Book* 1981 pp.27–31. 5. Sultana J., and Gauci C., 1982 p.27.
6. Mifsud, A. 1917 pp.116–122.
7. Libr. Ms 49 p.21, 90. I am indebted to Simon Mercieca for this reference.
8. AOM 117 Liber Conciliourum 1650–1651 f3. I am indebted to Stephen Degiorgio for this reference.
9. Libr. Ms 429 (3) f.124, f.132; (4) f.4, f.115,f.120; (5) f.50; (6) f.88.
10. Libr Ms 149 p.65.
11. Mifsud, A. 1917 p.117.
12. Libr Ms 149 pp.162–3.
13. Libr Ms 149 p.172.
14. Libr Ms 355 f.10; Libr Ms 429 (9) f.29; Liber. Ms 355 p.10
15. Libr Ms430(1) f.108.
16. Government Notice published in The Malta Government Gazette No. 2520, of the 22nd May, 1872 at p.173.
17. Government Notice No. 262 published in The Malta Government Gazette No. 5852 of the 13th October, 1916 at pp.666–668.
18. Government Notice No. 447 published in The Malta Government Gazette No. 8230 of the 3rd November, 1936 at p.1028.
19. Government Notice No. 448 published in The Malta Government Gazette No. 8230 of the 3rd November, 1936 at pp.1028–1029.
20. *Times of Malta* Protection of birds – meeting of sportsmen, December 4 1936.
21. Domnic Cutajar and Joe Attard pers. comm.
22. Gauci, A. Hard facts *Times of Malta*, December 16 1974.
23. Pratesi, F. & Chelini A. *Osservazzioni al 'Code of Police Laws – Cap. 13 – Protection of Birds and Wild Rabbit Regulations. 1977'.* Rome, April 1977 pp.6.
24. Act No. XVII of 1980 published in the Suppliment to the Malta Government Gazette 13736 of the 30th May 1980 at pp.A 173–177.
25. Debates of the House of Representatives Sitting No. 370, 17th March 1980.

26. Legal notice 25 of 1983 published in the Supplement to the Malta Government Gazette No 14120 of 15th April, 1987 at p B228.

27. Legal Notice 18 of 1987 published in the Supplement to the Malta Government Gazette No 14735 of 17th February, 1987 at pp.B39–40.

28. Case Law Louis F. Cassar et noe vs. Onorevoli Prim Ministru et. Civil Court, First Hall, 29.7.1988 per Mr. Justice V. Borg Costanzi, LL.D.

29. *Needs and Deeds* (SPCA) The Law Vol II (4) 1969.

30. *Needs and Deeds* (SPCA) Cruelty Cases Vol III(3) 1970.

31. *The Times* Fined Lm 10 for shooting protected bird, April 9 1987.

32. Alternattiva *Ta' Cancu u l-Griffon*, October 19 1991.

33. *Il-Passa Il-proposti tal-ghaqda* May 1984.

34. Gauci, A. The sport of shooting *Times of Malta* July 9 1984.

35. Scicluna, J.R. (1986 ?) *Comments on the ICBP study report on the shooting and catching in Malta.* (undated report sent to FACE in 1986.)

36. Kalchreuter, H. 1991 *Report on the first fact-finding mission about bird hunting on Malta, 30 April – 5 May 1991* European Wildlife Research Institute, University of Saar landes, Germany (unpublished) p.3.

37. Dr Y. Lecocq letter dated 9th May 1990.

38. Doublet, J. Public money given to shooters *The Sunday Times*, 23 December 1990.

39. *The Times* Hunters accuse ornithologists of violating gentleman's agreement, January 29 1991.

40. Farrugia, C.L. MOS-Hunters association meetings *The Sunday Times*, 6 January 1991.

41. *The Times* Hunters want public apology from MOS President, February 25 1991.

42. Portelli, P. Public apology *The Times* 4 March 1991.

43. Perici Calscione, J. Clarification preferred to apologies, *The Times* 4 April 1991.

44. *The Times* Equitable solution, 23 September 1991.

45. *Il-Helsien* Tajr u kaċċaturi, 4 October 1991.

46. *Il-Mument* Il-Gvern m'hux kontra d-delizzju tal-kaċċa, 16 February 1992.

47. *In-nazzjon taghna* Is-soċjalisti jinsabu f'paniku, 18 February 1992.

48. *The Times* MLP resorting to tales- PM, 18 February 1992.

49. Kalchreuter, H. 1991 p.6.

50. *Report by the EC Directorate to the Prime Minister and Minister of Foreign Affairs regarding Malta's membership of the European Community.* DOI Malta 1990 pp.183–4.

51. Bertelsen, J. & Simonsen, N.H. 1986 *Documentation on bird hunting and the conservation status of the species involved situation in 1986.* Game and Wildlife Administration, Denmark. pp.1323.

52. *The Times* Protecting Wildlife December 14 1990.

53. Act No. V of 1991 published in the Supplement to the Malta Government Gazette 15,399 of the 26th February 1991 at pp.A 65–96.

Tables

Tables 9 to 11 illustrate annual numbers of birds, stuffed by taxidermists.
Table 12 lists annual bag records of ten Maltese Shooters.

TABLE 9

List of birds stuffed by Taxidermist A during the years 1958–1977. Note that the records for 1970 and 1971 do not cover the whole years. The records for 1970 cover the months January to April only, while for the year 1971, the records from May to August, were not available.

year	58	59	60	61	62	63	64	65
Little grebe	1	–	1	1	–	–	1	2
Great crested grebe	1	1	–	2	–	–	2	3
Black necked grebe	2	–	–	1	–	1	1	–
Cory's shearwater	–	1	–	8	1	3	8	7
Manx shearwater	–	–	–	–	2	2	–	–
Storm petrel	–	–	–	1	–	–	–	1
Gannet	–	1	–	–	–	–	2	–
Cormorant	–	–	–	–	–	–	–	–
Bittern	–	–	–	–	1	–	–	–
Little bittern	–	–	–	2	3	5	4	3
Night heron	1	10	8	10	11	14	19	24
Squacco heron	–	5	11	22	11	16	34	18
Cattle egret	–	–	–	–	–	–	–	–
Great white egret	–	–	–	–	2	4	–	–
Little egret	–	–	9	12	18	17	16	18
Grey heron	–	3	–	–	–	6	2	–
Purple heron	1	7	6	13	14	18	18	14
Glossy ibis	–	–	1	–	–	1	2	3
Spoonbill	–	1	–	–	–	–	1	–
White stork	–	–	–	–	–	–	–	–
Black stork	–	–	–	–	–	–	–	–
Pink-footed goose	–	–	–	–	–	–	–	–
Grey-lag goose	–	–	–	–	–	–	–	–
Bean goose	–	–	–	–	–	–	–	–
Shelduck	–	–	–	–	–	–	1	–
Wigeon	–	–	–	–	–	–	1	–
Teal	–	–	–	–	–	1	1	–
Mallard	–	2	1	1	–	2	–	2
Pintail	1	–	–	–	–	–	–	–
Garganey	–	–	–	–	–	–	–	3
Shoveler	–	–	–	–	–	–	–	–
Pochard	–	–	–	–	1	–	–	–
Ferruginous duck	–	–	–	–	–	–	–	1
Red-breasted merganser	–	–	–	–	–	–	–	–
Honey buzzard	–	3	5	4	3	6	7	9
Black kite	–	–	–	–	–	–	–	–
Lesser-spotted eagle	–	–	–	–	–	1	–	–
Booted eagle	–	–	–	–	–	–	1	–
Egyptian vulture	–	–	–	–	–	–	–	–
Short-toed eagle	–	–	–	–	–	–	1	–
Marsh harrier	–	4	7	9	8	9	7	7
Ringtails (harriers)	–	1	1	–	–	2	1	1
Sparrowhawk	–	3	–	–	–	–	–	1
Osprey	–	–	–	–	–	1	–	1
Kestrel/lesser kestrel	2	10	24	25	32	23	38	31
Red-footed falcon	–	–	–	13	3	3	5	2
Merlin	–	–	–	–	1	–	–	–
Hobby	–	–	–	7	2	5	5	5
Eleonora's falcon	–	–	1	–	2	–	1	–
Saker falcon	–	–	–	–	–	–	1	–

TABLE 9

66	67	68	69	70	71	72	73	74	75	76	77	tot
1	1	3	1	2	1	3	–	–	–	–	–	18
1	1	–	1	1	–	–	2	–	2	1	2	20
3	–	2	–	–	7	3	8	7	11	9	2	57
14	9	11	23	2	4	19	13	9	15	20	12	179
1	2	1	1	–	–	–	–	–	1	1	1	12
3	2	–	–	–	–	–	–	–	1	–	–	8
1	–	2	–	–	–	1	1	–	–	–	–	8
–	–	1	–	–	–	4	1	5	1	1	–	13
–	–	4	2	2	–	7	1	1	3	1	1	23
8	10	18	14	16	11	13	10	25	18	19	32	211
26	24	25	45	32	32	77	42	38	87	55	106	686
16	17	19	17	14	16	14	35	16	25	29	40	375
–	–	–	–	–	–	–	–	–	–	1	–	1
–	–	–	–	–	–	1	–	–	1	1	1	10
14	15	11	18	13	14	10	10	13	16	15	22	261
2	–	5	–	–	6	8	11	10	6	27	9	95
21	14	39	28	15	18	40	42	29	38	60	51	486
–	–	–	1	2	2	–	4	12	–	1	3	32
–	–	–	–	–	–	1	1	–	–	–	–	4
–	–	–	–	–	–	–	1	1	–	–	–	1
–	–	–	–	–	–	–	1	–	–	–	1	2
1	4	–	–	–	–	1	1	–	–	–	–	7
–	–	3	–	–	–	–	–	–	–	–	–	3
–	2	–	–	–	–	–	–	–	–	–	–	2
–	1	–	1	–	–	3	1	2	–	–	–	9
3	–	3	2	–	–	–	–	–	–	–	–	9
–	–	–	4	–	2	1	2	4	2	–	–	17
1	3	–	2	–	2	4	13	3	5	10	17	68
–	–	–	1	–	1	8	4	7	3	1	1	27
2	3	1	1	–	6	4	87	27	7	3	2	146
–	–	–	–	1	1	1	3	2	1	2	–	11
–	–	–	–	–	1	1	4	3	1	1	–	12
–	1	–	–	–	–	–	–	–	–	–	–	2
–	–	1	2	–	–	2	–	–	4	–	4	13
13	16	37	24	5	30	21	22	30	23	35	31	324
–	–	–	–	–	–	–	–	1	–	4	3	8
–	–	–	–	–	–	–	–	–	–	–	–	1
–	–	–	–	–	–	–	–	–	–	–	1	
–	–	–	–	–	–	–	–	–	–	1	–	1
–	–	–	–	–	–	–	–	1	–	1	1	4
13	5	13	23	11	17	37	19	43	52	36	67	387
5	4	3	4	3	1	–	–	–	2	–	4	32
–	–	–	1	–	1	1	1	2	1	1	–	12
–	–	2	–	–	–	–	–	1	2	2	1	10
43	38	36	57	22	28	71	28	60	60	95	54	777
–	10	4	7	–	–	1	14	–	5	1	42	110
–	–	–	–	1	–	–	–	–	–	–	1	3
6	9	3	15	–	–	4	17	15	33	11	28	165
2	2	1	1	–	2	1	3	1	2	1	1	21
–	–	1	1	–	–	–	–	–	–	–	–	3

TABLE 9 (contd.)

year	58	59	60	61	62	63	64	65
Peregrine falcon	–	–	–	–	–	–	1	–
Quail	–	–	1	1	2	–	2	3
Spotted crake	–	–	–	–	–	–	–	–
Little crake	–	1	–	1	–	–	1	1
Baillon's crake	–	–	–	–	–	–	–	3
Corncrake	–	–	–	–	–	–	–	1
Moorhen	–	5	8	6	11	10	12	19
Coot	1	–	–	–	–	–	–	–
Crane	–	–	1	1	–	1	–	–
Little bustard	–	–	–	–	–	–	–	1
Black-winged stilt	–	–	–	–	–	–	–	2
Avocet	–	–	–	–	–	–	–	–
Stone curlew	–	1	1	–	6	2	3	1
Cream-coloured courser	–	–	–	–	–	–	–	2
Pratincole	–	–	–	–	–	1	–	–
Little Ringed plover	–	–	–	–	–	1	–	1
Ringed plover	–	–	–	–	–	1	4	3
Dottorel	–	1	–	–	–	1	4	3
Golden plover	–	1	3	4	–	4	4	12
Grey plover	–	–	–	–	–	–	1	–
Lapwing	1	1	4	3	1	7	12	14
Little stint	–	–	–	–	–	1	–	1
Curlew sandpiper	–	4	1	3	–	2	–	–
Ruff	–	2	–	1	–	–	4	3
Jack snipe	–	–	–	–	–	–	–	–
Snipe	–	3	2	–	2	1	4	6
Great snipe	–	–	–	–	–	–	–	–
Woodcock	3	1	4	2	1	5	3	11
Black-tailed godwit	–	–	–	–	–	–	–	1
Whimbrel	–	–	–	–	–	–	–	–
Curlew	–	–	–	–	–	–	–	–
Spotted redshank	–	–	–	1	–	–	3	1
Redshank	–	–	–	–	–	–	–	1
Marsh sandpiper	–	–	–	–	–	–	–	1
Greenshank	–	1	–	1	–	–	1	1
Green sandpiper	–	–	–	–	–	–	1	–
Wood sandpiper	–	–	–	–	–	–	2	–
Common sandpiper	–	1	1	4	2	6	7	7
Turnstone	–	–	–	–	–	–	4	–
Arctic skua	–	–	–	–	–	–	–	–
Little gull	1	–	–	–	–	–	2	–
Black-headed gull	–	–	–	–	–	–	2	–
Slender-billed gull	–	–	–	–	–	1	–	–
Herring gull	–	2	1	–	1	4	8	2
Sandwich tern	1	–	–	6	–	3	6	–
Black tern	–	–	–	–	–	1	1	–
Woodpigeon	–	–	2	–	–	–	1	–
Turtle dove	–	–	–	–	2	2	4	7
Palm dove	–	–	–	–	–	–	–	–
Great spotted cuckoo	–	–	–	–	–	–	1	–
Cuckoo	–	1	1	1	1	4	6	11
Barn owl	5	6	12	5	3	7	9	14
Scops owl	–	–	6	3	3	1	7	8
Long-eared owl	–	–	–	–	2	2	1	–
Short-eared owl	2	5	7	5	1	6	5	9

TABLE 9 (contd.)

66	67	68	69	70	71	72	73	74	75	76	77	tot
—	—	—	—	—	—	—	1	2	2	1	—	7
8	6	4	1	1	5	9	3	9	14	15	16	100
—	—	6	—	—	—	—	—	—	—	—	—	6
—	—	1	1	—	1	1	—	—	—	—	—	8
—	—	—	—	—	—	—	—	—	—	—	—	3
—	—	—	—	—	—	—	—	—	—	—	—	1
6	11	27	28	2	13	23	24	19	28	26	11	289
—	—	—	2	—	5	2 13	1	26	19	18	87	
7	1	—	1	—	—	—	1	1	—	5	—	19
—	—	—	—	—	—	—	—	—	—	—	—	1
1	2	1	—	1	—	1	1	10	2	—	2	23
—	—	—	—	—	—	—	—	—	1	—	—	1
5	1	7	4	5	3 15	7	9	2	6	13	91	
1	—	—	—	—	2	2	2	—	—	—	3	12
—	—	2	4	—	1	—	1	2	5	3	1	20
—	—	—	—	—	—	—	—	—	3	2	2	7
—	—	—	—	—	—	—	5	—	—	1	8	
3	4	2	4	4	8	11	10	8	8	21	10	102
7	9	4	12	1	4	20	46	6	40	20	35	232
—	—	—	—	—	—	—	—	—	2	1	—	4
9	27	12	6	2	7	4	40	12	17	24	46	249
—	1	—	—	—	—	—	—	1	—	—	7	11
1	2	—	4	—	—	—	6	2	—	7	—	32
2	—	—	—	—	1	1	4	1	—	—	2	21
—	—	—	—	—	—	—	2	—	—	—	—	2
9	2	5	10	8	8	21	11	11	21	14	14	152
—	—	—	—	—	2	1	9	2	—	—	—	14
6	4	7	14	—	19	14	30	19	69	17	29	258
1	—	—	—	—	—	—	—	—	—	—	—	1
—	—	—	—	—	—	—	—	—	—	—	—	1
—	—	—	—	—	—	—	—	—	2	—	—	2
2	—	—	—	—	—	2	—	1	—	—	—	5
—	—	—	—	—	—	—	—	—	—	—	—	6
—	4	1	2	—	—	1	1	1	3	1	9	1
—	—	—	—	—	—	—	—	—	—	—	—	27
—	—	1	—	—	—	—	—	—	—	—	—	1
12	8	12	10	5	2	10	18	13	21	12	8	3
—	—	1	2	—	—	—	—	—	—	—	—	159
—	—	—	—	—	—	—	—	—	1	—	—	7
—	2	1	2	—	2	1	2	2	5	2	3	1
—	—	—	1	—	—	—	—	—	4	2	3	25
—	—	—	—	—	—	—	—	—	—	—	—	12
6	3	13	5	7	5	11	7	6	10	16	12	1
1	—	—	—	—	—	1	3	12	1	1	1	119
1	2	2	—	5	4	2	2	—	5	6	9	36
—	1	1	—	1	—	—	—	2	—	—	—	40
5	3	5	1	1	4	10	3	—	13	9	15	8
—	—	—	—	—	2	—	—	—	—	—	—	84
—	—	2	—	1	—	—	1	—	1	—	1	2
6	4	8	13	3	1	10	15	8	27	14	24	7
10	14	3	14	—	5	12	11	10	13	7	10	158
6	4	5	11	2	9	23	17	24	17	34	18	170
—	1	2	—	—	3	4	—	2	3	—	7	198
14	13	17	11	6	7	32	15	39	52	81	3	27
												330

TABLE 9 (contd.)

year	58	59	60	61	62	63	64	65
Nightjar	–	–	–	–	1	2	1	2
Swift	–	–	–	2	1	4	–	1
Alpine swift	–	–	–	–	–	2	2	3
Kingfisher	2	2	2	6	1	1	8	2
Bee-eater	–	5	10	8	10	16	34	30
Blue-cheeked bee-eater	–	–	–	–	–	–	–	–
Roller	–	20	20	11	17	23	27	13
Hoopoe	–	2	1	5	5	10	16	26
Wryneck	1	–	1	–	–	2	1	1
Calandra lark	–	–	–	–	–	–	–	–
Wood lark	–	–	–	–	–	–	1	–
Skylark	2	–	–	–	–	1	–	1
Red-throated pipit	–	–	–	–	–	–	1	–
Tawny pipit	–	–	–	–	–	1	1	–
Meadow pipit	–	–	–	–	–	–	2	–
Yellow wagtail	–	–	–	–	–	1	2	–
White wagtail	–	–	–	–	–	2	1	–
Dunnock	–	–	–	–	–	–	–	–
Wheatear	–	–	–	–	–	–	–	11
Rock thrush	–	–	–	1	1	2	–	3
Blue rock thrush	–	1	1	–	–	–	2	2
Ring ouzel	–	–	–	1	–	1	1	1
Blackbird	1	–	–	3	–	–	3	2
Fieldfare	–	–	–	1	–	–	1	19
Song thrush	2	–	2	3	–	–	4	8
Redwing	–	–	–	–	–	1	1	1
Sardinian warbler	–	1	–	–	–	–	3	1
Chiffchaff	–	–	–	–	–	–	2	–
Goldcrest	–	–	–	–	–	–	1	–
Golden oriole	–	19	18	56	43	63	53	29
Woodchat shrike	–	–	–	1	–	–	2	3
Starling	5	7	2	5	3	3	2	2
Rose-coloured starling	–	–	1	–	–	–	–	–
Spanish sparrow	1	1	–	–	–	2	1	–
Wren	–	–	–	–	–	–	–	–
Chaffinch	2	–	–	–	–	–	–	–
Greenfinch	2	–	–	–	–	–	1	1
Goldfinch	4	–	1	–	–	2	9	8
Siskin	–	–	–	–	–	1	–	2
Linnet	–	–	–	–	–	–	–	–
Hawfinch	–	–	–	–	–	–	–	1
Ortolan bunting	–	–	–	–	–	–	–	–
Corn bunting	–	1	–	–	–	–	1	1
Snow bunting	–	–	1	–	–	–	–	–
Yellow hammer	–	–	–	–	–	–	–	1
year	1958	59	60	61	62	63	64	65
total	45	147	190	282	235	352	486	479

TABLE 9 (contd.)

66	67	68	69	70	71	72	73	74	75	76	77	tot
–	2	1	7	–	1	–	3	6	2	1	2	31
1	1	1	1	–	1	–	–	2	–	2	–	17
2	1	2	2	1	2	1	2	3	2	3	5	33
5	1	2	2	3	5	2	4	1	22	8	7	86
31	17	19	21	19	17	27	29	27	24	28	38	410
–	2	–	–	–	–	–	–	–	–	–	–	2
17	37	16	45	12	10	21	15	33	44	14	12	407
22	12	20	31	8	13	12	7	27	16	14	22	269
6	2	2	6	6	2	1	1	1	12	1	4	50
–	–	–	–	–	–	–	1	–	–	1	1	3
–	–	–	–	–	–	–	–	–	–	–	–	1
–	1	2	–	–	–	1	–	–	1	2	7	18
–	–	–	–	–	–	–	–	–	–	–	–	1
–	–	–	–	–	–	–	–	–	–	–	–	2
1	–	–	–	–	–	–	1	–	–	–	–	2
–	–	–	–	–	–	–	–	–	–	–	–	5
–	1	–	–	–	–	–	–	–	–	–	–	3
–	–	2	–	–	–	–	–	–	–	–	–	1
4	3	2	1	3	2	3	2	2	2	7	1	43
8	–	14	14	5	4	16	4	6	6	7	4	95
3	3	4	6	4	1	4	3	3	6	1	3	47
1	1	1	2	1	–	1	4	–	1	2	1	19
3	–	–	4	–	4	1	–	1	–	–	–	22
7	2	4	3	2	4	7	11	17	43	9	11	141
2	2	7	9	1	7	6	13	8	31	5	7	117
1	–	–	1	–	–	–	–	–	1	–	2	8
–	–	–	–	–	–	–	–	–	–	–	–	5
1	–	2	–	–	–	–	–	–	–	–	–	5
–	–	–	–	–	–	–	–	–	–	–	–	1
41	38	29	70	15	12	31	58	33	64	23	103	798
4	7	3	1	–	1	–	–	5	4	–	6	37
8	15	10	11	2	8	28	15	21	15	10	26	198
–	–	–	–	–	–	–	–	–	–	–	–	1
–	–	–	–	–	–	–	–	–	–	–	2	7
–	–	–	–	–	–	3	–	–	–	–	–	3
2	–	–	1	1	–	–	–	–	–	–	–	6
3	4	–	1	–	–	–	–	–	–	2	5	19
6	2	2	1	–	–	–	–	–	–	–	4	39
–	–	–	–	–	–	–	–	–	–	–	–	3
–	–	2	–	–	–	–	–	–	–	–	–	2
2	–	–	1	–	4	–	–	4	2	1	–	15
1	–	–	–	–	–	–	–	–	–	–	–	1
1	–	–	–	–	–	–	–	–	–	–	–	4
–	–	–	–	–	–	–	–	–	–	–	–	1
–	–	–	–	–	–	–	–	–	–	–	–	1
66	67	68	69	70	71	72	73	74	75	76	77	tot
512	476	546	701	280	424	768	883	808	1144	953	1146	10,857

TABLE 10

A list of birds which were stuffed by Taxidermists B and C during the years 1976–1986

Taxidermist B used to stuff and mount birds for an average of 35 shooters between the years 1976 and 1982, while Taxidermist C, who catered for 30 shooters, stuffed birds between 1983 and 1986.

Years	1976	77	78	79	80	81	82	83	84	85	86	Total
Little grebe	–	–	–	–	–	–	–	–	–	1	1	2
Great crested grebe	–	1	–	–	3	–	–	1	–	1	1	7
Black-necked grebe	3	2	2	2	2	3	2	5	5	3	4	33
Cory's shearwater	1	1	2	4	1	7	5	7	1	2	1	32
Manx shearwater	1	2	1	2	7	4	6	3	2	2	1	31
Storm petrel	1	–	–	–	–	–	–	1	–	–	–	2
Gannet	–	–	1	1	–	1	–	3	–	1	5	12
Cormorant	1	–	–	–	–	1	1	3	–	1	5	12
Bittern	2	–	–	–	–	–	1	1	–	2	–	6
Little bittern	5	6	3	3	3	3	3	14	6	5	7	58
Night heron *	16	15	14	19	16	18	17	21	16	14	16	182
Squacco heron *	5	4	2	3	7	7	11	4	2	2	3	50
Little egret *	3	5	3	5	5	6	14	8	4	6	6	65
Grey heron *	4	2	3	5	3	3	7	6	3	7	6	49
Purple heron *	5	18	10	7	6	5	8	8	3	8	4	82
Glossy ibis	–	–	–	–	3	–	–	–	2	2	1	8
Spoonbill	1	–	–	–	–	–	–	–	–	–	–	1
Flamingo	–	–	–	–	–	–	–	–	1	–	–	1
Goose sp.	–	–	–	–	–	–	–	1	–	–	–	1
Shelduck*	–	–	–	–	–	–	–	2	2	–	–	4
Widgeon *	–	–	–	–	–	2	–	–	2	1	1	6
Teal *	2	2	–	–	–	2	2	2	4	4	4	22
Mallard *	–	–	2	–	–	–	–	6	–	2	1	11
Pintail *	–	1	–	–	–	2	–	2	4	2	–	11
Garganey *	1	–	–	–	6	3	12	20	7	7	5	61
Shoveler *	–	–	–	–	–	–	–	–	–	3	–	3
Pochard *	–	–	–	–	–	–	–	1	–	–	–	1
Ferruginous duck *	–	–	1	–	–	–	–	2	2	5	2	12
Honey buzzard	11	9	12	29	15	12	14	23	25	14	22	186
Black kite	–	–	1	1	–	1	–	–	–	1	1	5
Red kite	–	–	–	–	–	–	–	1	–	–	–	1
Short-toed eagle	–	–	1	–	–	–	–	–	–	–	–	1
Marsh harrier	12	10	14	11	9	16	18	24	20	26	26	186
Hen harrier	1	1	–	–	1	–	3	–	2	–	–	8
Pallid harrier	1	–	1	1	–	2	1	6	1	–	–	13
Montagu's harrier	2	3	2	2	2	3	2	10	9	5	9	49
Sparrowhawk	1	–	1	2	1	1	1	3	1	1	1	13
Buzzard	–	–	–	–	–	–	–	–	1	1	1	3
Osprey	–	–	–	2	–	–	–	–	1	–	1	4
Lesser kestrel	3	2	2	4	3	4	3	3	1	1	2	28
Kestrel	28	21	24	45	26	22	18	22	27	18	23	274
Red-footed falcon	6	8	10	8	12	7	23	48	19	10	18	169
Merlin	–	–	–	–	1	–	–	–	3	–	1	5
Hobby	4	4	5	8	4	7	10	19	10	8	12	91
Eleonora's falcon	–	–	–	–	1	–	2	–	1	3	1	8
Peregrine falcon	1	–	–	–	–	–	–	1	–	–	–	1
Quail *	2	2	1	4	1	2	8	8	2	1	2	33
Water rail *	–	–	–	–	1	1	1	1	–	7	3	14
Spotted crake *	–	1	–	–	3	–	–	1	–	–	1	6
Little crake *	–	–	–	–	–	–	1	–	–	–	–	1
Corncrake *	–	–	–	–	2	–	–	3	–	–	–	5
Moorhen *	4	3	5	7	9	7	12	9	5	5	7	73
Coot *	1	–	–	–	2	1	1	4	3	3	3	18

TABLE 10 (*contd.*)

Years	1976	77	78	79	80	81	82	83	84	85	86	Total
Crane	–	–	–	–	1	–	–	–	1	–	–	2
Black-winged stilt	1	2	1	3	1	2	1	9	5	3	3	31
Stone curlew *	–	3	1	2	1	1	1	1	2	3	2	17
Avocet	–	–	–	–	–	–	–	–	–	1	–	1
Cream-coloured courser	–	–	–	–	–	–	–	1	–	1	–	2
Pratincole	1	1	–	–	1	–	2	–	1	–	1	7
Little ringed plover	3	–	–	2	2	3	5	1	–	–	–	16
Ringed plover	1	4	–	1	–	–	1	4	4	2	–	17
Kentish plover	–	1	1	1	–	–	–	–	1	–	–	4
Dottorel *	5	1	2	6	2	1	4	2	3	5	4	35
Golden plover *	2	3	3	8	1	6	5	2	6	8	7	51
Grey plover	1	1	–	2	–	–	1	3	–	–	4	12
Lapwing *	4	1	5	3	4	10	1	2	3	4	3	40
Sanderling	–	–	–	3	–	–	–	–	–	–	–	3
Little stint	5	–	1	5	1	1	5	1	2	1	1	23
Curlew sandpiper	–	1	–	–	3	3	1	–	–	–	–	8
Dunlin	–	–	2	–	–	1	1	2	4	1	2	13
Ruff	2	4	2	4	5	2	3	2	2	12	7	45
Jack snipe *	–	–	–	3	–	–	–	2	2	6	5	18
Snipe *	4	1	4	1	1	5	8	7	3	5	4	43
Great snipe *	1	–	–	–	2	–	1	7	1	1	1	14
Woodcock *	3	2	5	6	5	6	7	10	6	5	7	62
Black-tailed godwit	1	–	–	–	–	–	–	–	–	–	–	1
Whimbrel	1	1	–	–	–	–	–	–	–	1	–	3
Curlew	–	–	3	–	–	–	–	1	3	1	1	9
Spotted redshank	–	1	1	–	–	–	–	–	2	–	–	4
Redshank	2	–	–	3	1	–	1	1	1	2	1	12
Marsh sandpiper	–	–	–	–	1	–	–	–	–	–	–	1
Greenshank	2	2	–	–	1	–	–	–	–	3	1	9
Green sandpiper	–	–	1	–	4	1	3	2	2	1	–	14
Wood sandpiper	3	2	3	3	1	1	4	2	1	4	1	25
Common sandpiper	4	3	9	9	4	9	7	3	6	4	3	61
Turnstone	1	–	–	–	–	–	2	1	–	–	–	4
Pomarine skua	–	–	–	–	1	–	–	1	–	1	–	3
Long-tailed skua	–	–	–	1	–	–	–	–	–	–	–	1
Mediterranean gull	1	1	–	4	5	3	1	1	1	4	2	23
Little gull	1	2	3	2	2	2	2	2	3	1	2	22
Black-headed gull	4	2	3	3	5	8	6	8	3	6	7	55
Slender-billed gull	–	–	–	–	7	–	–	2	2	1	1	13
Lesser black-backed gull	–	–	1	–	–	–	–	–	–	–	–	1
Herring gull	7	1	2	3	11	4	4	4	4	6	6	52
Kittiwake	–	–	–	–	–	–	–	–	1	–	–	1
Caspian tern	1	–	–	2	–	–	–	1	–	1	–	5
Sandwich tern	1	2	–	–	4	2	1	5	5	2	4	26
Roseate tern	1	–	–	–	–	–	–	–	–	–	–	1
Black tern	3	1	1	2	1	1	1	1	2	1	1	15
White-winged black tern	–	1	–	1	–	–	–	3	1	2	–	8
Turtle dove *	3	2	4	8	8	5	10	5	3	5	6	59
Great spotted cuckoo	–	–	1	–	1	–	–	–	1	–	–	3
Cuckoo	10	10	11	10	11	10	19	10	16	20	24	151
Barn owl	–	–	–	–	–	1	–	–	–	–	–	1
Scops owl	2	8	2	15	8	5	1	8	9	4	7	69
Long-eared owl	1	2	1	1	–	1	–	1	–	2	1	10
Short-eared owl	10	5	7	12	5	11	11	10	16	20	18	125
Nightjar *	9	3	1	4	5	8	11	3	2	4	3	53
Swift	1	3	1	4	2	1	2	2	1	1	2	20
Alpine swift	2	2	2	3	2	4	4	2	4	2	3	30

TABLE 10 (contd.)

Years	1976	77	78	79	80	81	82	83	84	85	86	Total
Kingfisher	3	3	1	1	2	1	2	13	5	6	9	46
Bee-eater	7	5	5	5	7	9	9	11	24	18	19	119
Roller	2	2	2	1	–	1	3	4	3	4	4	26
Hoopoe	10	12	11	12	18	15	18	25	13	29	28	191
Wryneck	1	1	1	8	2	4	4	3	2	3	2	31
Short-toed lark	–	–	–	1	1	–	–	–	1	–	–	3
Skylark *	–	–	1	1	4	5	1	–	1	1	2	16
Swallow	–	1	–	–	–	1	–	–	2	1	–	5
Red-rumped swallow	–	–	1	–	–	–	–	1	–	1	–	3
Tree pipit	–	–	–	–	1	–	1	–	–	1	–	3
Tree pipit	–	–	–	–	–	1	–	1	–	–	–	2
Meadow pipit	–	–	2	3	1	1	–	1	–	1	1	10
Yellow wagtail	–	–	–	–	–	1	–	–	1	–	–	2
White wagtail	–	–	–	1	–	–	–	2	1	–	2	6
Alpine accentor	–	–	–	–	–	–	1	–	–	–	–	1
Robin	–	–	–	1	–	1	–	1	1	2	1	7
Nightingale	–	–	–	3	1	–	–	1	–	1	–	6
Bluethroat	–	–	–	–	–	–	1	–	–	–	–	1
Black redstart	–	–	1	–	1	–	–	1	–	1	1	5
Redstart	1	–	–	1	–	1	–	1	1	2	1	8
Stonechat	–	–	–	1	1	–	–	2	1	–	1	6
Wheatear	–	1	1	5	–	3	2	2	2	1	2	19
Black-eared wheatear	1	–	–	1	1	1	1	–	1	–	1	7
Rock thrush *	2	5	3	7	3	7	12	7	5	7	6	64
Blue rock thrush	5	2	4	6	2	2	1	1	2	1	3	29
Ring ouzel *	1	–	–	1	3	4	2	–	–	2	4	42
Blackbird *	3	2	2	7	4	8	2	3	2	5	4	42
Fieldfare *	1	1	2	2	2	7	2	4	4	3	3	31
Song thrush *	4	2	3	4	2	6	1	5	3	9	6	45
Redwing *	2	1	1	3	3	3	3	2	1	1	2	22
Mistle thrush *	–	–	–	1	–	1	1	4	1	6	2	16
Great reed warbler	–	–	–	1	–	–	–	1	–	1	–	3
Dartford's warbler	–	–	1	1	–	–	–	–	–	–	–	2
Spectacled warbler	–	–	2	2	–	–	–	–	1	–	–	5
Sardinian warbler	–	1	–	–	–	1	–	–	–	1	–3	
Chiffchaff	–	–	–	–	–	1	–	–	1	–	–	2
Firecrest	–	1	2	3	–	1	1	–	1	–	–	9
Spotted flycatcher	–	–	–	1	–	–	–	1	–	–	–	2
Pied flycatcher	–	–	–	–	2	–	–	2	–	1	–	5
Golden oriole	10	14	14	12	18	16	33	39	24	22	26	228
Red-backed shrike	–	–	–	1	–	–	–	–	1	–	–	2
Woodchat shrike	1	2	2	13	3	19	12	5	4	6	6	73
Starling *	4	4	5	6	4	7	2	1	1	5	3	42
Spanish sparrow *	–	–	2	2	2	–	1	1	1	2	–	11
Tree sparrow	1	–	2	–	–	–	–	1	–	1	–	5
Chaffinch *	–	–	–	1	–	–	–	2	–	1	1	5
Brambling	–	–	–	1	–	–	–	–	1	–	–	2
Greenfinch *	–	–	–	4	3	–	1	2	2	1	1	14
Goldfinch *	2	–	2	–	–	–	1	3	2	1	1	12
Siskin *	–	–	–	1	–	–	1	–	1	1	–	4
Linnet *	–	–	–	–	1	–	1	–	3	1	–	6
Crossbill	–	–	–	1	–	–	–	–	–	–	–	1
Hawfinch	–	–	–	3	–	–	–	1	1	1	1	7
Ortolan bunting *	–	–	–	–	–	1	–	–	–	–	–	1
Reed bunting	–	–	–	–	1	–	–	–	1	–	–	2
Corn bunting	–	–	1	4	1	–	2	1	2	2	1	14
Totals	293	262	281	448	369	399	467	597	454	496	494	4560

* denotes that the bird is not protected by the Bird Protection Regulations of 1980.

TABLE 11

Birds that are known to have been imported from abroad and which were stuffed by Taxidermist C.

Species	1983	1984	1985	1986	Total
Pink-footed goose	1	–	–	–	1
Pochard	1	–	–	–	1
Tufted duck	3	4	–	–	7
Goldeneye	2	–	–	–	2
Goosander	1	–	–	–	1
Grouse	1	–	–	–	1
Curlew	2	–	–	–	2
Woodpigeon	1	1	1	–	3
Collared dove	1	–	–	–	1
Tawny owl	2	–	–	–	2
Desert lark	–	–	1	–	1
Jay	–	2	–	–	2
Magpie	–	1	–	–	1
Crow	1	–	–	–	1
Raven	–	1	–	–	1
total:15 species	16	7	3	1	27

TABLE 12

Bag records of shooter 1

Although quite a large number of shooters keep a diary of what they shoot, bag records of shooters are not easily available. One of the reasons why bag records are not given is because shooters do not want to show how much they kill, especially to people who do not form part of the shooting community.

Species year	1972	73	74	75	76	77	78	79	80	81	82	83	Total
Little grebe	–	–	–	–	–	–	–	1	–	–	–	–	1
Black-necked grebe	–	–	–	1	–	–	–	1	–	–	–	2	4
Cormorant	–	–	–	–	–	–	1	–	–	–	–	–	1
Little bittern	1	–	–	–	–	–	–	2	–	–	1	–	4
Night heron	1	1	1	1	6	1	2	1	5	2	1	2	24
Squacco heron	–	–	–	–	–	–	–	–	2	–	–	–	2
Little egret	–	–	–	–	–	–	–	1	2	2	–	–	5
Grey heron	–	–	–	–	–	–	–	–	1	–	–	–	1
Purple heron	1	–	–	–	1	–	–	–	–	–	–	–	2
Shelduck	–	–	–	–	–	1	1	–	–	–	–	–	2
Mallard	–	–	–	–	–	–	–	1	–	–	–	–	1
Teal	–	–	–	–	–	1	1	1	–	–	–	–	3
Wigeon	–	–	1	1	–	1	–	1	2	–	–	–	6
Pintail	–	–	–	1	–	–	–	1	–	–	10	–	12
Garganey	–	1	–	–	–	–	–	–	6	6	2	–	15
Shoveler	–	–	–	–	–	2	–	–	–	11	–	–	13
Pochard	–	–	–	–	–	–	–	–	3	–	–	–	3
Ferruginous duck	1	–	–	–	–	–	–	–	–	–	5	–	6
Red-breasted merganser	–	–	–	1	–	1	–	–	–	–	–	–	2
Honey buzzard	–	–	–	–	–	–	–	1	–	1	1	1	4
Black kite	–	–	–	–	–	–	–	–	–	1	–	1	2
Pallid harrier	–	–	–	–	–	–	–	–	–	–	1	–	1

Bag records of shooter 1 (*contd.*)

Species year	1972	73	74	75	76	77	78	79	80	81	82	83	Total
Montagu's harrier	1	–	–	–	1	–	–	–	–	1	2	–	5
Marsh harrier	–	–	1	–	–	–	–	1	1	3	1	–	7
Hobby	1	–	–	1	1	–	1	1	1	1	3	2	12
Red-footed falcon	–	–	–	–	–	4	–	–	–	1	1	3	2	9
Lesser kestrel	–	–	–	–	–	–	–	–	1	1	–	–	2
Kestrel	1	1	1	2	13	1	1	3	7	1	5	4	40
Quail	3	1	1	1	1	1	1	1	1	1	2	1	15
Water rail	–	–	1	–	–	–	–	1	–	–	–	–	2
Crake sp.	–	–	–	–	–	–	–	1	–	–	–	1
Moorhen	–	–	1	–	1	2	1	–	1	–	1	–	7
Coot	–	–	–	–	–	–	1	1	1	–	–	–	3
Ringed plover	–	–	–	–	–	–	–	–	–	1	–	–	1
Little ringed plover	–	–	–	–	1	–	–	–	1	–	–	–	2
Dottorel	–	–	–	–	–	–	1	–	–	–	–	–	1
Golden plover	–	–	–	1	1	–	–	1	–	1	–	–	4
Grey plover	–	–	–	–	–	–	–	2	–	–	1	–	3
Lapwing	–	1	–	–	1	–	–	–	–	1	1	–	4
Turnstone	–	–	–	–	–	–	–	–	1	1	–	–	2
Ruff	1	–	1	–	–	1	2	–	1	–	1	–	7
Common sandpiper	2	1	3	2	1	–	1	1	–	–	2	1	14
Spotted redshank	–	–	–	–	–	1	–	–	–	1	–	–	2
Redshank	1	–	–	–	1	–	–	–	1	–	2	–	5
Greenshank	–	–	–	–	–	1	–	–	–	6	1	–	8
Bar-tailed godwit	–	–	–	–	–	–	–	1	–	–	–	–	1
Curlew	–	–	–	–	–	–	–	1	–	–	3	–	4
Whimbrel	–	–	–	–	–	–	–	–	3	–	–	–	3
Woodcock	–	–	–	1	–	1	1	–	–	–	2	–	5
Snipe	–	–	1	1	1	1	1	3	1	1	1	–	11
Jack snipe	–	–	–	–	–	–	1	–	–	1	–	–	2
Black-winged stilt	–	–	–	–	–	–	–	1	–	–	–	–	1
Avocet	–	–	–	–	–	–	–	2	–	7	–	–	9
Stone curlew	–	–	–	–	–	–	–	–	1	1	1	–	3
Mediterranean gull	–	–	–	–	–	–	1	–	1	–	–	–	2
Black-headed gull	1	1	2	3	1	1	3	1	2	1	1	1	18
Slender-billed gull	–	–	–	–	–	–	–	–	1	1	–	–	2
Herring gull	–	–	1	–	–	–	–	2	1	–	–	–	4
Audouin's gull	–	–	–	–	–	–	–	–	1	–	–	–	1
Black tern	–	–	–	–	–	–	–	–	2	–	–	–	2
Caspian tern	–	–	–	–	–	–	–	1	–	–	–	–	1
Sandwich tern	–	–	–	–	6	1	–	1	–	1	–	–	9
Little tern	–	–	–	–	–	–	–	–	1	–	–	–	1
Pigeon	1	–	–	1	–	–	1	1	–	–	1	–	5
Collared dove	–	–	–	–	–	–	1	–	–	–	–	–	1
Turtle dove	13	12	7	33	40	57	18	46	19	21	33	51	350
Cuckoo	1	1	1	1	2	7	3	2	1	2	1	1	23
Short-eared owl	–	–	–	1	–	–	–	–	1	–	–	–	2
Long-eared owl	–	–	–	–	–	–	–	–	–	–	1	1
Nightjar	2	2	1	4	2	2	1	2	1	2	1	1	21
Kingfisher	–	–	–	–	–	1	–	–	–	–	–	–	1
Bee-eater	–	–	1	–	3	–	–	–	–	–	–	4
Roller	–	–	1	–	–	–	–	–	2	–	–	–	3
Hoopoe	3	1	2	1	2	2	2	1	2	2	1	3	22
Rock thrush	–	–	–	–	–	–	–	–	2	–	1	–	3
Ring otzel	–	–	1	–	–	–	–	–	–	–	–	–	1
Blackbird	–	1	1	–	–	–	3	2	1	–	–	–	8

Bag records of shooter 1 (contd.)

Species year	1972	73	74	75	76	77	78	79	80	81	82	83	Total
Redwing	–	–	–	–	–	–	–	1	–	–	–	–	1
Song thrush	7	9	28	29	10	13	13	47	3	2	13	5	179
Rose-coloured starling	–	–	–	–	–	–	–	–	–	1	–	–	1
Starling	34	2	21	20	17	7	8	12	1	9	11	5	147
Golden oriole	4	5	7	4	5	6	4	3	5	9	5	5	62
Totals:	80	40	86	111	118	116	75	154	91	103	121	89	1184

Bag records of shooter 2

years	82	83	84	85	86	87	Total	Average (on 5.5 yrs)
Manx shearwater	–	–	6	–	2	–	8	1.45
Black-necked grebe	–	–	–	–	1	1	2	.36
Little bittern	1	–	–	1	–	–	2	.36
Night heron	–	1	–	1	–	–	2	.36
Squacco heron	1	–	–	–	–	–	1	.18
Little egret	–	1	1	–	–	–	2	.36
Purple heron	–	1	–	–	–	–	1	.18
Mallard	–	1	–	–	–	–	1	.18
Honey buzzard	2	1	2	–	–	1	6	1.09
Pallid harrier	–	–	–	1	–	–	1	.18
Montagu's harrier	–	1	1	–	1	–	3	.54
Marsh harrier	2	1	–	1	2	–	6	1.09
Hobby	–	3	2	–	–	–	5	.9
Red-footed falcon	–	–	–	–	–	5	5	.9
Kestrel	4	1	1	2	2	3	13	2.4
Merlin	–	–	1	–	–	–	1	.18
Quail	5	1	2	–	–	–	8	1.45
Water rail	–	–	–	1	–	–	1	1.18
Moorhen	1	1	–	1	–	1	4	.73
Coot	–	1	–	–	–	–	1	.18
Ringed plover	–	–	–	–	–	2	2	.36
Little ringed plover	–	–	–	–	–	2	2	.36
Dottorel	–	–	–	2	–	–	2	.36
Golden plover	–	–	1	–	1	–	2	.36
Lapwing	–	–	–	1	–	1	2	.36
Ruff	–	–	2	–	1	–	3	.54
Common sandpiper	–	–	3	–	–	3	6	.91
Woodcock	2	2	2	–	–	–	6	1.9
Snipe	1	1	–	2	–	1	5	.9
Jack snipe	1	–	–	1	–	–	2	.36
Great snipe	–	–	–	–	–	1	1	.18
Black-winged stilt	–	–	–	–	–	1	–	.18
Stone curlew	1	–	–	–	–	–	1	.18
Mediterranean gull	–	1	–	–	–	–	1	.18
Black-headed gull	1	1	–	1	–	–	3	.54
Slender-billed gull	–	–	1	–	–	–	1	.18
Herring gull	–	–	1	–	–	–	1	.18
Turtle dove	11	47	28	29	8	8	131	23.9
Cuckoo	–	5	22	4	4	7	42	7.6
Scops owl	4	4	4	5	–	3	20	3.64
Short-eared owl	1	–	2	–	–	–	3	.54

Bag records of shooter 2 (*contd.*)

years	82	83	84	85	86	87	Total	Average (on 5.5 yrs)
Nightjar	4	3	2	8	–	–	17	3
Alpine swift	–	–	3	–	–	–	3	.55
Kingfisher	–	1	–	–	–	–	1	.18
Bee-eater	–	–	–	6	–	–	6	1.1
Roller	–	–	2	–	–	–	2	.3
Hoopoe	1	3	4	2	5	1	16	3
Rock thrush	–	–	–	2	1	1	4	.73
Blue rock thrush	–	1	–	–	–	–	1	.18
Blackbird	1	4	1	–	–	–	6	1.09
Mistle thrush	–	1	–	–	–	–	1	.18
Fieldfare	–	–	–	1	–	2	3	.54
Redwing	–	1	1	–	–	–	2	.36
Song thrush	71	150	80	66	8	7	332	60.3
Starling	1	27	12	11	11	5	67	12.18
Golden oriole	1	23	12	11	4	3	54	10

Note that the records of 1982 include only the months of September to December

Bag records of shooter 3

years	82	83	84	85	86	87	88	89	Total	Average/yr (7.5 yrs)
Manx shearwater	–	–	5	–	–	–	–	–	5	.67
Great crested grebe	–	–	–	–	–	–	–	1	1	.13
Black necked grebe	–	–	–	–	–	–	–	2	2	.26
Cormorant	–	–	–	–	–	–	–	1	1	.13
Little bittern	–	–	1	–	–	1	–	1	3	.4
Night heron	4	1	–	–	–	–	–	–	5	.67
Squacco heron	–	1	–	–	–	–	–	–	1	.13
Little egret	–	2	–	–	–	–	–	3	5	.67
Grey heron	1	–	–	–	–	2	–	2	5	.67
Mallard	1	–	–	–	–	–	–	–	1	.13
Teal	1	–	–	–	–	–	–	–	1	.13
Wigeon	1	–	–	–	–	–	1	–	2	.26
Osprey	–	–	–	–	–	–	1	1	1	.13
Buzzard	–	–	–	–	–	1	–	–	1	.13
Honey buzzard	–	1	1	1	1	–	1	2	7	1.6
Pallid harrier	–	1	–	–	–	–	–	–	1	.13
Montagu's harrier	–	–	1	1	–	1	–	–	3	.4
Marsh harrier	–	–	2	1	1	–	2	4	10	1.33
Hobby	2	1	1	1	–	1	–	–	6	.8
Eleonora's falcon	–	–	–	–	–	–	–	1	1	.13
Red-footed falcon	–	–	–	–	–	10	–	–	10	1.33
Lesser kestrel	–	–	–	–	1	–	–	–	1	.13
Kestrel	1	1	3	3	5	7	4	3	27	3.6
Merlin	–	1	–	–	–	–	–	–	1	.13
Quail	2	1	1	3	3	–	–	1	11	1.47
Water rail	–	–	–	–	–	–	–	–	1	.13
Moorhen	–	1	–	1	1	–	–	1	4	.53
Coot	5	–	–	–	–	–	–	–	5	.66
Little ringed plover	–	–	–	1	–	1	–	–	2	.26
Common sandpiper	–	–	2	2	2	2	1	–	9	1.2

Bag records of shooter 3 (contd.)

years	82	83	84	85	86	87	88	89	Total	Average/yr (7.5 yrs)
Golden plover	4	–	–	–	–	–	–	–	4	.53
Grey plover	–	–	–	–	–	–	–	1	1	.13
Lapwing	–	–	–	–	–	1	–	–	1	.13
Ruff	–	1	–	3	–	–	1	–	5	.66
Curlew	–	–	–	–	–	–	–	1	1	.13
Woodcock	1	1	2	–	–	–	1	1	6	.8
Snipe	4	1	2	–	4	–	–	1	12	1.6
Jack snipe	4	–	–	–	–	–	–	–	4	.53
Black-winged stilt	–	1	–	–	–	–	–	–	1	.13
Stone curlew	1	–	–	–	–	–	–	–	1	.13
Black-headed gull	–	3	19	–	–	–	–	–	22	3
Slender-billed gull	–	–	1	–	–	–	–	–	1	.13
Herring gull	–	–	–	–	2	–	–	–	2	.27
Black tern	–	–	–	–	–	–	–	1	1	.13
Sandwich tern	–	–	–	–	–	–	–	1	1	.13
Turtle dove	8	32	30	39	19	20	31	27	206	27.5
Cuckoo	–	3	9	3	12	16	5	1	49	6.5
Short-eared owl	–	–	2	–	–	1	–	–	3	.4
Scops owl	4	1	7	3	–	3	4	3	25	3.33
Nightjar	1	3	5	1	3	3	1	4	21	2.8
Alpine swift	–	–	1	–	–	1	1	–	3	.4
Kingfisher	–	–	–	–	1	–	–	–	1	.13
Bee-eater	1	–	–	–	–	–	–	–	1	.13
Hoopoe	–	1	1	7	3	3	1	–	16	2.13
Rock thrush	–	–	–	–	1	–	–	–	–	.13
Blue rock thrush	–	1	–	–	–	–	–	–	1	.13
Ring ouzel	–	–	1	–	1	–	–	–	2	.27
Blackbird	–	6	6	2	1	–	1	–	16	2.13
Fieldfare	–	1	–	–	–	–	2	1	4	.5
Mistle thrush	1	1	–	–	–	–	–	–	2	.27
Redwing	1	6	4	1	–	1	4	2	19	2.5
Song thrush	33	113	95	115	50	90	87	46	629	84
Starling	1	14	29	42	10	109	45	9	259	35
Golden oriole	3	10	11	7	7	8	6	2	54	7.2

Bag records of shooter 4

years	82	83	84	85	86	Total	Average/yr (4.5 yrs)
Black-necked grebe	–	–	–	–	2	2	.44
Little bittern	–	1	–	1	–	2	.44
Night heron	1	2	–	2	2	7	1.56
Squacco heron	–	–	–	1	–	1	.2
Little egret	–	1	–	1	–	2	.4
Grey heron	–	–	–	–	1	1	.2
Purple heron	–	–	1	–	–	1	.2
Honey buzzard	–	1	–	1	–	2	.44
Montagu's harrier	–	1	–	–	–	1	.2
Marsh harrier	–	–	1	–	1	2	.44
Hobby	–	2	–	–	–	2	.4
Red-footed falcon	–	1	–	3	–	4	.88
Kestrel	2	2	1	2	2	9	2

Bag records of shooter 4 (*contd.*)

years	82	83	84	85	86	Total	Average/yr (4.5 yrs)
Quail	2	–	–	1	–	3	.66
Moorhen	1	–	–	1	1	3	.6
Coot	–	1	–	–	–	1	.2
Golden plover	1	–	1	–	1	3	.6
Lapwing	–	1	–	1	–	2	.44
Ruff	1	–	–	1	–	2	.44
Woodcock	–	1	3	1	–	5	1.11
Snipe	2	–	1	–	1	4	.88
Common sandpiper	2	2	1	1	1	7	1.56
Mediterranean gull	–	1	1	–	–	2	.44
Black-headed gull	–	2	2	2	1	7	1.56
Herring gull	–	–	–	1	–	1	.2
Black tern	–	–	–	1	–	1	.2
Turtle dove	7	18	8	23	11	67	14.88
Cuckoo	–	1	9	1	2	13	2.88
Short-eared owl	–	1	–	1	1	3	.66
Scops owl	2	2	1	4	–	9	2
Nightjar	1	3	5	2	2	13	2.88
Kingfisher	–	–	1	–	–	1	.2
Bee-eater	–	2	–	–	–	2	.44
Hoopoe	1	1	1	1	1	5	1.1
Blue rock thrush	1	–	1	1	–	3	.66
Blackbird	–	1	–	–	2	3	.66
Redwing	–	1	–	–	–	1	.2
Song thrush	14	56	59	38	47	214	47.5
Mistle thrush	1	–	–	–	–	1	.2
Starling	6	15	1	5	1	28	6.2
Golden oriole	–	13	13	4	–	30	6.66

Bag records of shooter 5

years	84	85	86	87	Total	Average/yr (3.5 yrs)
Night heron	1	–	1	1	3	.85
Squacco heron	1	–	–	–	1	.29
Little egret	–	–	–	1	1	.29
Purple heron	–	–	1	–	1	.29
Honey buzzard	2	–	–	–	2	.57
Montagu's harrier	–	1	–	–	1	.29
Marsh harrier	–	–	1	–	1	.29
Hobby	1	–	–	–	1	.29
Red-footed falcon	–	–	–	5	5	1.43
Kestrel	2	1	1	1	5	1.43
Quail	2	2	1	2	7	.57
Moorhen	1	–	1	–	2	.57
Ringed plover	–	–	1	–	1	.29
Golden plover	–	1	–	–	1	.29
Lapwing	1	–	–	–	1	.29
Woodcock	3	1	1	–	56	1.43
Snipe	1	1	1	1	4	1.14
Common sandpiper	3	–	–	–	3	.86
Stone curlew	–	–	1	–	1	.29
Black-headed gull	–	1	–	1	2	.57

Bag records of shooter 5 (*contd.*)

years	84	85	86	87	Total	Average/yr (3.5 yrs)
Herring gull	–	1	–	–	1	.29
Turtle dove	7	13	16	8	44	12.6
Cuckoo	6	2	2	2	12	3.43
Scops owl	3	3	4	–	10	2.86
Short-eared owl	–	–	1	–	1	.29
Nightjar	6	2	2	–	10	2.86
Kingfisher	1	–	–	–	1	.29
Bee-eater	–	1	–	–	1	.29
Hoopoe	1	1	1	1	4	1.14
Rock thrush	1	–	–	–	1	.29
Blue rock thrush	1	–	–	–	1	.29
Blackbird	–	3	1	–	4	1.14
Song thrush	26	56	35	–	117	33.4
Fieldfare	–	2	1	–	3	.86
Starling	–	7	3	–	10	2.86
Golden oriole	6	8	6	4	24	6.9

Bag records of shooter 6

years	84	85	86	87	Total	Average/yr (/ 3yrs)
Little bittern	–	1	–	–	1	.33
Night heron	–	–	2	–	2	.6
Squacco heron	1	–	–	–	1	1.33
Little egret	–	1	–	–	1	.33
Honey buzzard	–	–	–	1	1	.33
Montagu's harrier	1	–	–	–	1	.33
Hobby	–	2	–	–	2	.66
Red-footed falcon	–	1	–	–	1	.33
Kestrel	–	1	1	–	2	.66
Quail	1	2	1	–	4	1.33
Moorhen	1	–	1	–	2	.66
Dottorel	–	1	–	–	1	.33
Lapwing	–	1	–	–	1	.33
Woodcock	1	1	–	–	2	.66
Snipe	1	1	–	1	3	1
Great snipe	1	–	–	–	1	.33
Common sandpiper	2	–	1	1	4	1.33
Black-headed gull	2	–	1	–	3	1
Turtle dove	5	3	4	3	15	5
Cuckoo	7	1	–	–	8	2.66
Scops owl	1	3	–	–	4	1.33
Long-eared owl	1	–	–	–	1	.33
Nightjar	5	–	–	1	6	2
Bee-eater	1	–	–	–	1	.33
Hoopoe	1	–	2	–	1	1
Song thrush	5	3	2	4	14	4.66
Starling	3	–	–	–	3	1
Golden oriole	2	3	2	4	5	5.33

Note: the records for 1984 are for September—Dec, while those for 1986 are the records of the month of April only

Bag records of shooter 7

years	84	85	Total	Average/yr (tot = av)
Night heron	1	–	1	1
Purple heron	1	–	1	1
Marsh harrier	–	1	1	1
Red-footed falcon	–	1	1	1
Kestrel	–	1	1	1
Sparrowhawk	1	–	1	1
Quail	1	1	2	2
Woodcock	1	–	1	1
Snipe	–	1	1	1
Turtle dove	1	10	11	11
Cuckoo	–	5	5	5
Scops owl	3	1	4	4
Nightjar	–	3	3	3
Alpine swift	1	–	1	1
Hoopoe	–	4	4	4
Blue rock thrush	1	–	1	1
Blackbird	1	–	1	1
Song thrush	57	11	68	68
Fieldfare	–	1	1	1
Starling	11	6	17	17
Golden oriole	1	1	2	2

Note that the records for the year 1984 are for the months of September to December, while those for 1985 are for the months January-May; hence the total = average.

Bag records of shooter 8

years	84	85	86	87	Total	Average/yr (/ 3yrs)
Black-necked grebe	–	1	–	–	1	.33
Little bittern	–	–	1	–	1	.33
Night heron	–	2	–	–	2	.57
Little egret	–	1	–	–	1	.33
Mallard	–	1	–	–	1	.33
Honey buzzard	–	–	1	1	2	.57
Montagu's harrier	–	1	–	–	1	.33
Marsh harrier	1	1	–	–	2	1.57
Red-footed falcon	–	2	–	–	2	.57
Lesser kestrel	–	1	–	–	1	.33
Kestrel	–	1	–	1	2	.57
Quail	2	2	–	–	4	1.14
Moorhen	1	2	–	–	3	.85
Little-ringed plover	1	–	–	–	1	.33
Golden plover	1	1	–	–	2	.57
Lapwing	–	–	1	–	1	.33
Ruff	–	–	–	–	2	.57
Woodcock	2	1	–	–	3	.86
Snipe	1	1	1	1	1	1.33
Great snipe	1	–	–	–	1	.33
Black-headed gull	1	–	1	–	2	.66
Turtle dove	12	21	14	14	61	20.33
Cuckoo	3	1	1	1	6	1.71

Bag records of shooter 8 (*contd.*)

years	84	85	86	87	Total	Average/yr (/ 3yrs)
Short-eared owl	–	1	–	–	1	.33
Scops owl	–	3	–	–	3	.86
Nightjar	–	1	1	–	2	.57
Alpine swift	–	–	–	1	1	.33
Kingfisher	–	–	1	–	1	.33
Bee-eater	1	–	–	–	1	.33
Hoopoe	1	3	1	1	6	2
Song thrush	6	7	6	–	19	6.33
Starling	1	–	–	–	1	.3
Golden oriole	1	9	5	3	18	6

Note that the records for 1986 and 87 are partial, hence I divided the total by 3 as the number of years.

Bag records of shooter 9

years	84	85	86	87	Total	Average (/ 2.5yrs)
Night heron	2	–	–	–	1	.8
Little egret	1	–	–	–	1	.4
Grey heron	1	–	–	–	1	.4
Red-footed falcon	–	2	–	–	2	.8
Kestrel	1	–	–	1	2	.8
Golden plover	1	–	–	–	1	.4
Lapwing	1	–	–	–	1	.4
Ruff	1	–	–	–	1	.4
Woodcock	2	–	–	–	2	.8
Snipe	1	–	1	–	2	.8
Jack snipe	–	1	–	–	1	.8
Turtle dove	10	3	9	8	30	12
Cuckoo	2	1	2	3	8	3.2
Scops owl	1	–	–	–	1	.4
Short-eared owl	1	–	–	–	1	.4
Nightjar	4	–	–	–	4	1.6
Hoopoe	1	1	1	1	4	1.6
Song thrush	10	9	11	–	30	12
Starling	2	3	2	2	9	3.6
Golden oriole	2	3	2	1	8	3.2

1985 Sept–Oct only, 1987 Apr–May only, 1986, Apr, Sept, Oct Only.

Bag records of shooter 10

years	84	85	86	87	Total	Average/yr (4yrs)
Little egret	–	1	–	–	1	.25
Night heron	2	–	1	–	3	.75
Short-toed eagle	–	1	–	–	1	.25
Marsh harrier	–	–	1	–	1	.5
Red-footed falcon	–	1	–	–	1	.25

Bag records of shooter 10 (*contd.*)

years	84	85	86	87	Total	Average/yr (4yrs)
Kestrel	–	–	–	1	1	.5
Quail	–	2	–	1	3	.75
Moorhen	–	1	1	–	2	.5
Ruff	1	1	–	–	2	.5
Snipe	1	1	1	1	4	1
Great snipe	–	1	–	–	1	.25
Turtle dove	1	7	2	2	18	3
Cuckoo	1	–	1	–	2	.5
Scops owl	1	1	–	3	5	1.25
Short-eared owl	–	–	1	–	1	.25
Nightjar	1	–	–	–	1	.25
Hoopoe	1	1	1	2	5	1.25
Song thrush	6	9	–	–	15	3.75
Starling	2	2	1	3	8	2
Golden oriole	2	2	2	3	9	2.25